EVERYTHING

QUICKBOOKS 2023

All-In-One Guide That Teaches Everything You Need to Know to Master Bookkeeping and QuickBooks Accounting for All Users + Professional Hacks, Tips & Tricks for Organized and Effortless Accounting

CARTY BINN

Disclaimer and Terms of Use

The author and publisher of this book and the accompanying materials have used their best efforts in preparing this book. The author and publisher make no representation or warranties with respect to the accuracy, applicability, fitness, or completeness of the contents of this book. The information contained in this book is strictly for informational purposes. Therefore, if you wish to apply the ideas contained in this book, you are taking full responsibility for your actions.

Printed in the United States of America

CONTENTS

INTRODUCTION

If you are a new small business owner and you're just starting to research accounting software, you would have seen the name QuickBooks everywhere. So, this book will help you understand what exactly QuickBooks is and what it can do for you.

To use this book to benefit the most, you should know that this book is broken into **Several sections** and each section has **several chapters**. The first section is all about how to set up QuickBooks, after that, you will learn about how to manage customers and receivables regarding sales and income, then you will know all about vendors and accounts payable for things like expenses and the last main section is all about banking features so that you can become an absolute expert in QuickBooks desktop.

You should be aware that each section has several of its chapters within that section and each chapter is a separate topic that you can learn separately from the whole book. When you finish learning each of the chapters in one section, you can then move on to the next section. Keep doing that a little bit each day until you finish all the sections and you are one step closer to becoming an expert in QuickBooks desktop. Constant Practice perfects your learning and in no time, you eventually become a QuickBooks Pro.

SECTION ONE
THE FOUNDATION OF ACCOUNTING

CHAPTER 1
PRINCIPLES OF ACCOUNTING

In the first section of this chapter, we will answer three main questions: what is accounting, why do we need it and what areas of accounting are out there? As we proceed, we will explain the four main purposes of accounting. Also, we'll briefly cover the common financial statements so you become familiar with or refresh your knowledge of these terms. We will cover some practical examples by looking at an overview of the financial statements of a company to give you some background on financial statements, their layout, and what they're used for.

Introducing you to the world of accounting

Some might think that accounting is only a boring and unnecessary redundancy and that it exists only due to regulations and legal requirements but the opposite is true. Accounting exists because it plays an extremely important role in running a business.

Let's illustrate this with a simple example:

Meet Ken. he lives in a small village where there are no convenience stores and its residents have to travel to a nearby town to go shopping for essential goods which are a few miles away. Ken came up with the idea that he could open his own small store where he would sell the most necessary products. He rented and renovated a garage in his neighbor's house and built several shelves and a counter with the materials he had on hand, then he went to the wholesaler and bought goods for a total amount of 2000 dollars. He knew the prices of items from the store in town and he set his prices at the same level; he expected that his potential customers will be more willing to buy from him than drive a few miles since the prices are the same, of course, these prices were higher than the prices at which he bought his merchandise. Ken bought the same goods every week and sold them at the same prices. However, after a month when he checked his account, it turned out that he had 500 less than a month earlier. Initially, he thought he had been robbed; however, all account activity was in order and nobody attacked him in the store either so what went wrong? Later, Ken sat down and took his bills and notes he had kept during work. He wrote down all the expenses on one side adding up four bills from the warehouse for 2000 dollars each, then he took bills from the gas stations (there were five of them for the amount of 200). In the end, he added the amount for the monthly rental of the premises which is 1000;

The total was 8000. On the other side, he wrote down his total sales by week. Ken realized that even though he was getting more money for the goods than he paid for them, the store had brought him a loss. He began to wonder what to do; not only does he have to break even, but he also has to make a living from this business.

We can see that if someone wants to run a business without even the simplest of calculations, he will be at the mercy of fate. It might as well turn out that Ken gained a lot from his company but without any calculations, he would not be able to analyze and optimize his business. Also, when in a crisis he would have a problem finding the reason why he suddenly stopped earning money. So, Ken started counting; as we saw, he learned that his business took losses but he didn't yet know why so he started to look for a reason. At the very beginning, he checked how individual products were selling and it turned out that every three days he was selling all the bread he bought, every four days all the vegetables, and every five days all the fruit. He also realized that some of the cleaning products didn't sell because they are longer-lasting products so people don't buy them every week. At the same time, some products such as juices went bad rather quickly which caused Ken to throw away half of them every week. After counting everything up, Ken made a shopping list but this time he decided he would buy more prepackaged bread, vegetables, and fruits so he wouldn't run out so quickly. He also bought half as many juices and did not buy cleaning products at all because he still had a supply from previous purchases (he decided that he would only buy it when he would have a week's supply of cleaning products left). This time he paid only 850 to the wholesaler. After a week, when people saw that Ken's store was better stocked and had more products actually needed on a daily basis, they started to buy there more willingly, after all, Ken's well-stocked store saved them time and fuel money. Sales became higher and more stable. Ken's clients spent 2500 dollars in his store every week. Every week Ken would go to the wholesaler and buy best-selling products and once every four weeks he would also buy cleaning products; this meant that he bought products for 850 dollars three times a month and once a month he bought for 2000 dollars.

At the end of the month, Ken calculated his sales and expenses again. This time, thanks to Ken's analysis he earned 2850 which covered last month's losses and generated profit; however, it would not be possible if it were not for the calculations he made.

4

A few years passed, and during this time Ken expanded his business and his profits grew. After a while, he opened a second store in the town nearby and finally expanded his business to a whole network of small shops. Simple calculations made on a piece of paper are no longer sufficient for Ken's needs, now his accountant prepares a complete report for him every month to give him an overall view of the operation of the entire company. On the basis of this report and comparing it with the reports from previous periods Ken is able to initially assess whether the business is going well or badly, whether the company is profitable or whether it has adequate financial liquidity. If the company would underperform, the reports would help Ken to determine why or at least where to look for a problem. If for example the company is no longer profitable or its profitability declines, Ken could request reports for individual stores, look at their performance and see which one is profitable and which one is losing money, then he will look for reasons why this store is not profitable, analyze its income and costs. There can be various reasons for a store to underperform; for example, Ken can find out that the sales have dropped significantly, and to find out why it dropped he will need to talk to the store manager. However, thanks to his analysis, he knows what the problem is and what to ask about to sum up.

Ken from 10 years ago who did everything by himself in his small convenience store needed only the simplest calculations. He certainly didn't need complicated reports because he personally knew about everything that was happening in his store. However, with the growth of the business, when Ken stopped participating personally in most of the processes in his company, efficient management of the company is possible thanks to accounting which provides him with crucial knowledge.

What is Accounting?

Accounting is an information science that is used to collect and organize financial data for organizations and individuals.

Let's break down this definition:

First of all, we said that accounting is information science. It is concerned with analyzing, collecting, and organizing information, but what type of information? Accounting organizes financial information; it is about money, it is quantitative in nature, and measures money. Accounting isn't an abstract science; it is much more practical than theoretical and one of those things that you'll learn best by doing.

The last part of the definition says that accounting serves organizations and individuals. How come?

Well, as one can imagine, every firm needs to be able to organize the financial information related to its business. A firm has to know how much of a product it was able to sell, how much it costs to produce the product and how much money it has in the bank. Similarly, an individual needs to be aware of their personal finances. If they don't pay attention to how much comes in and how much goes out, they may soon be in deep trouble.

Accounting is a science that helps us organize and represent financial information and it helps corporations and individuals understand their finances and make decisions about the future. Accounting helps you to use the past in order to take action in the present and change the future.

Areas of Accounting

There are four main areas of accounting which we will discuss in this section.

Bookkeeping

First of all, we have **Bookkeeping**. Without bookkeeping, we wouldn't be able to do anything because bookkeepers are responsible for all of the information that is collected and taken into consideration. Bookkeeping is a fundamental activity as it ensures that financial information has been gathered systematically.

Financial Accounting

Then we have financial accounting which focuses on the three main statements: income statement, balance sheet, and cash flow. It is prepared for the company's ownership, its lenders, financial analysts, and other external stakeholders. It is highly regulated given that the information is prepared for third-party users and they should be able to read it without having inside information. The fact that the information is designed according to a specific set of rules renders it comparable with the one prepared by other companies which in turn facilitates investors and lenders. Financial statements are prepared according to a uniform set of rules called accounting principles. The aim of these reports is to allow externals like banks and investors to get an idea of your business, how much sales you had, was the company profitable, how is it financed, and so on.

Managerial Accounting

The third type of accounting is **Managerial accounting**. It is available only for insiders, it is not defined by accounting principles, and is in most cases more detailed than financial accounting. It contains strategic information that shouldn't be seen by the firm's competitors. Managerial accounting looks into topics like pricing, competition marginality, budgeting, and so on. The company does not want to reveal this information to outsiders because outsiders will prepare a counter plan and gain a strategic advantage. Of course, Managerial and Financial accounting are often interrelated and it is a frequent practice to reconcile managerial and financial accounting figures.

Tax Accounting

The fourth type of accounting that we need to mention is **Tax accounting**. This is the accounting that will determine the amount of taxes that a company has to pay. Tax accounting is a very technical field that varies for every single legislation in the world.

In this book, our main focus will be on bookkeeping and financial accounting as they are the solid foundation that one needs in order to understand financial transactions.

Purpose of Accounting

As individuals, we tend to keep a record of our finances and we have different reasons for this. We compare what we have received against what we have spent, we look at if we have paid off all the individuals that we are owing, we may look at if we have enough money saved for probably a trip that we are saving for whether within your country or not or it may just be a case where you want to surprise someone or you want to get a gadget for yourself. Similarly, businesses do the same. The owners of businesses do what is called accounting and, in this section, we are going to look at the purpose of accounting.

Ascertain profit

Why is this important? As a trading firm, the main reason for engaging in business is to make a profit, and accounting is done to know whether a business is making a profit. To achieve this, proper records must be kept of all transactions that take place daily.

Ascertain the value of assets and liabilities

This is important to keep a proper record of assets (which are the things that the business owns) and liabilities (those things that are owed by a business) so that the value of each asset and liability can be known at any time to the owner.

Provide financial information about the business

At the end of each accounting period, financial statements are prepared and these are important to the users of accounting information which include the owners, bank, and lending agencies and those stakeholders can use this information to make proper decisions.

We will look at users of accounting information in another section.

Maintain proper financial control of the business

This is necessary as proper control must be exercised when dealing with expenses and revenues in a for-profit business. So, once you're running a business and your aim is to generate a profit, you have to ensure that you keep proper records of your expenses and your revenues. The accountant uses techniques such as forecasting and budgeting to ensure there is control. Financial statements can be analyzed using financial ratios to determine whether the business is profitable, whether it is running efficiently or if it is liquid and this creates a pathway in ensuring that they are able to pick up what measures can be taken to maintain efficiency and profitability of the business.

Reviewing the Common financial statements

This section is designed as an introductory module for those who may not have had any experience or exposure to financial statements.

The generally accepted accounting principles can change from time to time but in this section, we will look at what the generally accepted accounting principles are as regards financial statements.

Financial statements are basically a record of financial activity that has happened over a certain period of time. All publicly traded companies are required to file four basic financial statements: the Income statement, Balance sheet, Cash flow statement, and statement of shareholders equity.

The income statements

The income statement layout is basically your revenue minus expenses. What that means is revenue is all the money that a company or an organization brings in fewer expenses they incurred to arrive at Net Income.

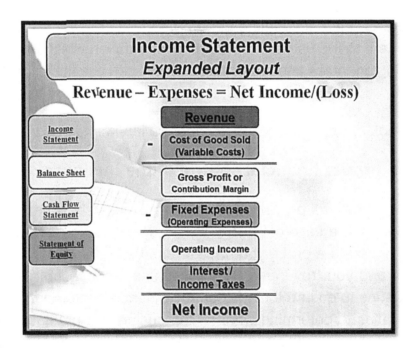

The Net Income statement may be broken out a little bit more and the expanded version starts out with Revenue and then it minuses the Cost of Goods Sold (this is the cost of the products or services that they're selling) to come up with either Gross Profit number or Contribution Margin number, less their Fixed Expenses or Operating Expenses to come up with Operating Income and then finally you subtract your Interest in Income Taxes to come up with Net Income.

9

So, if you were running a Coffee stand, you know you'd have Revenue from selling coffee minus the Cost of the coffee to give the Gross Profit. Now your Fixed Expenses could be things like buying a table or pitcher and you know they're fixed, so in subtracting your Fixed Expenses, you come up with Operating Income minus interest or income taxes to come up with Net Income. That's the basic layout of the Income statement. The income statement is what we call a temporary statement and what that means is that it's over a period of time and then it is usually reset to zero. So, you have an income statement for a month or an income statement for a quarter or a year and it measures the revenue and expenses for that time period but then it's reset to zero.

Balance sheet

The layout of the balance sheet is assets equals liabilities plus equity. This must always stay in balance.

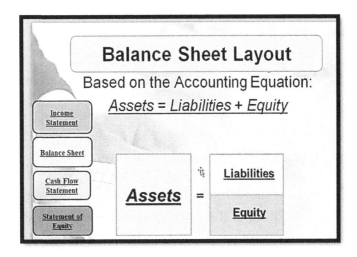

The balance sheet is basically a financial statement that shows what the company has (what its assets are) minus what it borrowed or what people have put into the company.

Some examples of assets would be cash, inventory, buildings, and land. These are all assets that a company could have. Liabilities on the other hand may be the amount they owe to the bank, amounts they borrowed from different vendors, and then equity is the owner's equity because this is the amount that the owners have contributed and it also represents the accumulation of all retained earnings.

The balance sheet is a permanent financial statement; it never goes away but it's only good for a certain date in time. Usually, you'll see the balance sheets as of a certain date and it just keeps going and going and going but it changes every day as different transactions occur.

Cash flow statement

This helps reconcile your Net Income to cash because for some companies, even though they may produce income, they run out of cash and so this helps you understand the cash flow from a company.

Statement of shareholders' equity

This is the Beginning Retained Earnings plus or minus some Equity Adjustments to equal the Ending Retained Earnings.

This helps analyze the different entries and adjustments that are going on in this payment shareholders' equity.

Putting it all together

Whenever we're making financial statements in financial accounting, we always start with the income statement. We make the statement of owner's equity next, the balance sheet, and then the cash flow statement.

At the top of every single financial statement that you make you are going to have three things: the first thing is the company name, the next thing you're going to put in the statement name, then you're going to write the date or the period of time. An income statement is always for a period of time so your income statement should either have "for the year ended" and then the date or "for the month ended" and then the date; it depends on what period of time you're looking at.

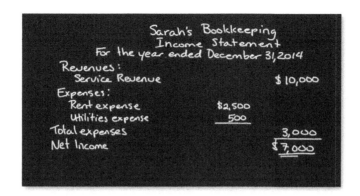

The income statement shows two major categories of accounts. It shows your revenues and expenses. Recall that revenues are the amount of money we charge per hour or per project or that's the amount you charge per product when you sell something. The income statement shows revenues minus expenses to give you net income.

Expenses are things that you have to pay for in the course of doing business so this includes your rent, utilities, your phone, if you have to pay employees' salaries; all sorts of things like that are considered to be expenses.

Note that you have to get your net income first because you're going to use this number for the statement of owner's equity, that's why it's very important that you make the income statement first. The statement of owner's equity and the income statement look almost the same and run through the same period. The statement of owner's equity always has the five same things: the opening balance, investment by the owner, net income or loss number, withdrawals by the owner, and the closing balance of the capital account.

We always make the statement of owner's equity second and the reason for that is that you are going to use that closing capital balance on your next statement which is the balance sheet.

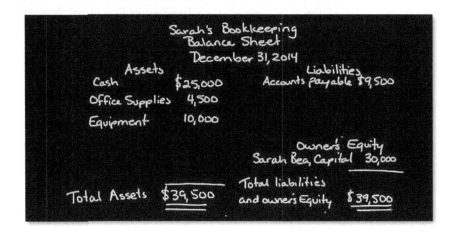

Notice that you don't put "for the period ended" because the balance sheet has accounts that we just look at a time. The balance sheet is concerned with the accounting equation. You'll remember the accounting equation which is assets equal liabilities plus owner's equity; that's exactly what the balance sheet is showing and that's what you're trying to balance. You're going to balance assets on one side and then liabilities and owner's equity on the other side.

You keep track of all your income and then what happens is at the end of the reporting period, your Net Income is posted into equity. So, you can think of the income statement as a subset of equity. You can see that your Net Income is going to be a piece of equity and that rolls into your retained earnings, so as the net income statement closes out it adjusts equity and that's how everything stays in balance. Your balance sheet should and must always balance; assets must always equal liabilities plus equity, right after your net income has been posted for the period.

Also, note that it's quite common for companies to use different terminologies for the income statement. Sometimes they call it a Statement of operations, a Statement, and OPs, the P&L which stands for a Profit and Loss statement (that's an older term but a lot of people still use P&L), OPs and some even refer to it as the Budget Line Item.

Some examples

Now let's look at a couple of examples: The image below shows the income statement for a company.

CONSOLIDATED STATEMENTS OF OPERATIONS
(In millions, except number of shares which are reflected in thousands and per share amounts)

		Years ended	
	September 27, 2014	September 28, 2013	September 29, 2012
Net sales	$ 182,795	$ 170,910	$ 156,508
Cost of sales	112,258	106,606	87,846
Gross margin	70,537	64,304	68,662
Operating expenses:			
Research and development	6,041	4,475	3,381
Selling, general and administrative	11,993	10,830	10,040
Total operating expenses	18,034	15,305	13,421
Operating income	52,503	48,999	55,241
Other income/(expense), net	980	1,156	522
Income before provision for income taxes	53,483	50,155	55,763
Provision for income taxes	13,973	13,118	14,030
Net income	$ 39,510	$ 37,037	$ 41,733
Earnings per share:			
Basic	$ 6.49	$ 5.72	$ 6.38
Diluted	$ 6.45	$ 5.68	$ 6.31
Shares used in computing earnings per share:			
Basic	6,085,572	6,477,320	6,543,726
Diluted	6,122,663	6,521,634	6,617,483

Looking at our example above, the first thing you want to look at with the income statement is that you can see it is for the year thus income statement goes for a full year and this company is in a fiscal year in this year 2014, and ended on September 27, 2014, so for a year, this is their income. It starts out with Net sales, has the cost of sales and then they have its Gross Margin or sometimes called Gross Profit.

Then you subtract their Operating Expenses to come up with their Operating Income and then you subtract their taxes, other interest, and expense items to come up with their Net income. This is the layout of the income statement for this company and you can see that it is in millions, so for the year ending on September 27, 2014, this company had sales of 182 billion, 795 million, as this is their cost of goods sold. Their operating income was 52 billion, 503 million. Their net income was 39 billion, 510 million.

Moving on to another example, let's look at a Balance sheet. This is as of a certain date when the balance sheet closed and you can see the list of their Assets first with total assets of 239 billion, 839 million.

Other current assets	9,806	6,882
Total current assets	68,531	73,286
Long-term marketable securities	130,162	106,215
Property, plant and equipment, net	20,624	16,597
Goodwill	4,616	1,577
Acquired intangible assets, net	4,142	4,179
Other assets	3,764	5,146
Total assets	$ 231,839	$ 207,000

LIABILITIES AND SHAREHOLDERS' EQUITY:

Current liabilities:		
Accounts payable	$ 30,196	$ 22,367
Accrued expenses	18,453	13,856
Deferred revenue	8,491	7,435
Commercial paper	6,308	0
Total current liabilities	63,448	43,658
Deferred revenue – non-current	3,031	2,625
Long-term debt	28,987	16,960
Other non-current liabilities	24,826	20,208
Total liabilities	120,292	83,451
Commitments and contingencies		
Shareholders' equity:		
Common stock and additional paid-in capital, $0.00001 par value; 12,600,000 shares authorized;		
5,866,161 and 6,294,494 shares issued and outstanding, respectively	23,313	19,764
Retained earnings	87,152	104,256
Accumulated other comprehensive income/(loss)	1,082	(471)
Total shareholders' equity	111,547	123,549
Total liabilities and shareholders' equity	$ 231,839	$ 207,000

See accompanying Notes to Consolidated Financial Statements.

You will also see that their total liabilities and equity equals their assets. You can see their Liabilities section right there and their Equity section. In this case, they didn't call it Owner's equity, instead, they called it Shareholders equity; whether it's Equity, Shareholders Equity, Stockholders Equity, or Owner's Equity, it's all the same.

Let's move over to an example of the statement of cash flows. The way the statement of cash flows works is that in most cases, you start with net income so it's going to be Net Income plus or minus all those adjustments to come up with this Increase in cash.

CONSOLIDATED STATEMENTS OF CASH FLOWS
(In millions)

	Years ended		
	September 27,	September 28,	September 29,
	2014	2013	2012
Cash and cash equivalents, beginning of the year	$ 14,259	$ 10,746	$ 9,815
Operating activities:			
Net income	39,510	37,037	41,733
Adjustments to reconcile net income to cash generated by operating activities:			
Depreciation and amortization	7,946	6,757	3,277
Share-based compensation expense	2,863	2,253	1,740
Deferred income tax expense	2,347	1,141	4,405
Changes in operating assets and liabilities:			
Accounts receivable, net	(4,232)	(2,172)	(5,551)
Inventories	(76)	(973)	(15)
Vendor non-trade receivables	(2,220)	223	(1,414)
Other current and non-current assets	167	1,080	(3,162)
Accounts payable	5,938	2,340	4,467
Deferred revenue	1,460	1,459	2,824
Other current and non-current liabilities	6,010	4,521	2,552
Cash generated by operating activities	59,713	53,666	50,856
Investing activities:			
Purchases of marketable securities	(217,128)	(148,489)	(151,232)
Proceeds from maturities of marketable securities	18,810	20,317	13,035
Proceeds from sales of marketable securities	189,301	104,130	99,770
Payments made in connection with business acquisitions, net	(3,765)	(496)	(350)
Payments for acquisition of property, plant and equipment	(9,571)	(8,165)	(8,295)
Payments for acquisition of intangible assets	(242)	(911)	(1,107)

When you look at it, if you remember right back on the income statement you saw that this company had 39 billion dollars of Net Income but when you look at their Balance sheet, they started the year with 14 billion in cash and cash went down to 13 billion. Now you may be wondering how come they made 39 billion dollars of net income and their cash went down, well, the Cash flow statement explains the change in cash.

You can scroll back up to see what caused their cash to go down and from their balance sheet, you can see that the biggest decrease in cash was that they spent 45 billion dollars in buying back some of their stock and that was one of the major draws on cash. They didn't have some marketable securities they invested in and pulled out which is up there but the main outflow of cash was for repurchasing common stock.

16

Other current and non-current assets	101	1,000	(5,102)
Accounts payable	5,938	2,340	4,467
Deferred revenue	1,460	1,459	2,824
Other current and non-current liabilities	6,010	4,521	2,552
Cash generated by operating activities	59,713	53,666	50,856
Investing activities:			
Purchases of marketable securities	(217,128)	(148,489)	(151,232)
Proceeds from maturities of marketable securities	18,810	20,317	13,035
Proceeds from sales of marketable securities	189,301	104,130	99,770
Payments made in connection with business acquisitions, net	(3,765)	(496)	(350)
Payments for acquisition of property, plant and equipment	(9,571)	(8,165)	(8,295)
Payments for acquisition of intangible assets	(242)	(911)	(1,107)
Other	16	(160)	(48)
Cash used in investing activities	(22,579)	(33,774)	(48,227)
Financing activities:			
Proceeds from issuance of common stock	730	530	665
Excess tax benefits from equity awards	739	701	1,351
Taxes paid related to net share settlement of equity awards	(1,158)	(1,082)	(1,226)
Dividends and dividend equivalents paid	(11,126)	(10,564)	(2,488)
Repurchase of common stock	(45,000)	(22,860)	0
Proceeds from issuance of long-term debt, net	11,960	16,896	0
Proceeds from issuance of commercial paper, net	6,306	0	0
Cash used in financing activities	(37,549)	(16,379)	(1,698)
Increase/(decrease) in cash and cash equivalents	(415)	3,513	931
Cash and cash equivalents, end of the year	$ 13,844	$ 14,259	$ 10,746
Supplemental cash flow disclosure:			
Cash paid for income taxes, net	$ 10,026	$ 9,128	$ 7,682
Cash paid for interest	$ 339	$ 0	$ 0

See accompanying Notes to Consolidated Financial Statements.

So, looking at the financial statements gives you an overview of the health of a company. You look at their Income statement to see how profitable they are for the year and how well their company is running their operations. The balance sheet is like their overall health and with it, you know how much cash they have on hand and how healthy they are financially. The cash flow statement helps explain where the cash went for the year. As the income statement shows revenue expense for the year, the cash flow shows the amount of cash and where it went for the year. Lastly, the statement of shareholders' equity would help you understand the changes in equity positions throughout the period.

Accounting Principles

In this section, we're going to be looking at accounting principles. We're going to explain what they are and give examples for each of the principles that we'll be explaining and we are done, you'll be able to get a grasp on how you can apply accounting principles when preparing financial data or financial information.

Accounting principles are the required rules and guidelines that companies are required to follow when producing their financial information.

If everyone was to produce their information however they wanted to then it would be very difficult for the users of financial information to make decisions because they would not know how they came about finalizing this financial information but because accounting principles are the rules and guidelines that are followed, that means that the financial information that is produced by a company can be relied on to make decisions. Financial information is of interest to various stakeholders of an entity; this information is used to make decisions, as such, how the financial information is presented may influence the decisions that are made by the stakeholders and that's why companies need to follow accounting principles when they are preparing their financial data or financial information. Let's go through some accounting principles now.

Consistency principle

This principle focuses on the consistency with which methods and policies are applied in the preparation of financial information in each period. This is to ensure that information is comparable. If methods and policies change this must be disclosed in the financial statements. So as the word consistency is, you have to be consistent in your preparation of financial information. If you're going to look at the set of financial information for a specific company over a few periods of, say two years, you should be confident that this information was prepared consistently from one period to another, and as it says here, if methods and policies change this must be disclosed in the financial statement so that the users can take that into account when they are analyzing the financial statements.

An example of a principle of consistency is that the method and rate of depreciation on vehicles are expected to be the same as the previous years. We know depreciation is the value of assets going down so the method that is used and the rate that is used to depreciate vehicles for instance should be the same from one year to another. If you're depreciating your vehicles using the straight-line method at 20 per annum, your stakeholders would expect to see the value for depreciation at 20 per annum this period as it was in the previous period. If it changes for any reason then this must be disclosed in the financial statements so that they can take that into account when analyzing the financial information.

Accrual principle

Regardless of cash movements, transactions must be recorded in the accounting records and shown in the financial statements in the financial period in which they occur. If you know the Accrual principle, you would know what is called prepaid income, prepaid expenses, and income received in advance as those accounts exist because of their Accrual principle that is applied.

What is the Accrual principle? This is just ensuring that all the income that is earned in a specific period and the expenses that are incurred must be recorded and shown in the financial statements in the financial period in which they occur. If you have received money that you have not earned in this period or paid out money for an expense you have not incurred in this period, you will not account for them as income or expenses but you will disclose it as the Accrual that it is whether it's income received in advance, prepaid expenses, accrued income or accrued expenses, you will account for them as such in the financial statement. This is just to ensure that every transaction that happens in this period is accounted for rightly.

In summary, the Accrual principle here is saying that it does not matter whether cash has changed hands, what matters i the transaction has happened and this must be shown in the financial statements in the financial period in which they occur.

An example here is that the rent expense for the last month of the financial year is recorded even though it has not been paid yet. So, the company has incurred rent expenses and it must record this expense even though the money may not have been paid yet. What we mean by saying "regardless of cash movements" is that as long as it has been incurred or an income has been earned, even though you have not received the money, it must be accounted for and it must be recorded.

Matching principle

The income earned and the related expenses that you have incurred in a specific period must be accounted for in the exact same period and financial statements.

An example here is that the cost of sale is paid for in cash but the sale is only received in the following period. The sales and the cost of sales are accounted for in the same accounting period. What this example is saying here is that if you have paid for your cost of sales in cash and you've made the sales but you have not received that money yet it does not matter, you have to record the sales and its cost of sales in the same accounting period because you would not have incurred the cost of sales if you did not make the sale so the fact that you made the sale and you incurred the cost of sale, they must both be accounted for in the same accounting period. You cannot account for the cost of sales alone in this period and then you say that in the next period or account for the sales, you have to make sure that you apply the Matching principle where the income earned and the expenses incurred as a result of earning that income is accounted for in the exact same period.

Prudence principle

This principal center on cautiously exercising judgment. When financial statements are prepared and uncertain results estimated, one must be conservative in the estimation of values. This is exercising judgment cautiously in making decisions with whatever transaction that you're dealing with.

An example here is that the account of a debtor who is experiencing financial challenges is written off. Here, you are exercising judgment to say this data is not going to pay you so you have to write it off and consider it a bad debt or a credit loss.

Realization principle

Income must be recorded as soon as it has been earned and realized. Likewise, expenses must be recorded as soon as they have been incurred and realized.

This is very important because if it's an income it must be earned and realized. What do we mean by realized? Well, if someone has paid you money for products, you must have delivered those products to the customer and that's what we mean by realizing. Likewise, expenses must be recorded as soon as they have been incurred and if you have incurred an expense, it must also be realized. If you paid for a service to someone, they must have delivered that service to you hence incurring the expense.

An example is that an entry is made immediately in the books for an invoice received for goods purchased. So, if you received an invoice for goods that you have purchased and you have received those goods, then that entry must be made immediately in the books.

Materiality principle

This principle states that information that is likely to influence a user's decision must be disclosed separately otherwise they may be grouped together with amounts of a similar nature. Here, you are looking at whatever information you are dealing with and you are asking if it is likely to influence a user's decision when looking at these financial statements. if the answer is yes, then it must be disclosed separately.

An example is that for a small company like counters for instance if you are looking at an amount of 20,000 rands that was incurred as a result of an accident that happened and you had to pay out a third party. That amount is definitely material for a small company so you'll have to account for that and record it separately or disclose it separately. But if you're looking at a multinational company, let's say Microsoft for instance, 20,000 rands or 1500 dollars would definitely not be material for them so they do not have to record it separately, instead, they can group it up with other expenses such as general expenses.

An amount is a material depending on the size of an entity and here's an example: a significant fine incurred by an entity is disclosed separately in the financial statements; it cannot just be grouped with general expenses. So, if a company has incurred a significant fine (let's say 40% of its revenue for that period), then it would have to be disclosed separately because of how big the amount is and it cannot be grouped with others.

Economic/Business entity principle

Also known as the Business entity concept, this states that the transaction of an entity is kept separately and does not include the transactions of the entity's owners or any other entity.

Going concern principle

This is a principle that states that financial statements are prepared under the assumption that the entity will continue to exist into the foreseeable future and thus all its data is kept using the going concern value.

Challenges to the Accounting Profession

In this chapter, we're going to discuss some challenges that the accounting profession is facing and at the end of the chapter, we will share some tips on how to manage these challenges.

Talent Shortage

The first challenge is talent shortages. As may know, baby boomers (people who were born in the mid-1940s and the mid-1960s) are retiring and so the profession needs people.

Dealing with Changes in technology

The first thing about technology changes is that it is cloud-based technology. This means all files and applications are saved on a shared server instead of a private device. The second thing about technology change is the Paperless office (you may feel familiar with this). It means that all documents are now digitally kept safe instead of paper.

The next one is text automation. This may sound familiar to you as nowadays people normally use text software to fight test returns.

Next, we have interactive artificial intelligence. People may interact with AI but may not know about that. For example, if you visit a website you may interact with AI but you may not recognize that.

Lastly, you may have heard a lot about cryptocurrencies.

With all these changes in our society today, the best way to manage challenges is to accept and adapt to these changes. This means that you will need to advance yourself. The Accounting professions still need you to be in this career but at a higher level. It just makes accounting less boring because you don't have to manually enter all the numbers since, we have software that helps out with that.

The recommendation to you is to advance yourself, understand the report, and provide advice and analysis to the client. By doing that you provide valuable services to the client.

Review Questions

1. What is Accounting?
2. Mention 4 areas of accounting
3. Why is accounting important?
4. Mention and define 3 financial statements

5. List and explain 5 principles of accounting

CHAPTER 2
DOUBLE-ENTRY BOOKKEEPING EXPLAINED

As with any other language, the accounting system has its own. In accounting, for you to record a transaction you have to use the double-entry system. What does it mean? Accountants use a visual aid, called T-entry. Due to its shape, the T-entry has two sides: debit and credit.

How does this all work? For each account entry, it must correspond to an opposite entry so that books will balance. Remember, the accounting equation says that assets must always equal liability plus equity.

An account is a record, and debit and credit under each account have different meanings. In some cases, debit increases the account, in other cases, it decreases the account. Therefore, a one-step transaction in the real world becomes a double entry in the accounting world.

The Accounting Equation

The accounting equation means the resources in the business equals the resources supplied by the owner. The resources in the business refer to the things the business owns such as fixtures, fittings, and computers and the resources supplied by the owner refer to the resources (such as money, etc.) that the owner should put into the business.

Now let's look at some of the terminologies here.

The amount of resources supplied by the owner is referred to as **capital**. The actual resources that are in the business are called **assets**, so the fixtures and fittings are referred to as assets. That gives us our accounting equation and in our accounting equation, assets (the resources that are actually in the business) are equal to capital (resources supplied by the owner). Now we can expand this by including liabilities. Liabilities represent the amount owing to people other than the owner or owners concerning the supply of the assets.

Therefore, our accounting equation now becomes

Assets = capital + liabilities

It is an equation so it must balance. This means a few very important things: firstly, every time there is a transaction it must have an impact in two areas and after that, the accounting equation must still balance. In other words, if capital goes up assets will go up or if an asset goes up another asset might go down.

Assets have a future benefit so those are accounts like cash, office supplies, and equipment and you're going to sum up your assets to show how much assets you have. Liabilities are things that you owe to outsiders of the company, so accounts payable, notes payable, and debt to the bank falls under liabilities and since we only have one account in liabilities you don't need to do a total. Then for the Owner's equity section, you're going to go back to that number that you had for closing capital balance and enter that amount.

Now you'll take the total of liabilities and owner's equity and check if it matches the total assets. If these two matches, in that your total assets equal total liabilities and owner's equity, that means your balance sheet works.

Double-entry Principle

Now we're going to look at how this will be recorded into the double-entry bookkeeping system so we start by looking at the double-entry principle. The double entry principle is basically as follows: every business transaction has a two-fold aspect. Both sides of the transaction must be recorded. The double entry system has an account for every asset, every liability, and capital, and when we say it has an account, we mean it has a ledger account so the transactions are recorded in the ledger and the ledger has a range of accounts.

In a ledger account, which is called a T-account, you have the name of the account (the name could be a computer account, fixtures and fittings account, or capital account), the left-hand side is referred to as the debit side (on the debit side you have three columns, one column for the date, one column for the details of the transaction and one column for the financial amount) and the right-hand side is referred to as the credit side (we have the same three columns for date, the details and the financial the amount).

DEBIT side		LEDGER ACCOUNT			CREDIT side
Date	Details	Amount	Date	Details	Amount

This means under the transaction there are two things that you have to decide: firstly, what are the two accounts involved? This is because as you've already seen, there will be two ledger accounts involved. Then secondly, which ledger account will be the debit account? And by that, we mean the ledger account in which you put the transaction on the debit side. Always keep in mind that if you put the transaction on the debit side of one account, you must put the transaction on the credit side of the other account. So, you need to pick the two accounts, while you debit one, you credit the other.

The debit-credit rules

Usually, identifying which of the two accounts is relatively straightforward but deciding which one to debit and which one to credit can be tricky, so we're going to look at that now. To decide which account, you're going to debit and which account you're going to credit, we have a list of rules as shown in the image below.

	Debit	Credit
Asset	Increase	Decrease
Liability	Decrease	Increase
Income	Decrease	Increase
Expense	Increase	Decrease
Equity/Capital	Decrease	Increase

Looking at the image above, we're going to explain this a little further.

If you're looking at an account that is an asset account and you want to record an increase in that asset account, you will put the transaction on the debit side of that account.

In other words, on the left-hand side.

- If you're looking at an asset account and you want to record a reduction or decrease in that account, you will put the amount on the credit side of that account, which is the right-hand side.
- Liabilities and capital in terms of debit and credit operate the same way. For liabilities, if you want to record an increase in liability you will put the transaction on the credit side of the account. Likewise for capital. To record an increase in the capital you will put the transaction on the right-hand side, which is also the credit side.

27

- To record a decrease in liability you will put the transaction on the debit side of the liability account and if you want to record a decrease in a capital account you will also put the transaction on the debit side of the capital account.

In addition, in accounting, we have five main accounts called an asset, liability, income, expense, and equity. Each one of them has a set of rules. Asset and Expense accounts will increase when debited and decrease when credited. Liability, Income, and Equity will decrease when debited and increase when credited.

You must know these rules so try to learn them. A handy little rule for remembering double-entry is that you **debit the receiver** and **you credit the giver**. In other words, the account that receives the benefit for the transaction is recorded on the debit side and the account with which that benefit came from is recorded on the credit side.

For example, if you put money into a business bank account, the bank account receives the money, you debit the bank and you will credit wherever the money came from.

To explain some of these rules and to show how the system works, we're going to do a quick little example. In this example, Ken started a business on the 1st of March by putting 100,000 pounds in the business bank account. On the 2nd of March, he bought premises for 70,000 paying by check, and on the 3rd of March, he purchased goods with 12,000 on credit from Adrian. What we're required to do here is to enter the above transactions into Ken's ledger accounts, so, we'd go down to each one of these in turn.

Starting off March 1st, Ken started the business by putting 100,000 into the business bank account. To record this, we need two accounts: we need a bank account and a capital account.

Since the money is going into the business bank account, on the debit side of the bank account, we'll put in the date, the reference to the other account (which in this case is the capital account), and the amount of money. Since we are debiting the bank account, we will credit the capital account. So, we do the same thing for the capital account by putting the date, reference, and amount.

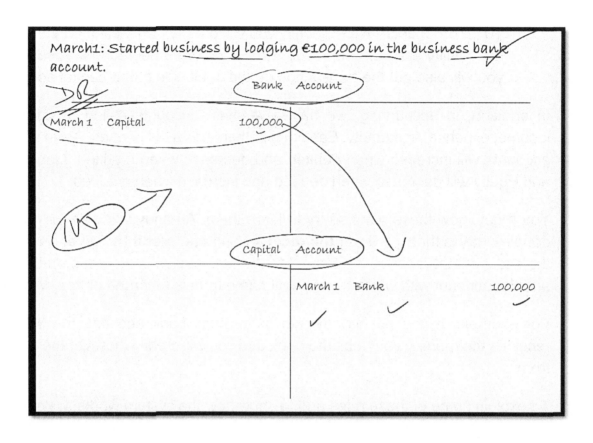

March1: Started business by lodging €100,000 in the business bank account.

Bank Account

March 1   Capital   100,000

Capital Account

March 1   Bank   100,000

Moving onto the second transaction, he bought premises for 70,000 and paid by check. We all know that a check implies a bank so we are going to use the bank account and since we have a new asset here which is "premises" we need to create a ledger account for Premises.

We already have the bank account and if you recall from earlier, you already have a transaction so we can proceed to create a Premises account. In this case, we're going to credit the bank because the money is going out with decreasing assets and because we're increasing the asset of Premises, we will debit the Premises account.

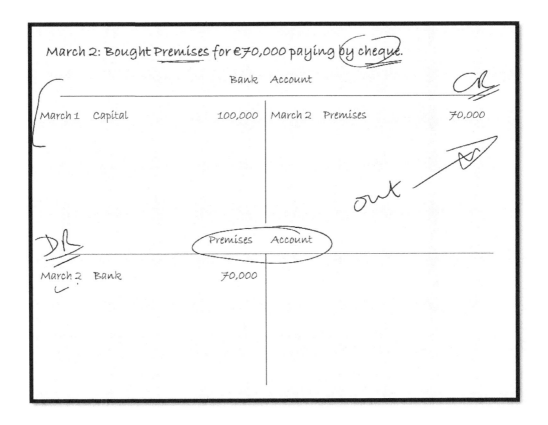

March 2: Bought Premises for €70,000 paying by cheque.

Bank Account | CR

March 1	Capital	100,000	March 2 Premises	70,000

out

DR | Premises Account

March 2	Bank	70,000

Lastly, he purchased goods costing 12,000 on credit from Adrian. Now what we need here is a Purchases account since there is a case of buying goods in an Adrian is going to be a creditor of the liability so we need two new ledger accounts here: The Purchase account and Adrian account.

The goods are coming in so what we will do is debit the Purchase account and of course, if we're debiting the Purchase account, we must be crediting the other account and that's because Adrian is a creditor, in other words, a liability.

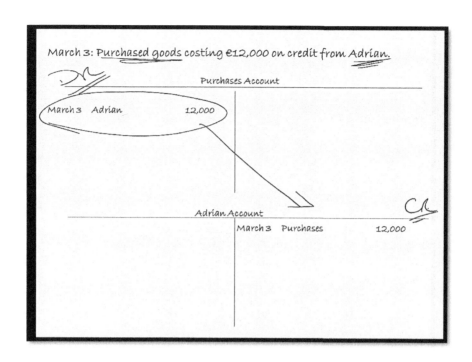

Now let's quickly summarize what we have discussed for better understanding.

- The T-account is a visual aid that helps to record double entries.
- A debit (Dr) represents an asset and a credit (CR) represents a liability or capital.
- If a transaction requires you to increase an asset account, you debit the asset account with the amount of the increase; to decrease an asset account you credit the asset account.
- If a transaction requires you to increase liabilities or the capital account, you credit the account with the amount of the increase; to decrease a liability or capital account, you debit the capital or liabilities account.
- Also remember: for every transaction, a debit will have a corresponding credit and vice versa.

Review Questions

1. Yesterday, you were at the restaurant and you ordered some food. You eventually paid your bill which was $100. How would this transaction look in the accounting world?

2.a) Your friend John just opened a clothing shop. He invested $100,000, so he is the only owner. What does this transaction look like in the accounting world?

31

b) Afterward, he had to pay $1000 for the first month's rent. Represent this transaction using the double-entry system.

c) Then, John had to pay $50,000 cash to furnish his store. What do you think this transaction would look like in the accounting world?

SECTION TWO
SETTING UP QUICKBOOKS

CHAPTER 3
SETTING UP QUICKBOOKS

Some of the steps you see will be the same basic QuickBooks setup steps to prepare a file for any type of company regardless. Please note that for the examples that would be used in this book, any other type of company would do these same steps plus any additional steps for that specific company type. For example, if we sold merchandise, you would do exactly what you see here plus the merchandise setup steps; if we had to collect sales tax, you would do exactly what you see here to begin setting up the file, and then you would add the extra steps to collect sales tax and so on.

What is QuickBooks?

QuickBooks is a small business accounting software. Its primary function is to simply compile your income and expenditure so that you can file the attachment and that's what the majority of small businesses do. However, QuickBooks does far more than primary necessary components; it also helps you manage your business.

QuickBooks deals with all things accounting, payroll, and bookkeeping. You can manage and pay bills, and you can accept payments, basically, QuickBooks is everything that you need to have your company's financials up and running and managed, and most importantly legal (because you don't ever want to know what the full wrath of the law is).

There are all kinds of offerings for pretty much any kind of small to medium-sized business that QuickBooks provides.

Why QuickBooks?

One of the biggest reasons that businesses fail is for a handful of things namely; mismanagement of funds or not understanding their cash flow meaning you may have a great product and even have a lot of demand but if you aren't managing properly where that money is going, how it's being spent, how it's being managed, what's going into labor taxes and all of that, if you can't look at your books and know exactly what your month-month is in costs versus revenue, you're in trouble. You can fix that definitely but that is some information that you should be able to access when you want it and QuickBooks is like the reigning champion of small and medium-sized businesses in taking care of their financials.

If you've got all those financial reports, those records, or documents that you need for your business, it can be a growing mess; this is where QuickBooks comes into the picture. QuickBooks comes along and it helps sort, organize and put all that information which is very important into one nice spot so you get all your nice little files here. What does it do with your finances? It allows you to look at all your purchases, and all your purchase orders starting from whenever you've kept your records for however long you want. For your sales, it keeps a record of what you've sold, what's popular, and most of all for your expenses, it also keeps a record of what you are spending and that's important to know so that you can cut out anything that will help with your revenue.

Your company may start out with you but as you expand you need to make sure that you're paying people on time and that you know who's doing what well. QuickBooks helps take care of that so you can monitor all those things, keep people happy and keep them paid. Whether you're having to downsize a little bit or hopefully expand because your business is growing QuickBooks grows with you and it allows for more users or space. QuickBooks makes sure that it has the capacity and the features that you want as your company continues to grow.

Downloading QuickBooks 2023

You can download the QuickBooks desktop 2023 software with Intuits (the official company of QuickBooks). At the end of the process, you want to download an installation software package which will then be installed to create the QuickBooks desktop 2023 software on your computer, that being the end objective. Remember that this software is not the data file but it's the software; it's similar to having Microsoft Word on the computer and then using Microsoft Word to open multiple different word documents. Once you have QuickBooks 2023 on the computer you can then use it to create multiple different company files.

There are three scenarios you might be in:

- You might not have the software at all and you might just try to be practicing with the software in which case you'll be looking to get the free 30-day trial download onto your system,

- or you might be purchasing the software for the first time in which case you'd have to go to the sales page for example to get access to the purchasing process and then download the software,
- or you may have purchased the software in a prior year remembering that the desktop version is now on a subscription basis so now that 2022 has passed, when you open up the software package it's usually going to be telling you that you have an update to the software and to update the software, you're going to have to go on to the Intuit website download the 2023 software and then just update your data file to the 2023 version.

Let's go over these three scenarios quickly and see what the differences are between them.

Downloading the Free-trial Version

First, let's say you don't have the software at all and you would like to download the free trial version to practice with along with this book. In that instance, instead of going to the Intuit site which is the owner of QuickBooks, it's easier to just go to a search page on your favorite browser such as Google and type in something like "**QuickBooks desktop free trial**" making sure that you're noting the desktop version as opposed to the online version and then searching for the free trial version. When this opens up, ensure that you're at the **quickbooks.intuit** website as that is the correct one and then you could go through the download process.

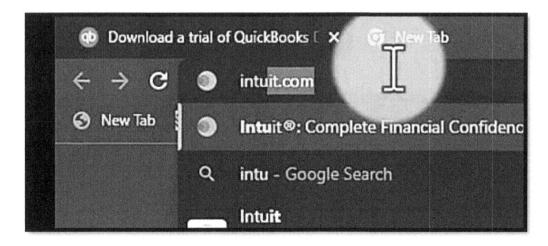

Notice that we have the QuickBooks Enterprise trial install file. You can't use the Enterprise version which is more of a level up than the version you'll be using because all of the things that you'll do will be at the lower version and you'll have a kind of software that can do that and more so that should be good.

> ## Download a 30-day trial of QuickBooks Desktop
>
> - QuickBooks Enterprise trial install file.
> - QuickBooks Desktop for Mac trial install file.
>
> Go ahead and purchase QuickBooks Pro and Premier Plus with our 60-day money back g
>
> Before you start, make sure your computer meets minimum requirements to install Quick
> Enterprise 22.0 or QuickBooks Desktop for Mac Plus 2022.
>
> Save the trial install file somewhere you can easily find it. You don't need any codes to op

If you download this installation, you're going to get an installation file that you're going to have to then open up and run on your desktop at which point you'll then end up with the actual software on your computer and you'll be ready to then open up another file within. So that's option number one.

QuickBook...

Updating to QuickBooks 2023

In this scenario, you already have the software and, in most cases, the 2022 software but when you open it, you might get a message that says something like this "**there's a new QuickBooks software update waiting for you**" and then you can go to the "**Install now**" option which will walk you through the installation process and which should still get you to the point where you go to download the software and you'll have another piece of software here which will be the 2023 version.

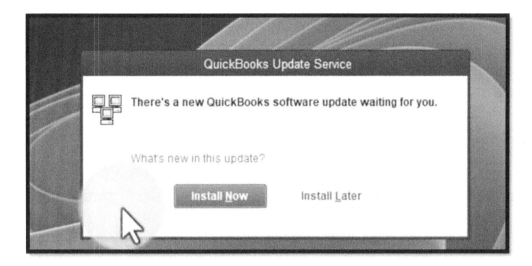

Then all you have to do is then open your data file in the 2023 version, like a Word document updating from an older version to a newer version, the data file will then hopefully update without any problems.

No matter which way you do it, the goal is to get the software on the computer then you can open up multiple data files with it and practice or work with it.

Buying the Software

The last option is that you're buying the software. Now if you're buying the software then you want to make sure that you're buying it for yourself (know you're going to be using the software for your purposes) but note that you can open up multiple Company files if you have the software. So, if you already have the software downloaded or if you're buying the software, you could still work through the practice problems in this book because the beauty of the desktop version is that you can open up multiple Company files with one download of the software.

The easiest way to get here would be to go to the owner of QuickBooks which is **intuit.com** and then go to QuickBooks. This way you're sure that you're at the Intuit website.

Now in the QuickBooks website within Intuit, you'll have to go all the way to the bottom to look at all the products and then you're going to make sure that you select the QuickBooks desktop.

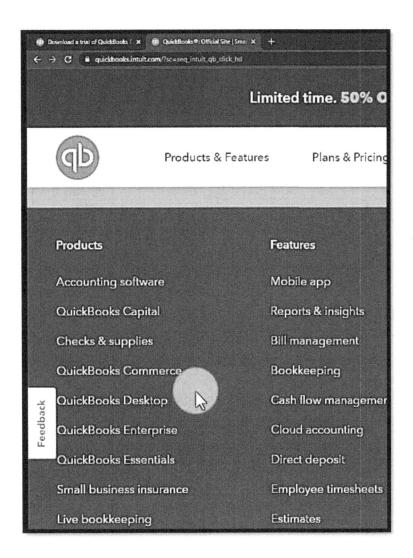

At this point, you select the version that you think would work best for you and if you purchase from the website then again, you'll go through the purchasing process after which you'll have to download the software which will be an installation software. Then once you install it you will once again get to your software on your computer.

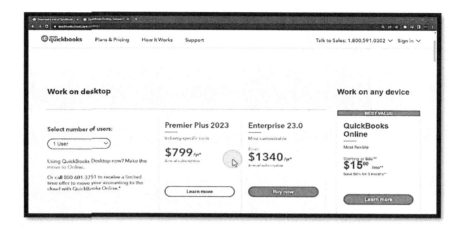

Install QuickBooks Desktop 2023

After downloading the QuickBooks Desktop from Intuit which is the owner of the QuickBooks website, you now have the Installation icon on the left-hand side. If you double-click on it and run it, this will result in the software with the QuickBooks icon appearing on your computer.

Running the installation wizard

If you double-click on the installation wizard it opens up the InstallShield welcome page. Once again, you might be using the Enterprise but if you're using the free software that will still be the desktop version of the software and you'll have everything that we're going to be using on it.

To continue, you go "**Next**" and then of course it's going to give you a little waiting screen.

41

The contents of this package are being extracted.

Please wait while the InstallShield Wizard extracts the files needed to install QuickBooks Financial Software PRO Plus Series 2023 R1 on your computer. This may take a few moments.

After that, you'll get a welcome screen asking you to complete your QuickBooks installation with just a few steps.

QuickBooks is a fairly large program so you want to make sure that you've got enough space on the computer to be able to handle QuickBooks. For smooth installation, it's a good idea to close any open programs with specialty virus protection programs. You might be able to still install it without closing your virus protection program but obviously if you have any problems with it that might be one of the things that's causing the problem.

Once the installer is done loading, accept the license agreement to continue then you've got to enter your license and product numbers.

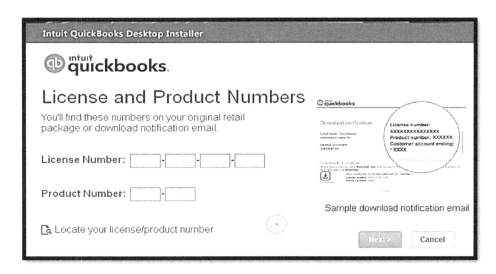

There are three ways that you might have gotten the software: you might have used the free version of the software in which case hopefully, they're going to give you the code for this or bypass the screen to needing those codes, you might be buying the software (if you buy the software it will give you these license codes within the purchasing process and you have to write them down or save them in some way so that you can enter them when you install them) or you can go into your account and within your account, you can find these two numbers (if you have the prior version 2022 and now you're renewing it, in that case, you could go to the account if you don't have the numbers still and you should be able to find these license numbers to be plugged in here).

Next, you've got the option to choose your installation type. "**Express**" which is the recommended option is the installation type that replaces the current version. Oftentimes, that's probably what most people want to do. You probably don't want the 2022 version still on your computer as that could save some space on the computer and will lead to less confusion then when you open up your data files they will automatically be updated.

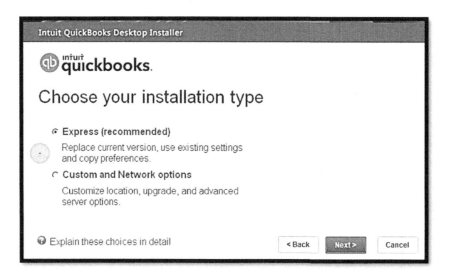

Keep in mind that you cannot go from a 2023 backup file for example to be opened in 2022. So, if you work with multiple companies as a bookkeeper, then you might still want the prior software 2022 on the computer so that you can share files possibly with people using an older version of the software. However, 2022 was the year they went subscription so anybody that bought 2022 and forward would have the latest version because all they have to do is update it but some people could still have older versions like that 2021 which was the last year that you could have a single purchase and not have a subscription so you might have people that still have those older versions of the software and if you're sharing data with them be aware of that. You've got the "**Custom and Network options**" for customized location upgrades and advanced server options. So, if you're just putting this onto your individual computer "**Express**" is the easier way to go. If you're working in a larger business or with multiple partners like multiple bookkeepers and you have servers involved then you have to consult your IT professional to help you out with that.

After selecting your installation type it's going to give you the "**Ready to Install**" page with one last check of the QuickBooks version and a recap of your license and your products (it tells you where the location is mapping it on your computer so if there are any problems with it that's where it's going to be).

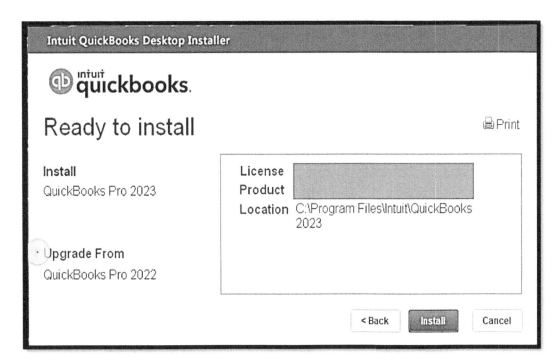

Then it's going to bring you to the QuickBooks desktop welcome page. The installation does take some time because again it's a fairly large program QuickBooks is so it gives you the little intro screen to organize and track your business finances as it uploads the process and then once it's done you should end up with the software on your computer.

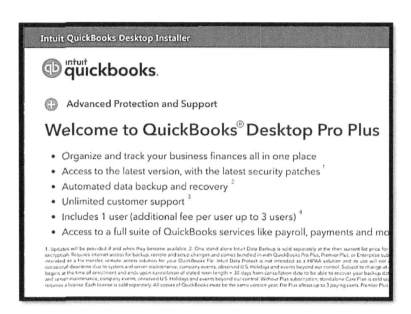

Now the 2023 software you'll see here is like having the Word software rather than the Word documents. As you can open up multiple Word documents for example with one Microsoft Word program, a similar thing works for QuickBooks; you can open up multiple company files with the one QuickBooks program.

Now if you're buying it just for the one company that you are working with, you will then have the company files that you typically open when you open up QuickBooks and it'll try to open that company file just like when you open the word document and it will then ask you to update that company file to the latest version that you have now installed in this case the 2023 version.

You have to make sure that you have an understanding of this installation and software. This is the actual software equivalent to Microsoft Word for example, and then we'll have other actual files that we will be opening similar to document files for Word. These will be the data files, the bookkeeping files, or the actual company files and then we'll also think about the backup files or zipped files that can be used to restore and so you've got to keep those things straight. You should also try to know where those different things are located (we saw the location of this actual file here when we went through the installation process). You also want to know the location of your data file and your backup files.

Creating and managing a QuickBooks company file

You may well ask, what is a company file? Well, a company file is in your computer and it is a data file in the computer that is represented by an icon just like a Microsoft Word document, an Excel file, or any other file that you can copy to a USB stick or send as an email attachment.

You have to know that all of your company's financial information is inside that one file that you can send as an attachment or copy to a USB stick. You have to keep it safe and make sure that it's easy to copy anywhere so you don't lose your accounting information.

When you go to physically create the file just answer the questions exactly as we do here or follow step by step and the answers that we give to the questions when we go to set up the file will be the simplest and the quickest so that you can get through the setup steps the easiest way and understand the most.

QuickBooks Setup

Here we are in QuickBooks with no company file open and just like any other software we go all the way to the top left and click the File menu and the very first choice in most of the common and popular software is File "**New Company**" and now here's where the answers to the questions come in.

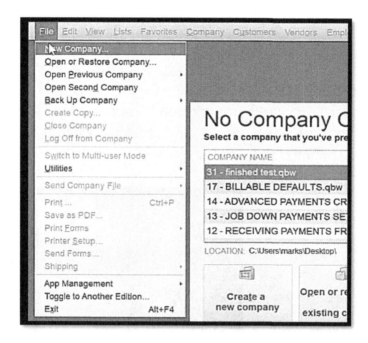

First, you have to tell QuickBooks that you're doing this for yourself and then you click "**Start setup**".

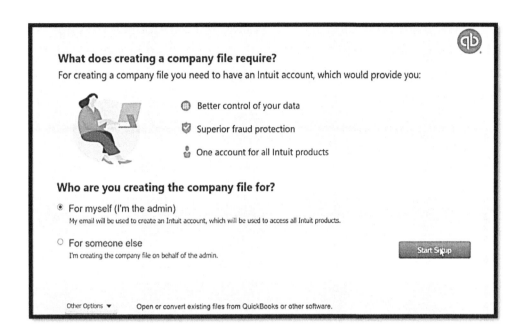

Now it's asking you to sign in to your Intuit account but you can come down here to the bottom left and click "**Sign in later**" when we click sign in later, the good option is seven days so it doesn't annoy you to sign in for a while. Click "**OK**" and this brings up a new window. Here, you are in the company information window.

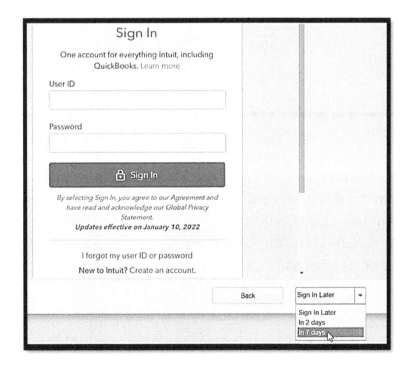

Notice, there are only four mandatory fields of information and normally you would put the company's name and address in these sections, however, we're going to skip the bottom part so you can see how to come back and change the company name and address anytime you need.

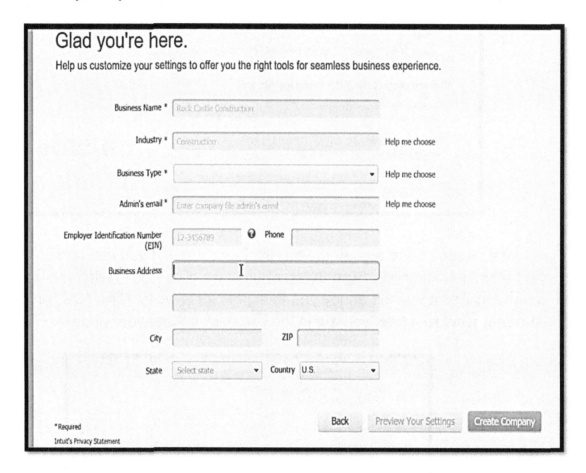

So now you can put in the four minimum pieces of information to make it the simplest setup that you can have. As far as industry type, you can click "**Help me choose**" and because we are doing an illustration, we're trying to do the quickest and easiest setup so we will not let QuickBooks put in a Chart of accounts for us. Instead, we will scroll to the bottom here and click "**Other/None**". This is because we want to show you how to put your chart of accounts so that you can learn it properly and understand it. So, after we click "**Other/None**" we click "**OK**".

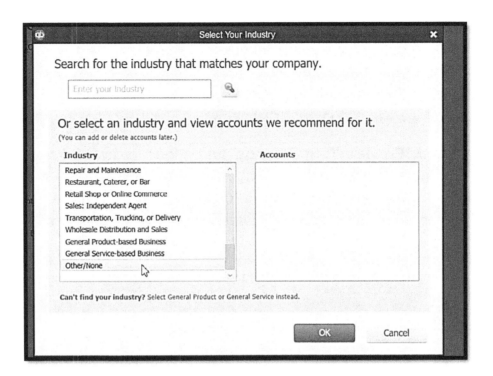

The same thing applies to your business type, you click "**Help me choose**" and then at the bottom to keep things as simple and clear as possible at the very beginning of Learning QuickBooks, you click "**Other/None**" and click "OK".

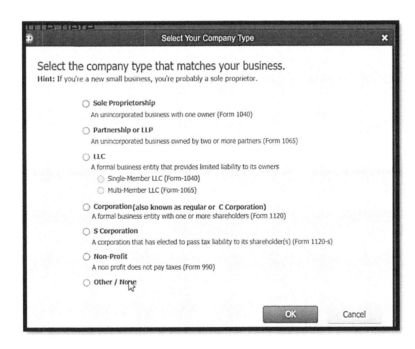

As far as an email address, you just have to put in any kind of valid email address that it will let you put, and then it will let you move on to the next piece. Now you have put the minimum information necessary to be able to create the file. Please note you must always click "Preview settings" before you save your file so that you can choose the location of the file, and in our example, we will make it easy by choosing the desktop.

So, we click "**Preview Your Settings**" and in the preview window we click "**Company file location**". QuickBooks remembers that the last file you created was on your desktop but you can click "**Change location**" and choose the location of the file so that you don't have to search for it later by name by using your search tool inside your windows.

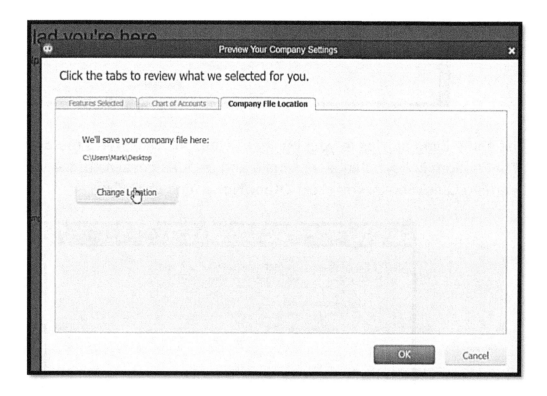

Now you know where it is once you create it and when you click "**OK**" and then click "**Create Company**". Now your company file is being physically created and placed on the desktop.

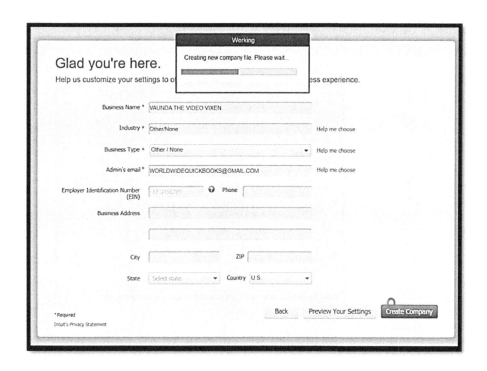

Once it gets created you can click the "**Start Working**" button and you'll be able to navigate around your new file.

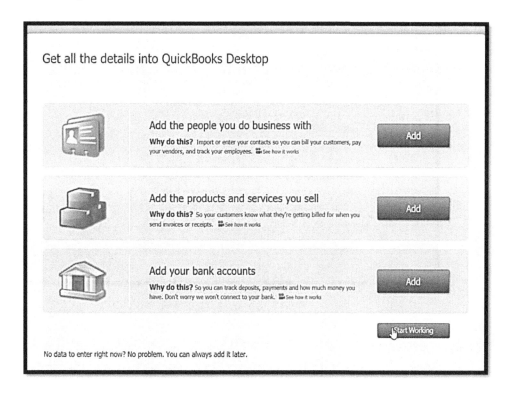

The image below shows the way your file should look on your desktop if it's outside any folder and just sitting on the desktop for the location that you just chose.

However, if you click on the file and drag it into a folder when you open that folder what you would see is that that file with the same name has then become two other files.

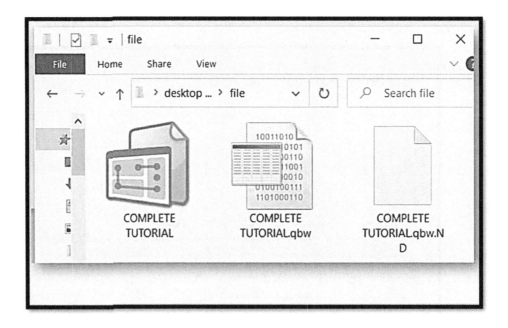

Why is that? That's because, from the computer's point of view, one QuickBooks file is physically several files but you don't have to worry, when you look at this in a folder, only the green ".qvw" file is the one that counts and that's the only one you have to click on if you want to copy it to a USB stick or copy it over the Internet or send it as an attachment. These other two files get automatically created every time the green file moves to a different location so you can just ignore and disregard them because when you move the green file, the computer will copy them over anyway.

Managing your company file

The last part of setting up your file physically is making sure you have the correct name and address in the "My Company" window. Let's say you already put in the proper name but did not put the proper address, now you have to put the name and address together so that they will show up properly on all the reports that you print and all the documents that you create when you record transactions and it's very simple to do that. From the main menu click "**Company**", and "**My Company**" and this opens up a new window. This is the "**My Company**" window.

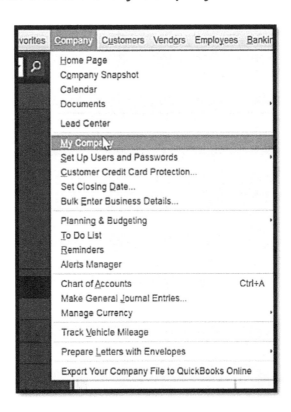

You may notice that it does not have an address or any of the other details because we skipped over that when we set up the file but we can put that in right now. If you click the pencil tool you see how to manage the company information.

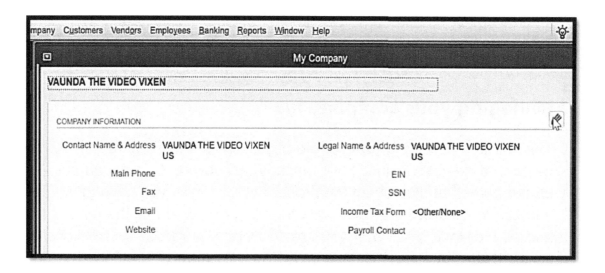

In the company information window, there are different sections that you can explore and experiment with but right now the contact information is the most important thing; let's make sure we put an address so that it will show up on reports and documents. And of course, you would normally put a phone number and so forth but if you just click **OK** and then click "**Yes**", you are then asked to confirm that that is your legal address.

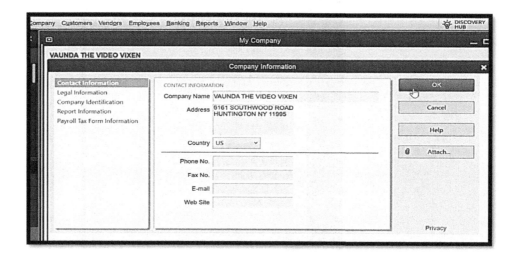

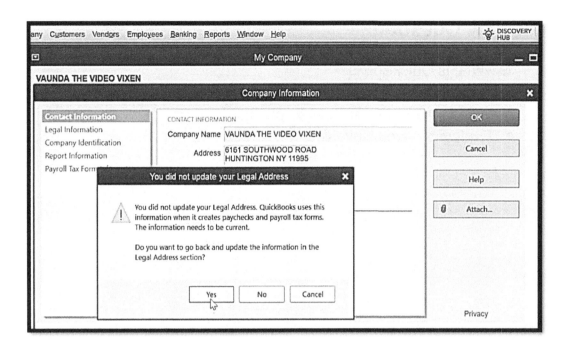

Then you click **OK** and your official address has changed. You can change this anytime your company moves or needs to print a different address on its documents and reports.

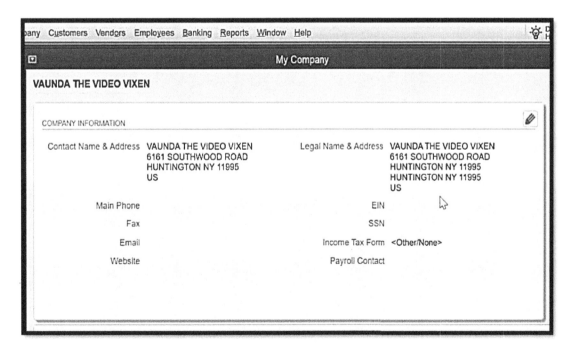

Review Questions

1. What is QuickBooks?
2. Why is QuickBooks important?
3. Who is the owner of QuickBooks?
4. Explain the steps involved in downloading QuickBooks

CHAPTER 4

PREFERENCES

Before you get started with entering and managing transactions in QuickBooks, you have to fine-tune your QuickBooks to carry out these processes with ease and Preferences is a way to do that. What are the preferences and how do you set the preferences? We will cover all that in this chapter.

What are Preferences?

Before we begin, you may be wondering what we mean by Preferences. They are the settings, the defaults, or the options. In other words, they are the automatic behavior of the software until you specifically tell the QuickBooks file to behave differently and they also tell you what features are available. You will learn how to navigate this Preferences window.

Locating your Preferences

From the main menu, click "**Edit**", and "**Preferences**" and the Preferences window opens up.

You'll notice that when you click anywhere in the left panel you change the category of Preferences. You may also notice that each category that you click has two sections: a "**My Preferences**" section and a "**Company Preferences**" section.

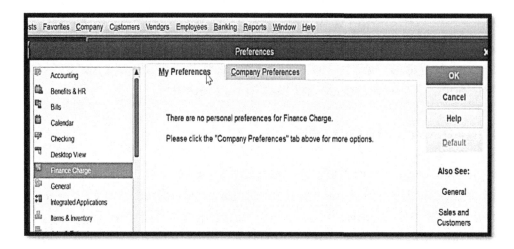

My Preferences

The "My Preferences" section is for things that help you make QuickBooks more convenient and that's just convenient for the user so what might be more convenient for you might not be more convenient for a different user, so they can set those personal preferences differently when they sit down to use QuickBooks.

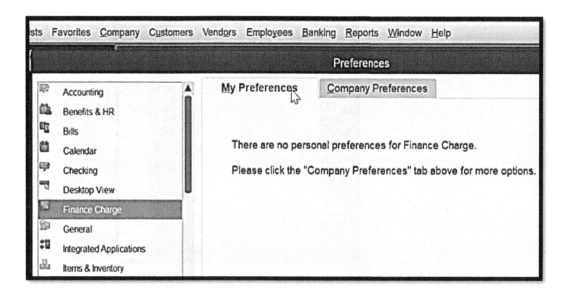

Company Preferences

The Company Preferences section controls how the file records transactions when doing business. That's the difference between this and the other section and we're going to do an example of each one.

Carrying out some preferential settings

First, let's learn some personal preferences. If you want to turn off all the pop-up messages for QuickBooks paid Services, well, that's very simple. You go to "**Edit**", and "**Preferences**", then click the "**General**" category.

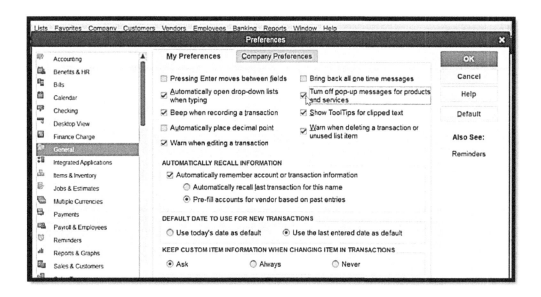

In the General category make sure you select "**My Preferences**". The checkmark is right here "Turn off pop-up messages for products and services" and by clicking to put the check mark in there, then click OK to make sure QuickBooks makes the change. Now you will not be distracted by commercials from the QuickBooks company as you do your business. Secondly, if you want to make sure that it auto refreshes the reports so you don't have to close and reopen reports if you added transactions, again, go to "**Edit**", "**Preferences**" and select the category of "**Reports & Graphs**" and again in the "My Preferences" tab you want the computer to "**Refresh the reports automatically**" so you don't have to reopen a report to get new numbers after transactions are recorded. Click OK and that preference has changed.

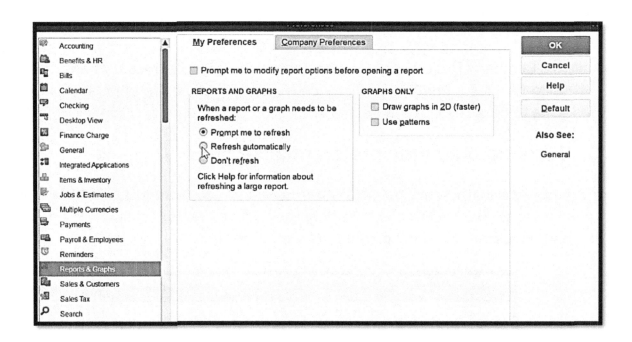

If you don't want QuickBooks to save the windows that were open from the previous session; some people do want it but you may not want it. To make sure the computer does not do that you click "Edit", and "Preferences", then you click the category of "**Desktop View**" and then click "**Don't save the desktop**".

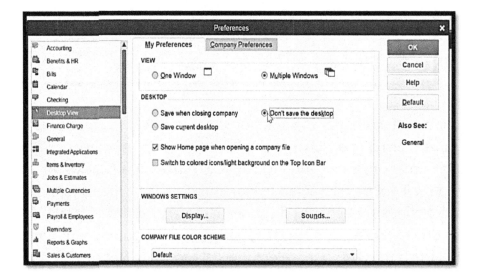

Also, if you don't want QuickBooks to pop up the home page every time you open the file that would be very distracting, in this very same window there's a right setting which is "**Show Home page when opening a company file**". You will click on the check mark to remove it.

61

So, it says "Don't save the desktop" and removes the check mark that says "show homepage when opening a company file" and then when you click OK you will no longer be distracted by the homepage that is always in front of you especially if you're not going to use that.

Now let's try changing some Company preferences so you can see how that would affect the QuickBooks file.

You can turn off the date warning for pop-ups for transactions you record on past or future dates that are extreme. In other words, QuickBooks constantly warns us that the transaction we're recording is more than 90 days in the past or more than 30 days in the future. So, you click "**Edit**", and "**Preferences**" and click the "**Accounting**" category of Preferences. Now you're changing a Company preference so under that category, remove these warning check marks because if you leave these check marks you will constantly get pop-up warnings every time you put in the sample transactions because the sample transactions are dated more than 90 days in the past and for some people or more than 30 days in the future so to make sure you save these preferences, we click OK.

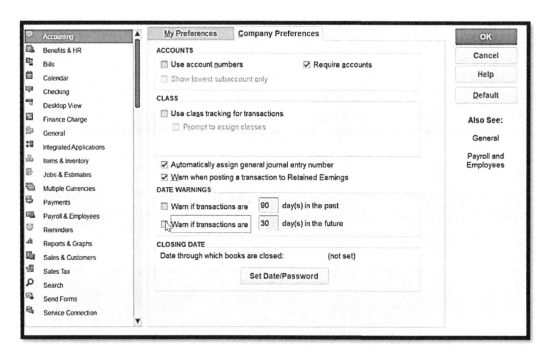

If you want to allow this file to record deposits when customers pay the money directly into the bank account, we will explain more about this in the banking section later, but believe it or not, the QuickBooks file is set up by default to not let you record receiving money from customers directly into the bank account. To fix that go to "Edit", and "Preferences" and in the category of "Payments" click the company preference and you remove the check mark that says "**Use undeposited funds as a default deposit to account**". We will not use this feature on deposited funds until much later in this book when we get to the banking section but by removing this check mark, QuickBooks will allow you to record transactions directly into the bank account. Click OK and congratulations you've set the preferences for your QuickBooks company file.

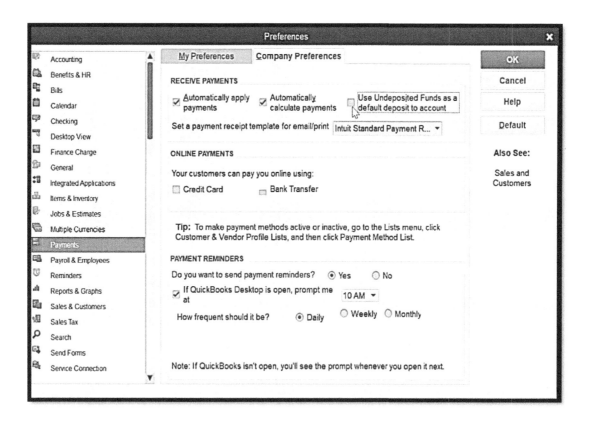

Review Questions

1. What are Preferences?
2. Where can you find Preferences?
3. What are the areas of Preferences?
4. What is the difference between "My Preferences" and "Company Preferences"?

CHAPTER 5

INPUT AND MANAGE THE QUICKBOOKS DESKTOP CHART OF ACCOUNTS

In the days before the computer, the Chart of Accounts was called General Ledger. It was simply a book where each page in the book represented a different account and an account was simply a category of transactions and you would categorize your transactions by recording them into the proper account on the proper page. For example, page one might be called Video Income, and every time you earned money from a Video service you would record that line by line on page one but if you also offered an editing service you might record each transaction with editing on page two and you would have an entire book of these pages to record everything you need to record for your transaction categories. Page six might be for Delivery Expense and every time you paid UPS or FedEx for delivery, you would record it in the Delivery Expense account page so that you could get the total and find out how much you paid for delivery regardless of who you paid. The image below is an example of what a company's Chart of Accounts looks like and these are the accounts we're going to put into QuickBooks desktop. You may notice that you have to put the account name and with the name, you also have to put an account type.

VAUNDA'S CHART OF ACCOUNTS

NAME	TYPE
CASH IN BANK	BANK
ACCOUNTS RECEIVABLE	ACCOUNTS RECEIVABLE
SUPPLIES	OTHER CURRENT ASSET
EQUIPMENT	FIXED ASSET
ACCOUNTS PAYABLE	ACCOUNTS PAYABLE
VIDEO INCOME	INCOME
EDITING INCOME	INCOME
DELIVERY EXPENSE	EXPENSE
ELECTRIC EXPENSE	EXPENSE
REPAIR EXPENSE	EXPENSE
TELEPHONE EXPENSE	EXPENSE

The account name is self-explanatory, you could name your accounts anything you want, however, what you type in when you name the account is exactly what will show on the financial statements so be careful how you spell them. Account type is something different; it doesn't matter what the account name is, the type of the account determines what kind of transactions can be recorded into it and it determines where it appears on the financial statements. For example, if you make one Bank type of account, it does not matter the name that you give, it matters that when you go to record a check that will be the account that the check gets recorded into no matter what name you give because it's the only account that is a bank type of account. It's the same thing with Accounts Payable; if you only have one Accounts Payable type of account, this account is where all the vendors' bills will be recorded and it does not matter what you name the account so when you first open the Chart of Accounts you should see only these four accounts because when we created the file, we told QuickBooks that we do not want a sample Chart of Accounts; we want to put the accounts ourselves.

Opening Chart of Accounts

To open the Chart of Accounts, click "List", and "Chart of Accounts", then you can see four accounts.

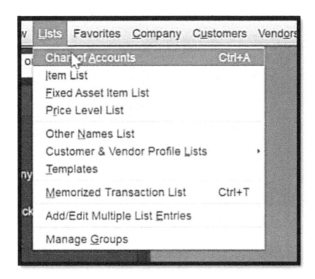

Now the two are in the middle we will use but for the two payroll-related accounts we will not and if we try to delete them QuickBooks won't let us. You want to conserve those two accounts in the middle because you will be using these or at least QuickBooks needs these.

66

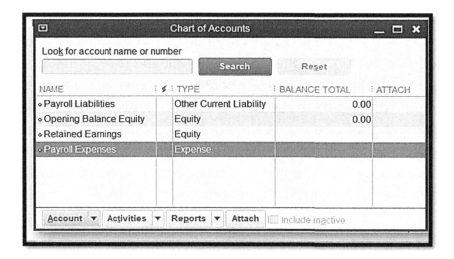

Getting Rid of an account

The bottom left button of the window controls the window and if you click "**Delete Account**," you'll get a message notifying you that you cannot complete that action so how do you remove the unwanted accounts if you can't delete them?

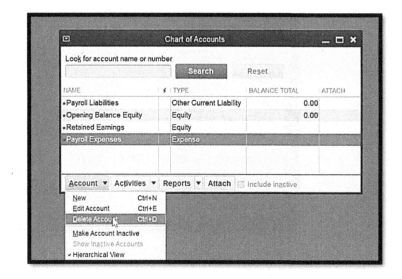

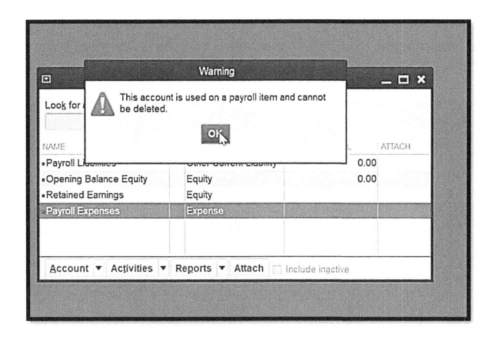

You do something called "**Make inactive**" which is the same thing as clicking on it and clicking delete and the only difference is you can always see the inactive accounts if you "**Include Inactive**".

So, for these accounts, what you can do is right-click and instead of clicking "**Delete**" you can click "**Make Account Inactive**" and you'll notice it disappears from the list.

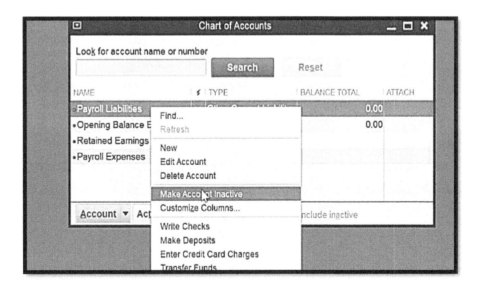

Right-click on the other payroll-related account, make it inactive and now it won't clutter up the list but then, if you click "**Include Inactive**", you can see that the ones with the X next to each other are inactive and if you want, you could right-click and make them active again so that when you remove the check mark they stay on the list.

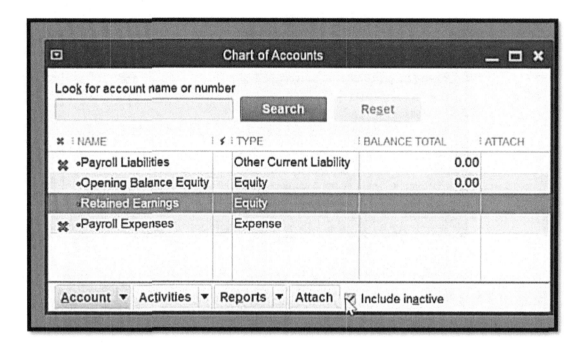

That's simply a way of getting rid of an account if QuickBooks does not let you delete the account. You will not be allowed to delete accounts that QuickBooks uses behind the scenes and you will not be able to delete accounts that already have transactions recorded in them; you would have to delete the transactions that are in the account before QuickBooks let you delete the account itself.

Adding a new account

Now it's just a question of data entry; Cash in Bank is a bank type of account. You click "**Account**", and "**New**" and the first one that you put in the New Account window comes up right here.

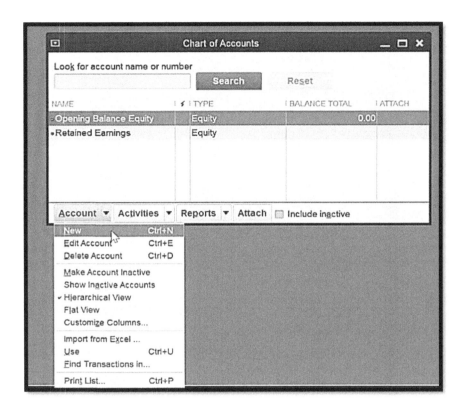

This window only shows up when you put in the first one and to put in several consecutively there's a different window but the first one is a Bank type of account, so you click on that checkbox and click "**Continue**".

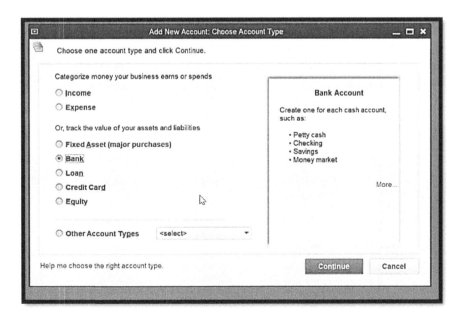

You now get the new account window and the new account window is the place that you stay until all the accounts are put in consecutively. If you close it and reopen it you would get that first window again. You can put in cap locks to make sure that you can see the difference between the accounts that you put in and the accounts that QuickBooks put in. For this illustration, "**CASH IN BANK**" is the name of the account that we just added.

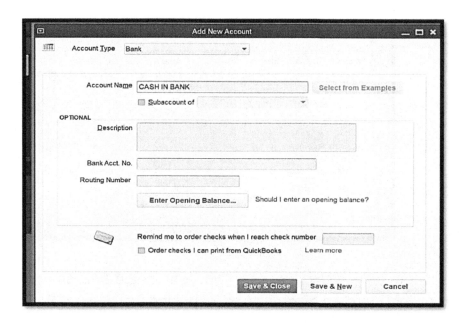

Now when we click "**Save & Close**", you can see that the name and the type have been put on the list.

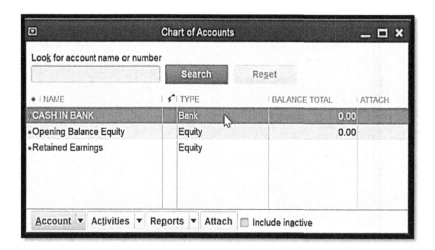

You don't have to do that every time because you keep getting back to this window; so, you can select the "**Account Receivable**" type of account, click "**Continue**" and that's both the name and the type in the second account on the list we are working with.

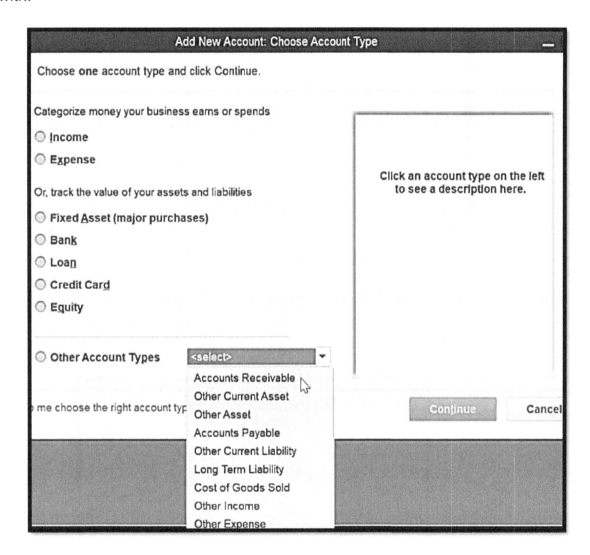

We will explain more about what Account Receivable is when we get to the customer section but this time you only click "**Save & New**" and that keeps the window open and it saves time.

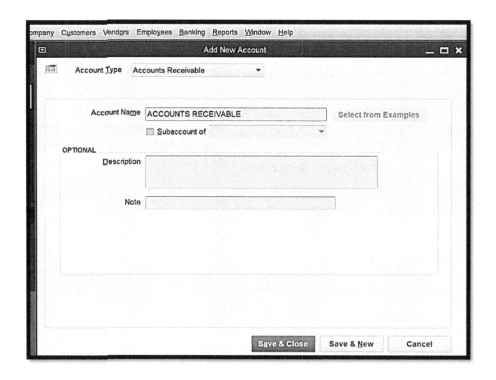

"**Other Current Assets**" and "**Supplies**" is the third one down on this list. So, you click the Account Type drop-down, select "**Other Current Asset**", enter the account name as "**SUPPLIES**" and then click "Save & New."

Equipment is a fixed asset. So, we choose "**Fixed Asset**" under the account type and type in "**EQUIPMENT**", then "**Save & New**".

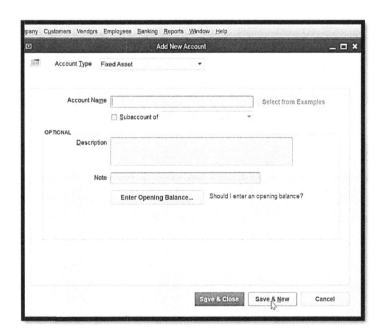

Accounts Payable is both the name and the type and of course, we will be explaining this more when we get to the vendors and accounts payable section. If you simply slide this down you can see that they are all being added to the Chart of Accounts and the ones in the capital are the ones that we added.

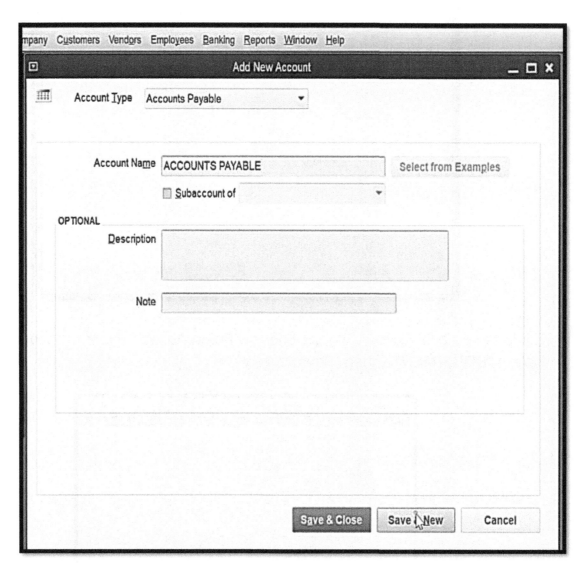

The income accounts are saved under the "**Income**" type of accounts and accounts such as delivery expense and other expenses fall under the "**Expense**" account type.

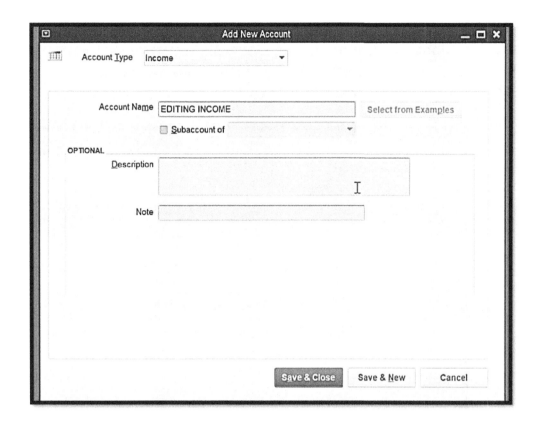

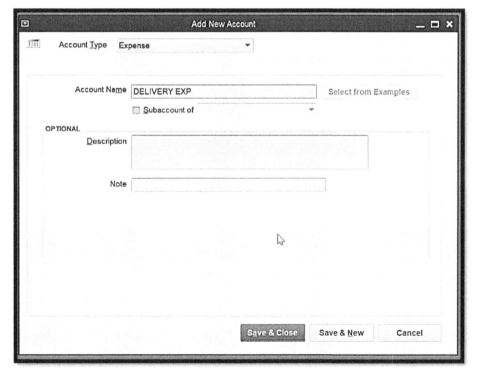

76

You can put the rest as it applies to your company and congratulations if you click "**Save & Close**," it reveals the full Chart of Accounts, and your Chart of Accounts should look similar to what you have in the image below and these are the accounts that we will use for the rest of this book.

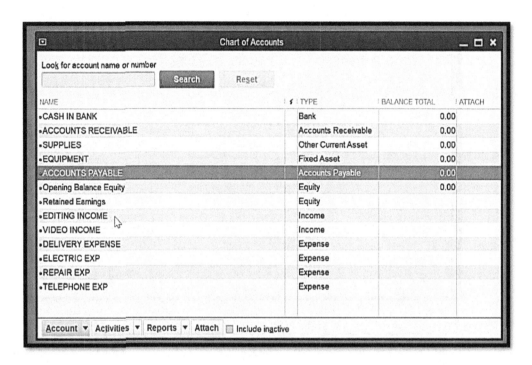

Input and manage customer information

We all know that customers are the ones who pay us for the services or products that we deliver and vendors are people or organizations whom we must pay for the products and services we need to service the customers. You need to have data on both however, QuickBooks gives you something like a little magic Rolodex that makes managing your customer and vendor data as easy as it could be.

Both customer and vendor data are managed in respective windows. The window that manages the customer data is called the Customer Center and the window that manages the vendor data is called the Vendor Center. They are both the same thing; they look the same way and they have the same functionality for both.

In the Customer Center, you can change and add the name and address of the customer, you can add notes about that customer and you can see all transactions organized in the way that you like them and add other functions as you get more advanced when using QuickBooks desktop. The vendor Center presents and makes available those same features when managing vendor data.

Customer Center

Let's just focus for now on the Customer Center and let's see what you can do with your current customers as you input their names and address. For example, we have three customers and the image below shows their names and addresses. Let's see how to record them on QuickBooks desktop.

To get to the Customer Center, click "**Customers**" from the main menu and the very first choice in the drop-down is the **Customer Center**.

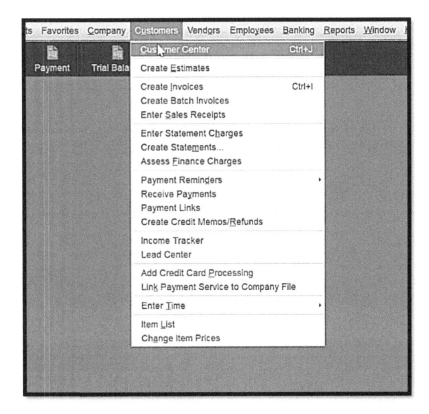

This is the section where you add the customer and see the customers on the list and when you choose a different customer from the list, you'll see all the information here. It's very simple to add a customer. If you click "**New Customer & Job**" and then click

"**New Customer**", you see the New Customer window open up for you to be able to put in the customer information.

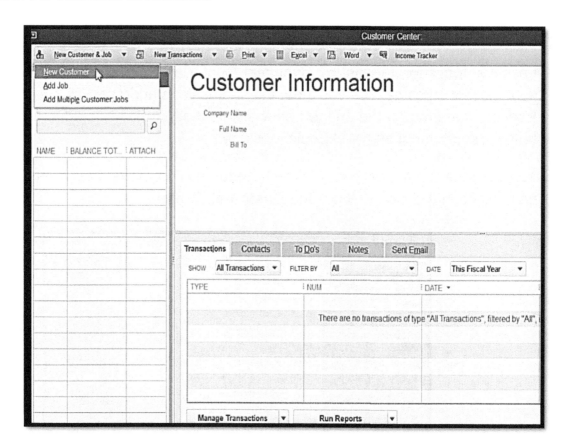

You'll see the field of customer name and you'll see that of a company name. Customer name can sometimes be a number that you identify the customer with and whatever you put here is what will print on whatever reports or whatever documents or statements you send them but you can also make it the same thing as the Company name. So, we type in the name of the customer and of course, the field for his address is down here; you can type it in or you could copy and paste it in.

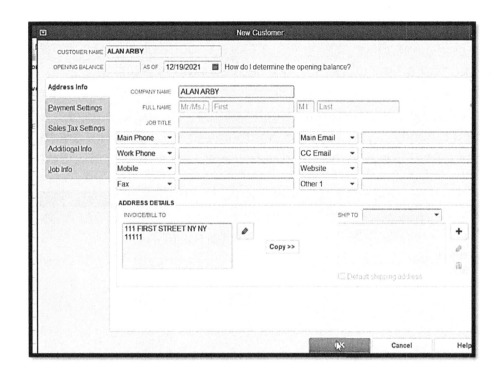

Now before you save this, you'll notice that there are five different tabs in the New Customer window. As you become more advanced in QuickBooks, you'll be utilizing these features but for now, you'll stick with address info and type in the address info accordingly. In some cases, you can put in the company name as the same name and after you click OK, you'll notice the customer has been added to the list.

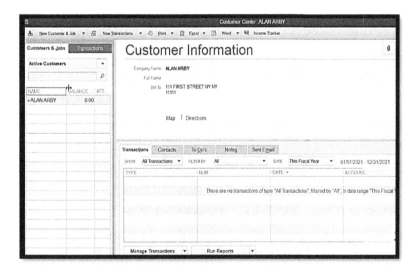

You can add another customer by going to **"New customer"**, entering the name (you can also type in the same name in the company name field), and entering the address.

Once again, please note that we're not using any of the other fields of data for now but you will use them as you learn more about QuickBooks. Now when you click OK after adding a new customer, notice the name is highlighted, so if the customer had prior transactions they will be listed here, the same thing happens if you click on another customer, his transactions would come up here as well. Also, if you click on the first customer, you'll see his address and if you click on another, you'll also get to see his/her address as well and you would see anything else that went on with them.

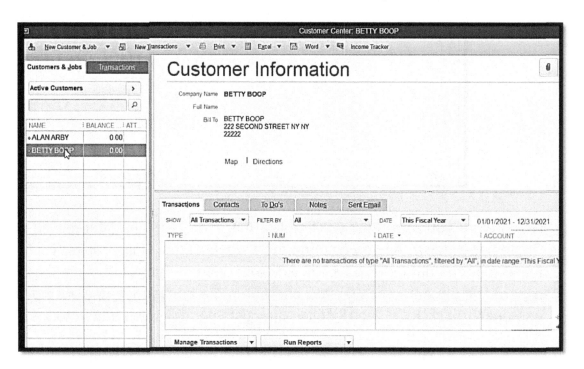

One thing that you should take advantage of from the beginning is being able to add **Customer Notes**. This is something important that you write down that doesn't have a specific field. For example, if you want to remember that one of your clients is allergic to peanuts so you don't kill them by showing up with a bag of peanuts during lunch, what you would do is you would click on that customer, click "**Notes**" and then down here you would click "**Manage notes**", "**Add new**" and then you just put "allergic to peanuts" or whatever you want to do but notice you can add date and time, stamp the note and then you can add it to the to-do list to remind you or whatever features you'd like to use. Click OK and there you have the notes.

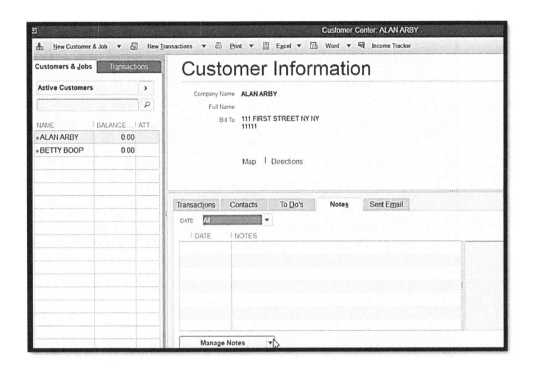

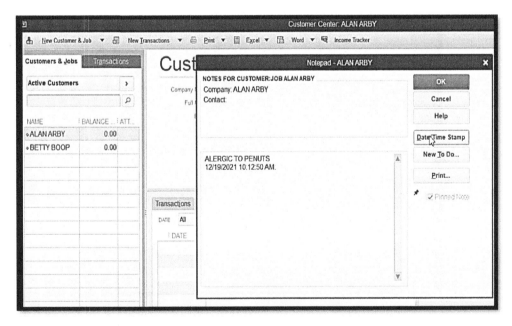

If you click for another customer, you see no notes but if you click for that particular customer and you choose the notes tab you can see all the notes that you might have made to make sure you're following up with any issue for that customer.

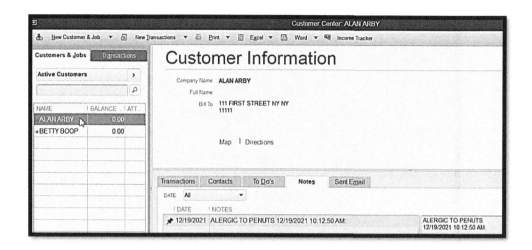

You can add as many customers as you want, including specific details about them and you'll see all of that on the list.

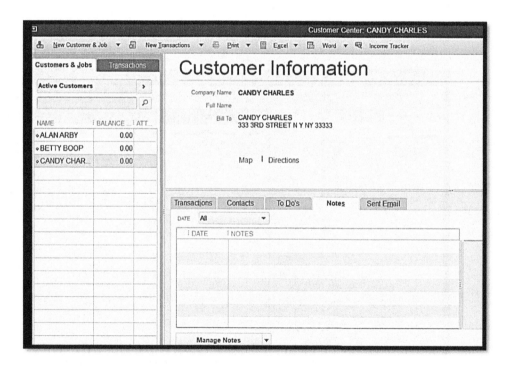

Vendor Center

Now let's go to the Vendor Center. The Vendor Center is exactly like the Customer Center except it says the word vendor Center across the top. Here, you also have to put in each vendor's address, phone number, email, and other details. To access this window, simply go to "**Vendor**", the "**Vendor Center**" and you will notice it looks the same as the Customer Center. You can also take notes on a vendor, see all their transactions, and so on.

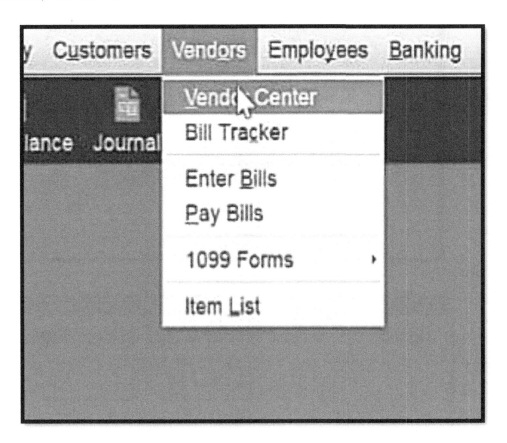

Adding a new vendor

To add a new vendor, go to "**New Vendor**", in the window that appears, add the details of the vendor and click OK.

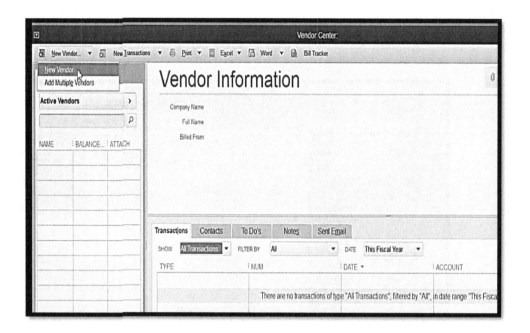

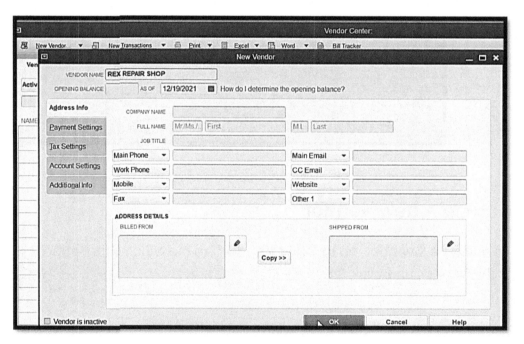

Do this for as many vendors as you wish to add and remember, you can always go back and add or edit any information you skipped or any wrong information. When you double-click one of the names the "**Edit vendor**" window opens and this window looks exactly like the "**New Vendor**" window with each of the different areas of functionality that you could input data into when you get more advanced in QuickBooks.

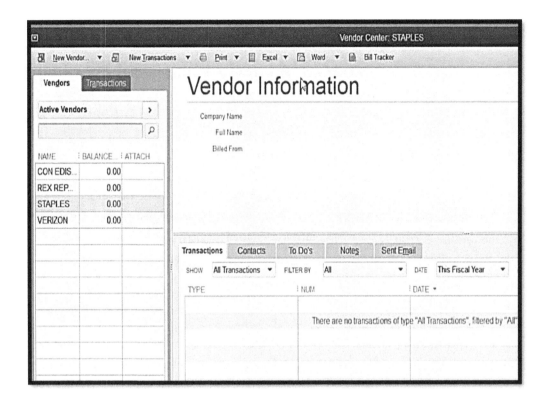

Review Questions

1. What is the Chart of Accounts formerly called?
2. Where is the Chart of Accounts located in QuickBooks?
3. Mention 5 names of accounts and their corresponding type in QuickBooks.
4. What is the difference between Customer Center and Vendor Center?

CHAPTER 6

PREPARING REPORTS

In this chapter, we will look at how you can set up and prepare the important reports you will need. We will also discuss the important shortcuts and icons in the QuickBooks desktop icon bar.

This is a special setup aimed to perfect what you are learning. You might not have to do this in your real company but it is strongly recommended that you see what this entails. You're going to learn about customizing reports and you're going to learn a little bit about the icon bar and you'll see how you can use them together to make using QuickBooks the easiest software ever.

You may as well ask, what makes QuickBooks challenging at the beginning when you first start learning? Well, the truth is there are too many menu choices to remember. For example, under "**Customers**" there are so many options and choices you can make and under Company, there are so many things you can choose such as **Banking reports** and so on but wouldn't it be nice to have one place for everything you need? That's what the icon bar is.

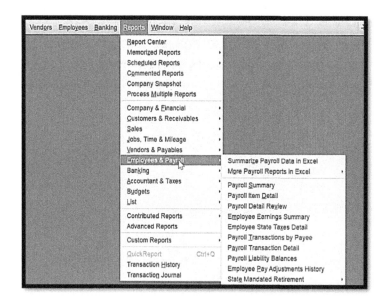

The Icon Bar

You can make the icon bar shortcuts to each of the different transaction windows that you open to input transactions and on that same icon bar you could put up reports that you need to see the results of those transactions. So instead of memorizing 200 menu choices, you only have to remember the few menu choices that you need in your specific company. For example, if you put up a shortcut to the "**Invoice**" window, that means when you click on the icon bar, the Invoice window opens up. If you put a shortcut to the "**Receipt**" window to record that type of transaction, if you click on it from the Icon bar the Receipt window would open up and so on.

Now let's see how you can add icons one by one but before we do that let's see how you can change the way the icon bar looks. First, you should know that everything that relates to the icon bar is in the "**View**" main menu and you can change it to the top icon bar because that's more of a traditional QuickBooks look.

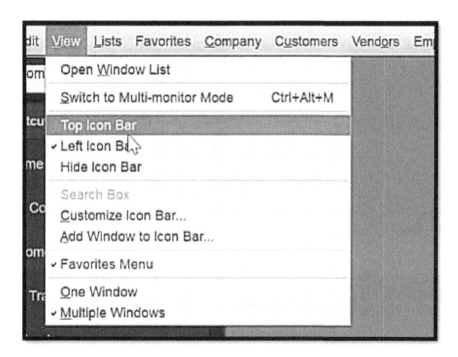

Then you will go to "**View**", and "**Customize icon bar**".

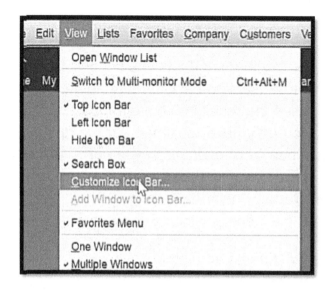

Now you can see that the items listed in the "**Customize**" window are the same items across the top, all you have to do is start at the bottom and click delete and they will all disappear. Now you must click OK because if you click "Cancel" they all come back. So go to "**View**", and "**Customize icon bar**" and keep clicking delete until they all go away. This way, when you click OK you now have a blank slate and you can add the shortcuts that you need.

You can add a shortcut to the Invoice window, so if you click "**Customers**", then "**Create invoice**", that would bring you to the invoice window. Instead of that, another way to do this is if at the moment the active window is in front of you, you click "**View**" and it will always be the name of the active window that you have the option to add to the icon bar.

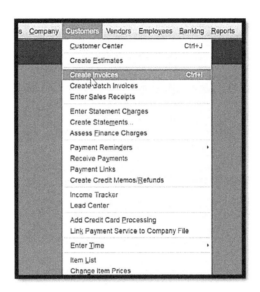

Now if you zoom in a little you can see that if you click "**View**" since the Invoice window is the active window you can click to **add "Create invoice" to the icon bar** and then click OK and now you have the shortcut up here.

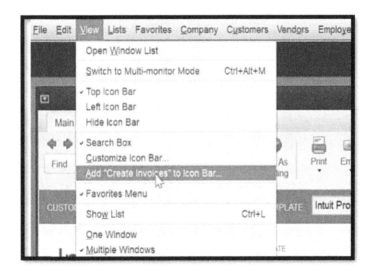

So now all you have to do is click the shortcut and the invoice window opens. The same thing applies to the **"Sales Receipt"** window; click **"Customers"**, and enter **"Sales Receipt"** now you don't have to worry about remembering that menu choice because at the moment the Sales Receipt window is the active window.

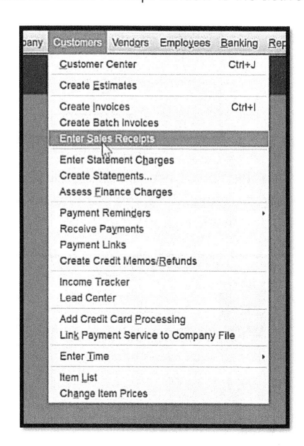

You can go to **"View"** click to **add "Enter Sales Receipt" into the icon bar**. We'll explain this in the next section but for now, click OK and now you can open the Sales Receipt window from the Icon bar.

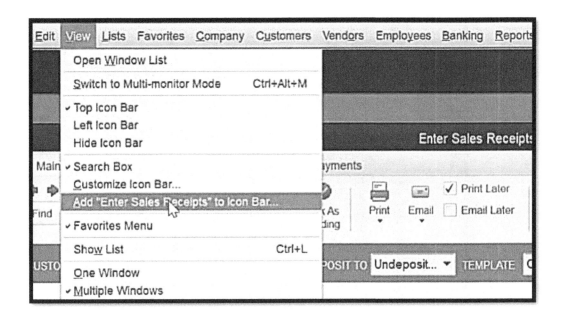

Customers receive payment which is recorded in the "Receive Payment" window and the same thing applies. With this window open, go to **"View"**, then add "**Receive Payments**" to the icon bar and click OK.

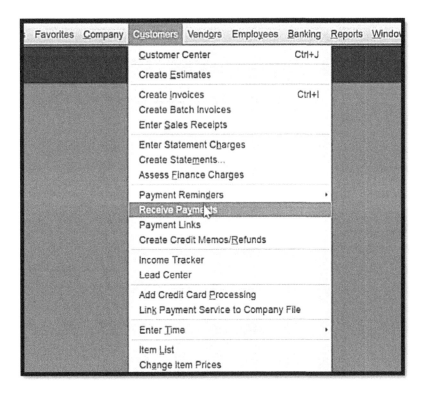

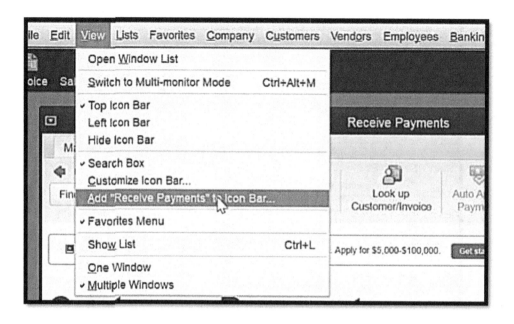

Now in the "**Customize icon bar**" window you can add three **separators** before you click OK and as you can see; this will separate the transaction windows from the report windows or any other window that you're about to open up.

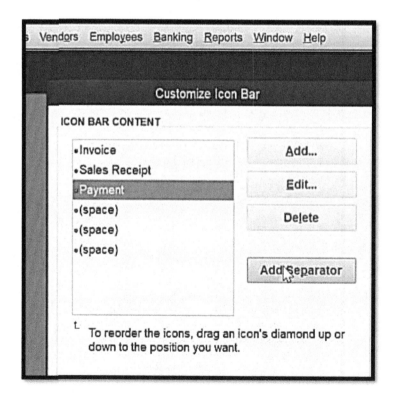

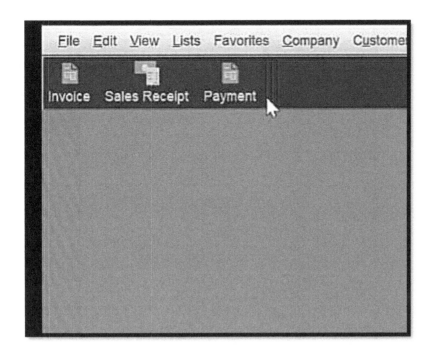

And now that will put up shortcuts for the transactions, to get out the results of the transactions in the reports so you will customize the reports that you need and then after you put them up in the icon bar, QuickBooks will remember the customization and remember that you like the way that it looks.

Trial balance

Your main report is the trial balance; it's considered the main financial report and we will be working with the trial balance in future sessions. It shows the totals and balances of each account in the Chart of Accounts that you had set up in an earlier chapter. You will customize the date so it shows the results of all transactions regardless of the date and then when you put it up in the icon bar, QuickBooks will remember how you wanted it to look.

From the main menu, you click "**Reports**", then go down to "**Accountant and taxes**" and click "**Trial balance**".

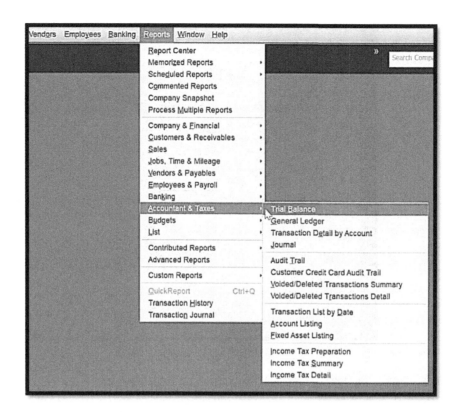

Now notice the trial balance opens automatically in the previous month to when you're opening it, this means if you're currently in December, by default what you'll see is from November 1 to November 30. You can zoom in and take a look.

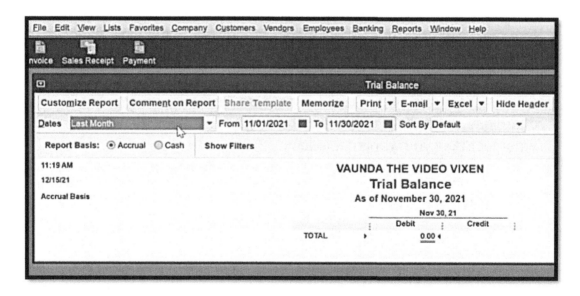

Now what you want to do is click the date, the drop-down, and then scroll up to the very top choice because you want your trial balance to show the results of all transactions regardless of date.

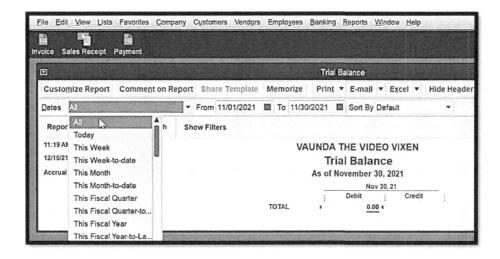

If you would also like to make the font a little bigger and thicker so that you can see things a little more clearly in your trial balance, what you'll do is click the "**Customize Report**" button and every report in QuickBooks has a customize button here that will open up the "**Modify Report**" window.

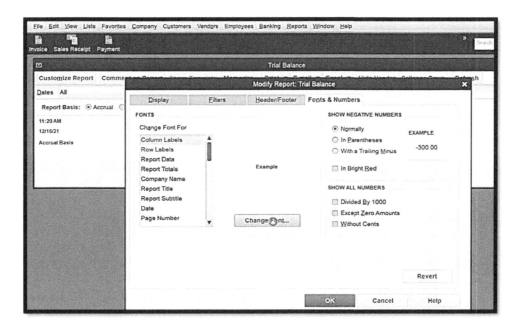

You may notice there are four tabs in the Modify Report window because there are four different ways that you can customize a report. In this example just click "**header/footer**" and where it's actually "**fonts and numbers**" change font and just make the font a little bigger, let's say about 12. Click OK, click "Yes" and then of course at the bottom of the customize window click OK.

Now to make the column a little bigger, click there, drag it over and you'll see the three dots; you have to click and you have to drag to make the column wider.

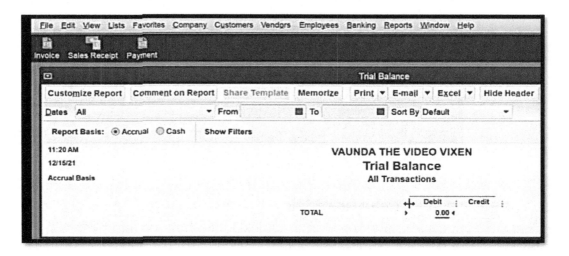

The trial balance is now nice and clear and it looks exactly the way you need it to look so at the moment that this is the active window, you go to "**View**", **add "Trial Balance" to the icon bar** and click OK.

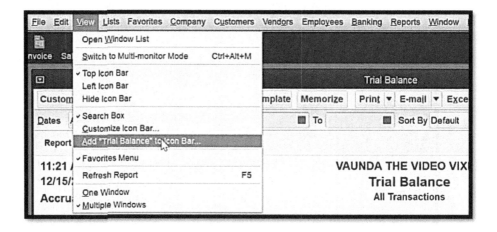

Now when you close it you may get a pop-up, just click the "do not display this message box" box and then click "No".

97

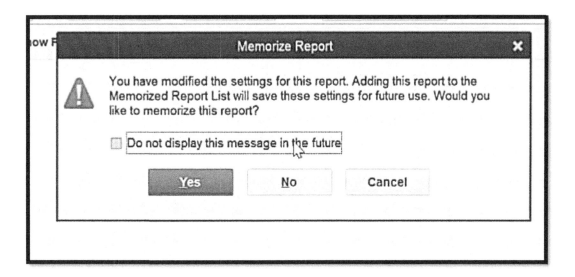

If you go back to the main menu and reopen it from the original main menu it may not look the way you want, it has a smaller font and it says last month but if you click on the shortcut in the icon bar it remembers and it opens up where it says "**All**" and it has the thicker font; that's why the icon bar is perfect for memorizing the reports that you need.

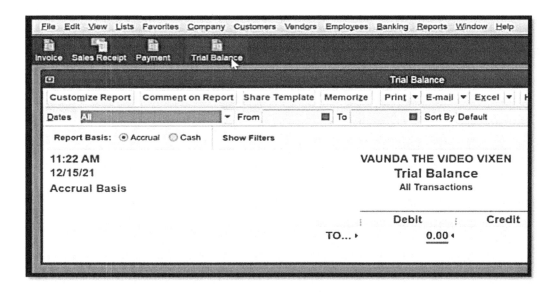

Journal report

The other report that you will put up right at the beginning is also one of the most important reports that you will use in QuickBooks and it's the Journal report. It lists every transaction ever recorded into the file. It's the only report that can show the

98

transactions in the order in which they were entered and not only just the date order. It can find any transaction's important details. After you open up the journal, you're going to add a column to see what date it was last entered or modified. You can remove the debit and credit columns and add a column that says just the amount and that'll make the journal a lot easier to work with. We will get to it in another section. So, from the main menu click "**Reports**", "**Accountant & Taxes**" and "**Journal**".

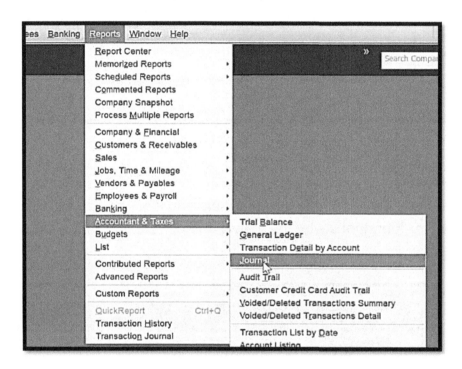

If there's something irrelevant that pops up you can just click OK. You'll notice it did not open with the date range "All" so that's the first thing you will put but if you make it a little wider you will see that it does not have the columns; you need to make sure it has the columns you need.

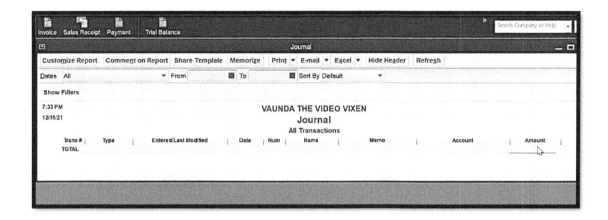

Now click "**Customize report**" and watch; you want to click a check mark here to add the column "**Last modified**" entered so you know the date and time that it was entered and then click OK.

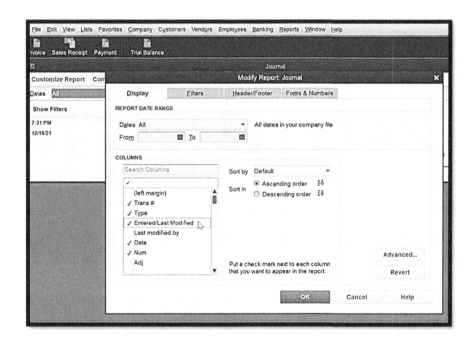

To make a column wider, you go to the three dots till the mouse becomes the cross, then click and drag to the right. You could also get rid of a column that you don't need something like the edge. If you want a very wide column, click and drag it very far and let it be. The same thing applies to the column of account: click the three dots to the right, click and drag and make it very wide. This way you will be able to read the account name and the memo.

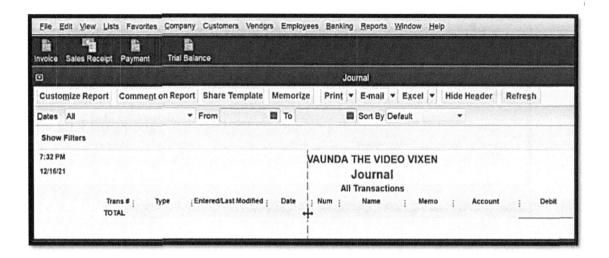

Also, if you don't want debit and credit and you just want one column for the amount, you can make this a little taller. Click "**Customize report**" and then come to the display tab of the "**Modify report**" window. Then click to remove the check marks for debit credit and click to put the amount. Now click OK and you can see that instead of debit credit you have one column for the money that says amount.

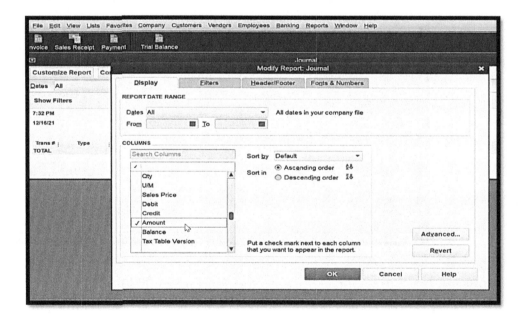

Now that the journal looks the way you need it to look, go to "**View**", **add "Journal" to the icon bar** and click OK, then close it out.

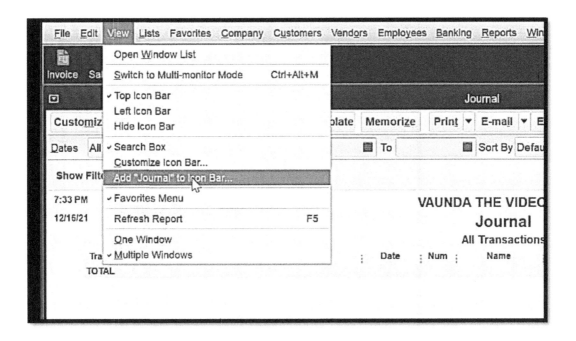

Now if you open it from the Icon bar it remembers; if you go back and open it from the main menu it will not remember and it will look the way it did in the first place so you can be using this one and it will help you.

Using the Journal report

In this section, you will learn how to use the best report on QuickBooks desktop.

The Journal report is the most helpful in QuickBooks. It lists all transactions in the entire file and all transaction types since the creation of the file and it's the only report that can do that. It's also the only report that shows transactions in the order in which they were entered into the computer regardless of date.

Now, why is that helpful? If you have a date mistake, if the piece of data that you made a mistake on when you entered a transaction was the date, that becomes the most difficult type of mistake to find and the reason it's difficult to find is that all of the other QuickBooks reports are displaying the transactions in date order. So, if you made a mistake on the date and you thought you recorded it in January, you're looking up here but if your mistake was that you put April instead of January as the date, the transaction is down there but you won't know that the transaction is down there because you don't know what the date is and that's the mistake.

102

Customer Balance Detail
All Transactions

	Date	Num	Account	
ACE				
	07/29/2016	14	ACCOUNTS R...	
	07/29/2016	15	ACCOUNTS R...	
	01/03/2017	1	ACCOUNTS R...	
	01/06/2017	2	ACCOUNTS R...	
	04/14/2017	20	ACCOUNTS R...	
N PLACE				
RD LANE				
	01/09/2017	3	ACCOUNTS R...	
	01/14/2017		ACCOUNTS R...	
	01/17/2017	5	ACCOUNTS...	
	01/20/2017	61	ACCOUNTS R...	
	01/23/2017	66	ACCOUNTS R...	
	03/14/2017	16	ACCOUNTS R...	
	03/22/2017	17	ACCOUNTS R...	
	04/05/2017	18	ACCOUNTS R...	
NGBIRD LANE				

However, if you go to the Journal and you open up the Journal here as we put from the icon bar in an earlier section you will see that the journal does not go in date order. It goes in this column order: transaction number and invoice number.

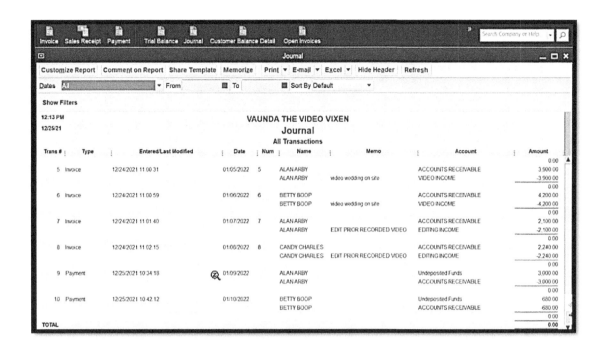

The first one shows the first transaction invoice number, the second shows transaction number two but when we scroll down you can see that the first payment was actually transaction number nine and the second payment was actually transaction number ten, and so on. So, it doesn't matter the date that you recorded the transaction; what matters is the order that it was entered.

Now if you're putting in a bunch of different kinds of transactions in one session such as invoices, payments, and so on, if you want to remember where you left off just scroll to the bottom of the journal where the most recent transactions are.

So, if you're putting in invoices, payments, and all other types of transactions and the phone rings and you can't remember which one you did enter and which one you did not enter, you open the journal, scroll to the bottom and you can see the last one entered, the one that was the one beforehand and so on. This will help you if you're putting in a bunch and you forgot where you left off or you're looking for a date mistake. You will also notice that you can compare the date of the transaction to the date and time that that specific transaction was recorded and these will be incredibly helpful as you approach more complex exercises you will rely more and more on the Journal.

Lastly, you can see exactly what transaction number was deleted and the approximate date. As we proceed, one of the chapters will be all about deleting transactions. However, the deleted transactions will show on a separate report that we will learn about soon but the Journal shows what was entered before and after the deleted transaction. This means if you delete a transaction or invoice number eight and then you re-enter it, you will see the transaction numbers we'll say 6, 7, 9, 10, and 8 will be gone.

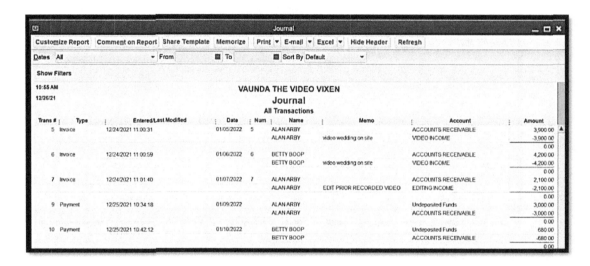

You will have to open the deleted report to see that transaction once it's deleted because it is removed from the journal. Think about how to use the Journal as effectively as you can.

Review Questions

1. What is the function of the Icon bar?
2. What is a Trial Balance?
3. Why is the Journal Report important in QuickBooks?
4. Mention 3 types of Reports in QuickBooks

SECTION THREE
MANAGING CUSTOMERS AND RECEIVABLES

CHAPTER 7

RECORDING TRANSACTIONS

We are now ready to record your first transaction. You've made it to the customers and receivables transaction section. This chapter will cover everything from creating invoices, recording payments, recording and managing sales receipts to exploring some practical examples.

Creating invoices

In this section, you will learn how to create and enter invoices. When we record any transaction such as an invoice, QuickBooks will automatically record that transaction into the proper accounts in the Chart of Accounts and the Chart of Accounts we know is the general ledger. So, you know that after you record this invoice, the results of recording one invoice will show up in the report that shows the results of the general ledger, which is our good friend the Trial Balance.

Now go ahead and open up the trial balance before you record the invoice. Remember you had set up your Trial Balance to be able to open it right here from the Icon bar but it does remember that you want to see the results of all transactions and it remembers the larger font that you had set up; if you did not do this earlier you would have to click "**Reports**", "**Accounting and taxes,**" choose the **Trial Balance** and then customize it the way you learned in a prior chapter and then save that customization right up here in the icon bar. However, you don't have to do that if you already did that because you've learned how to use the icon bar to memorize the customization of reports.

The example below is what a company's first transaction looks like.

On January 1, they performed 10 video hours on account of customer Alan; the word on account means Alan did not pay them on the day that they did the job. Therefore, the proper documentation to make for this transaction is an invoice and the amount of the invoice as we all know is equal to 3000 dollars and that's because each video hour is 300 dollars. On this invoice we're about to make, this company performed 10 video hours and is therefore going to bill Allen for those 10 video hours. Now we know the results and the Trial Balance will happen automatically if we earned 3000 dollars of video income which is what's indicated at the moment, we record the invoice then video income will be the first thing to show up on the Trial Balance for 3000 at the moment we record the invoice but we are also owed 3000 from Allen because Alan did not pay us on January 1 which is the day the service was performed.

Accounts Receivable

So, if we perform a service at the moment the client owes us the account that increases in the trial balance is called **Accounts receivable** and it will show up for 3000 dollars to indicate that the total of all customers that owe us all money together after January 1 would be 3000 dollars.

This is what the trial Balance would look similar to after opening the invoice window and recording the invoice. However, the Trial Balance is not the only area of data that gets affected when we record an invoice.

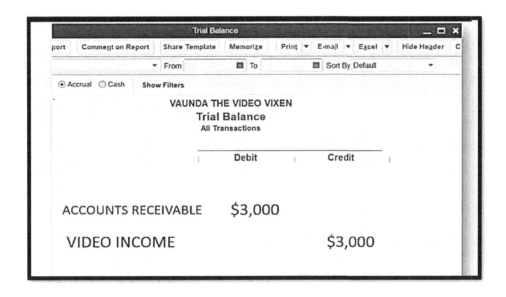

There's another area of data that the invoice gets recorded to and that area is the customer-specific records. You could call them the customer subsidiary ledger because that was the initial name but the name of the report that reflects the customer records and how much is owed from each customer is called the **customer balance detail**.

Let's go ahead and set that up before we record this transaction. From the main menu go to "**Reports**" and once you're in Reports go to the area of "**Customers and Receivables**" and open the "**Customer Balance Detail**".

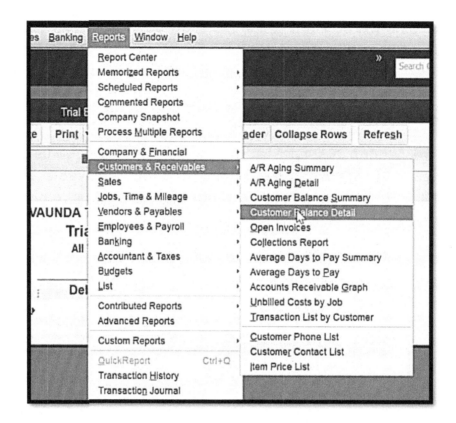

You may notice it's blank because you have not recorded any transactions yet but it will show the result as soon as you save your first invoice. So, let's go ahead and save it to the icon bar: go to **"View,"** **add "Customer Balance Detail" to the icon bar**, click OK, and now you don't have to go hunting through a million reports in the main menu, we can click right here to open the one that we need.

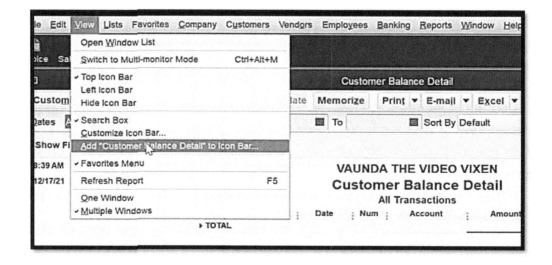

What will be the results in the Customer Balance Detail after we record one invoice for 10 video hours? Well, once we save the invoice, the customer records will reflect that only Alan Arby owes us 3000 dollars for the first invoice that we just recorded.

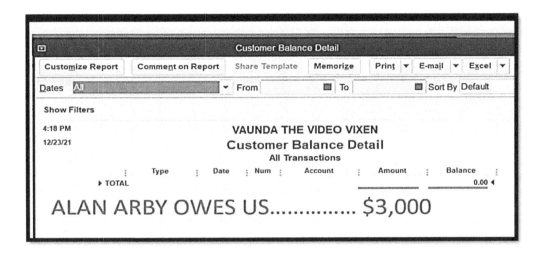

Now we have already set up a shortcut to clicking from the Icon bar to open the Invoice window. If you did not set up the shortcut you would have to click "**Customers**", then "**Create Invoice**" to open that window for that transaction. Now notice that the invoice window has a ribbon up top just like Microsoft Word and you can click here to collapse the ribbon and also click here to reopen it if you need any of these features that we will explore later.

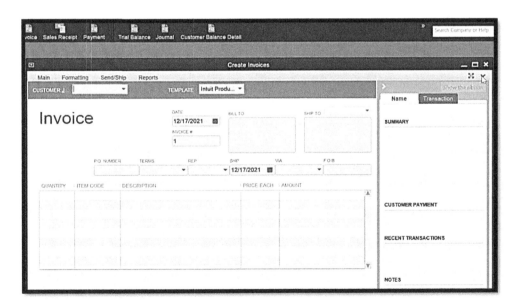

You may also notice that there's another arrow pointing to the left and if you click on that, a right-hand panel opens up with details about the customer's previous transactions. It may be blank at first especially if you don't have any previous transactions so you can hide the right panel and also hide the ribbon because those are the typical things in a transaction window and then only put the specific information about the transaction you're recording.

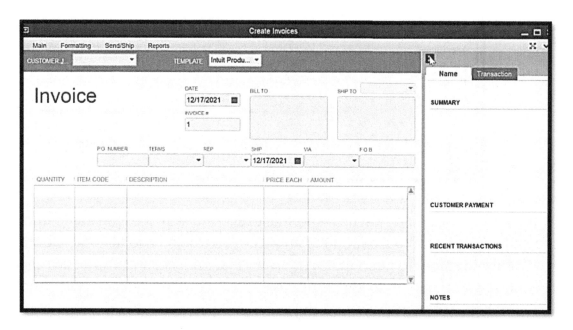

To choose the customer, you come to the top left and click the drop-down arrow you see here.

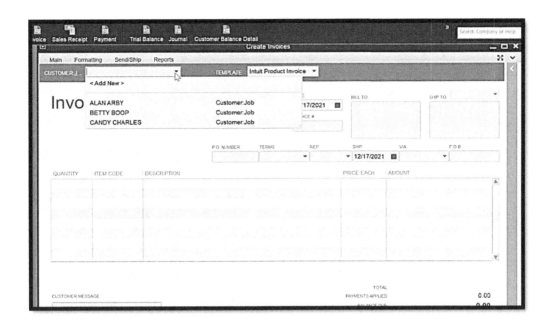

Once you click, you will see the customers that you put on the Customer List earlier, and when you click on the customer who you're making the transaction for, you'll notice that the address field gets populated with the same address that you put in when you set up customers.

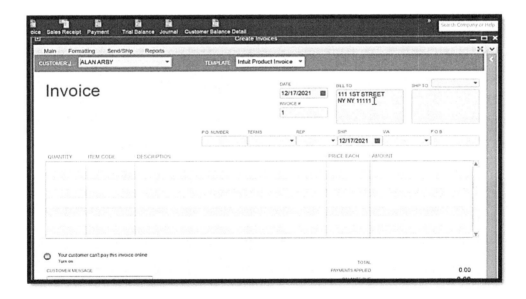

Now to change the date of a transaction, click the date box. You can click the characters and type them in one by one but it's much more convenient to click the date box and be able to go back when you click the month back arrow or forward.

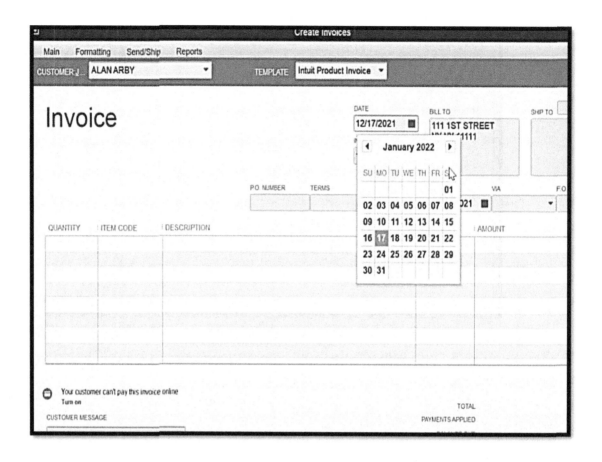

We're imagining that this is January 1 of 2022 in this example so that's what we put for the date. Notice QuickBooks automatically enumerates the invoices and tells you that this is invoice number one. The quantity of the items should go after you put the item; click directly under the word "**Item code**", and click once and that will bring the drop-down arrow. Click on the drop-down arrow to choose the specific service that you did, in this case, it's a video wedding. Notice when we click video wedding, 300 comes up automatically for the price because that's what we set up in the list window earlier when we talked about the Item list.

Now, all we have to do is click in the quantity field, and type the number 10 because the quantity of Video hours for this invoice is 10.

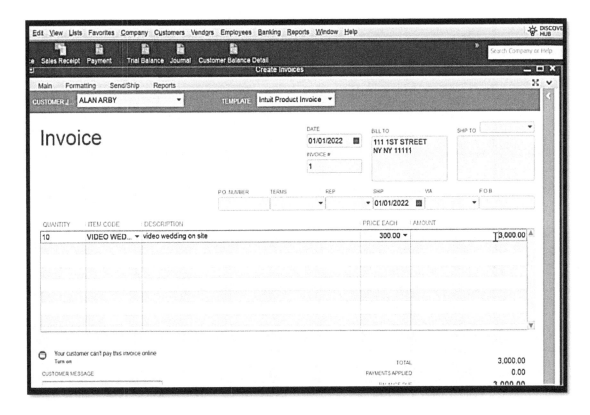

Please note: to get QuickBooks to save one field without closing the whole window, you go to the left of your keyboard and push the Tab Key and the moment you push the Tab Key, QuickBooks will save the quantity field and then multiply the quantity by the price for each item.

For our example, you can now see that the amount is 3000 dollars. That's how you make sure you save one field without closing the window. If you hit the enter key, the whole window will close so on the left of your keyboard you hit the tab key and now we have our first invoice where the total is 3000 dollars. Now we can click "**Save & Close**" and the transaction is recorded. We can immediately click to open our Trial balance and we can see that the results are exactly as we expected; video income showed up for the first time as 3000 dollars and Accounts Receivable also showed up for the first time as 3000 dollars.

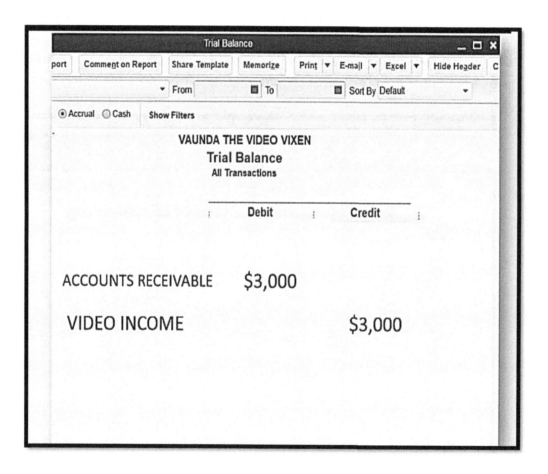

Well, we have just discussed the general ledger but what about our customer-specific records? Still using our example, if we click to open the customer balance detail, you can see that only the customer Alan owes us 3000 for the invoice that was made on January 22.

To fully understand this let's do a second example. Let's say on January 2 this same company did 10 editing hours on account for another customer Betty. Now you know that "**on account**" means we make an invoice and we know that each editing hour that we put on the items list was 140 dollars. Therefore, the amount of this invoice will be equal to 1400 dollars. So, after we make this invoice what will then be the result in the trial balance? Since this is our first editing invoice editing income, it will show up for the first time as 1400 dollars and because after this second invoice we will now receive more in the future from customers who owe us money, Accounts Receivable will increase by 1400 we are owed and after this second invoice Accounts Receivable will become 4400 dollars.

So we go back to QuickBooks, then to invoice, move this out of the way and record it the same way. Notice QuickBooks enumerates the invoices for you and this is invoice number two. We click the date box and choose January 2nd, then click the drop-down box to choose the customer and we choose Betty (notice her address populates the address field). Remember, we click directly under the word "Item code" to bring the drop-down arrow then click on the drop-down arrow to get the choices of items of service to put on the invoice, in this case, we're putting the editing item which means QuickBooks now remembers that each editing hour is 140 dollars. All we have to do is click in the quantity field, put 10, and hit the tab key and the moment we push the tab key, QuickBooks multiplies the quantity by 10 times the price of each editing hour and the total of the invoice is 1400 dollars. Now the moment we save the invoice, you will notice the results in the trial balance are exactly as we expected, Accounts Receivable increased to 4400, and editing income showed up for the first time as 1400.

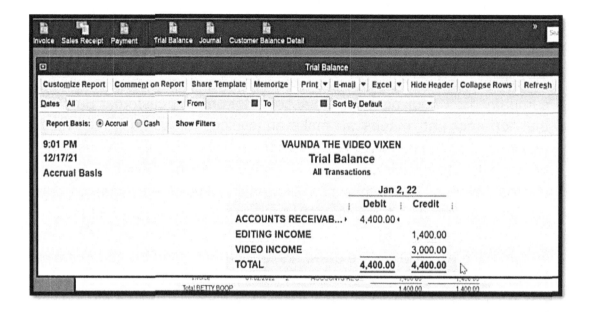

What else was affected? Well, the customer-specific records were also affected by this invoice and that means that we should see in our customer balance detail this invoice is listed for 1400 making the total of the customer balance detail equal to 4400 which is the same as the total Account Receivable in the trial balance. So when we come back to the customer balance detail or you could open it from the Icon bar, you see the first invoice that Allen owes is 3000 the other invoice that Betty owes is 1400 and that's why the bottom of the customer balance detail says 4400 which is equal to the total Accounts Receivable in the trial balance.

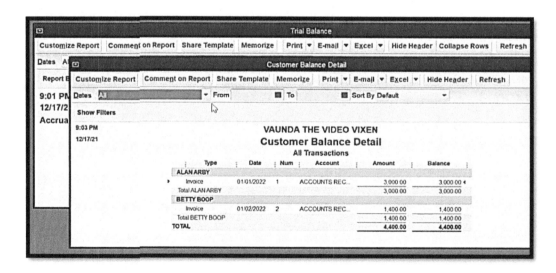

117

Invoice transactions

You will do your very first practice transaction set, so follow along as we will enter a batch of invoices and check the results together.

The image below is what the trial balance looks like or at least these are the numbers on the trial balance before we do the exercise.

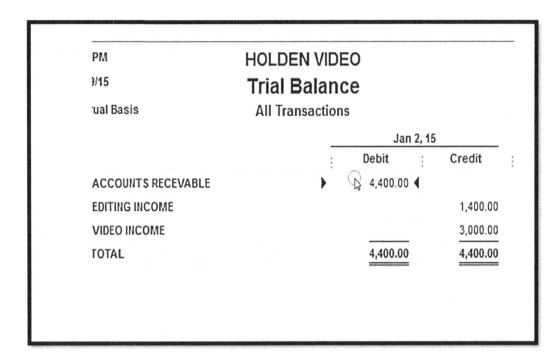

Here, you can also see the results after our first two invoices. The trial balance shows the date of the latest transaction. As we proceed, you will learn how to display your trial balance appropriately. So, you can see the results and this is what the numbers look like in the customer balance detail before this exercise set where only Allen owes us 3 000 and only Betty owes us 1400.

Below is an invoice list for practice, for which at a convenient time, you can enter it into your QuickBooks online account one by one. They are all invoices and here you can see the date, the quantity, the item, and the customer, and QuickBooks should automatically enumerate the invoice number.

DATE	QUANTITY	ITEM	CUSTOMER	INVOICE NUMBER
JANUARY 3	11	VIDEO	CANDY	3
JANUARY 4	12	EDITING	BETTY	4
JANUARY 5	13	VIDEO	ALAN	5
JANUARY 6	14	VIDEO	BETTY	6
JANUARY 7	15	EDITING	ALAN	7
JANUARY 8	16	EDITING	CANDY	8

If you enter these invoices properly, that means your final trial balance after the exercise should have these numbers: total Accounts Receivable should be 21,820, and editing income and video income should be these numbers accordingly.

HOLDEN VIDEO
Customer Balance Detail
All Transactions

PM
3/15

Type	Date	Num	Account	Amount	Balance
ALAN ARBY					
Invoice	01/01/2015	1	ACCOUNTS RECEV...	3,000.00	3,000.00 ◀
Invoice	01/05/2015	5	ACCOUNTS RECEV...	3,900.00	6,900.00
Invoice	01/07/2015	7	ACCOUNTS RECEV...	2,100.00	9,000.00
Total ALAN ARBY				9,000.00	9,000.00
BETTY BOOP					
Invoice	01/02/2015	2	ACCOUNTS RECEV...	1,400.00	1,400.00
Invoice	01/04/2015	4	ACCOUNTS RECEV...	1,680.00	3,080.00
Invoice	01/06/2015	6	ACCOUNTS RECEV...	4,200.00	7,280.00
Total BETTY BOOP				7,280.00	7,280.00
CANDY CHARLES					
Invoice	01/03/2015	3	ACCOUNTS RECEV...	3,300.00	3,300.00
Invoice	01/08/2015	8	ACCOUNTS RECEV...	2,240.00	5,540.00
Total CANDY CHARLES				5,540.00	5,540.00
TOTAL				21,820.00	21,820.00

Also, after this exercise, the balance of RB should be 9000, Betty's balance should be 7280 and the balance of Candy's should be 5540. If these are not your numbers after the exercise you may have missed out on something and not to worry, the next section will be all about finding and fixing mistakes.

119

Learning how to find and fix QuickBooks mistakes

The trial balance is a summary report; which means it shows the results of the transactions that have accumulated for each of the summary numbers on the report. The Customer Balance Detail however is a detailed report; that means that it lists the transactions one by one and every report in QuickBooks is either a summary or a detail.

For any transaction you see, you can edit the transaction just by clicking right on the transaction from the face of any detailed report. For example, if you open the Customer Balance Detail you can look up whatever you have there but if you pick one transaction on the line on the report and you double-click, the window that opens is the same window that you used to record that transaction in the first place. You can change any of the pieces of data that you originally put into the transaction when you first recorded it and the moment you save your changes, all of the reports will change accordingly. For example, if you come here and you change this to 1111 hours and then you push the Tab Key, you see you get a crazy giant number here in this invoice so you have changed the quantity and as a result, you change the amount.

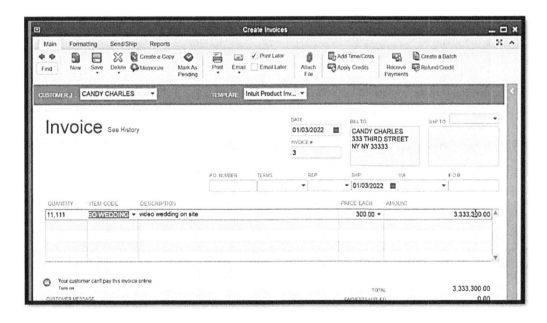

The moment you click "**save**", all of the reports will be updated for the new numbers. When you click "Save & Close" you get a warning message informing you that you have changed this and asking to confirm you want to save the changes if you click "Yes" all of the numbers and the reports are now different.

120

Looking at the transaction that we just opened, notice it has that big number and of course, it shows up here but did you know that every place that this transaction shows up will affect it? That means if you open the trial balance you can see that video income has exploded into a big giant number much bigger than it was before because it was a video invoice that you changed and you will also notice that Accounts Receivable have blown up into a giant number because that invoice affects the total of the video income and affects the total of the Accounts Receivable.

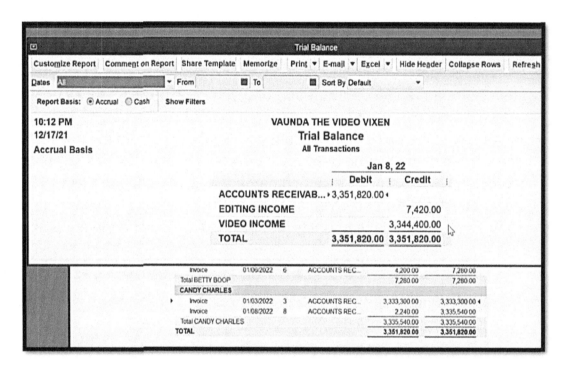

Now if you double-click on any summary number, you can see all of the transactions that the number includes. What does this mean? It means if you don't like the size of this Accounts Receivable number you can double-click and you can open up a detailed report that shows you how you got that summary number.

So, the summary number you double-clicked is here at the bottom and this detailed list shows every single transaction that adds up to that summary number just like on the customer balance detail this detailed report that lists every transaction in the Accounts Receivable account shows you clearly that this is the transaction with the problem and just like with the other report you can double-click and you can fix the number that is the problem.

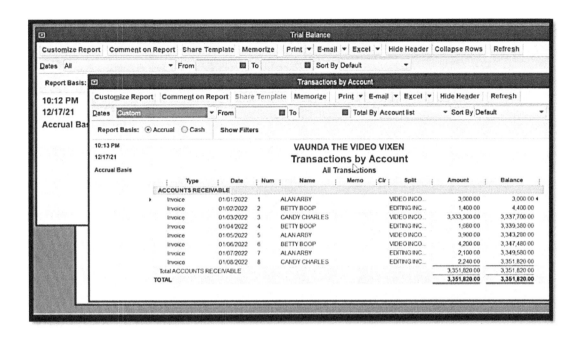

Hit the tab key to save the field, and you'll notice the number corrects itself, and the moment you click "**Save & close**" and then of course "**yes**", all of the numbers in all of the reports go back to exactly what they are supposed to be. That's the method of finding and fixing mistakes.

Record receiving payments for past invoices

You know that we record the customer payments in the customer payment window and you know that any transaction that we record affects the numbers in your Chart of Accounts because that's your general ledger and the report that immediately shows the changes to any account in the general ledger is the trial balance.

For example, let's say we received 3000 from Alan for the January 1 invoice that we recorded in a prior section. Let's also imagine that the money was deposited directly into the bank account so what will happen when they pay? If they pay us directly into the bank account then cash and bank go up because we now have the cash so that account in the Chart of Accounts will increase and if the reason, we got the cash was for a past invoice, we know that Accounts Receivable represents what was owed. So, if they pay, the number of Accounts Receivable will go down because now the customer owes less.

122

So, in this example of a 3000-dollar invoice what will be the results? Well, we just got paid for the first time in this course so Cash in Bank will show up for the first time in the amount. We got paid 3000 dollars and we know Accounts Receivable represents what customers owe us if they just paid us 3000, that means they owe us 3000 less, and Accounts Receivable will decrease by 3000 and become 18,820.

VAUNDA THE VIDEO VIXEN
Trial Balance
All Transactions

	Jan 8, 22	
	Debit	Credit
CASH IN BANK	3,000	
ACCOUNTS RECEIVABLE	18,820	
EDITING INCOME		7,420.00
VIDEO INCOME		14,400.00

This should be the results in the trial balance after we record our first payment from past invoices. However, we know from experience that there is another area of data that will also change when we receive payment from a customer. In this case, that will also change our subsidiary customer records and that payment should also show up on the Customer Balance Detail. If you look at the Customer Balance Detail now you see only invoices but if we record a transaction that affects the customer's balance it will be additionally listed right here on the Customer Balance Detail and of course because it's payment it will decrease what that specific customer owes.

This is what the Customer Balance Details should mostly look like after we record receiving 3000 dollars for the January 1 invoice, however, what you might notice is that it's not exactly clear the way it's written now in terms of which specific invoice was that particular payment being paid for.

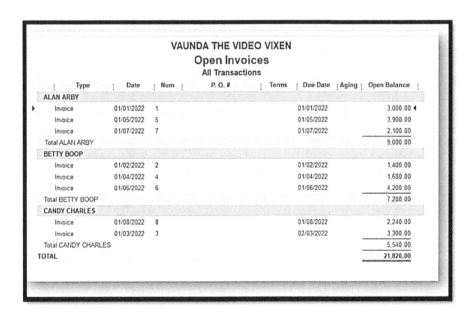

VAUNDA THE VIDEO VIXEN
Customer Balance Detail
All Transactions

	Type	Date	Num	Account	Amount	Balance	
ALAN ARBY							
▶	Invoice	01/01/2022	1	ACCOUNTS REC...	3,000.00	3,000.00 ◀
	Invoice	01/05/2022	5	ACCOUNTS REC...	3,900.00	6,900.00
	Invoice	01/07/2022	7	ACCOUNTS REC...	2,100.00	9,000.00
	PAYMENT	01/09/2022			-3,000	6,000

In other words, the fact that it's 3000 doesn't mean we can assume that it was paying for invoice number one therefore, we need an additional Customer Report.

We need a customer report that shows us only the unpaid invoices and the name of the report that shows us only the unpaid invoices are called the **Open Invoice report**.

VAUNDA THE VIDEO VIXEN
Open Invoices
All Transactions

	Type	Date	Num	P. O. #	Terms	Due Date	Aging	Open Balance	
ALAN ARBY									
▶	Invoice	01/01/2022	1			01/01/2022		3,000.00 ◀
	Invoice	01/05/2022	5			01/05/2022		3,900.00
	Invoice	01/07/2022	7			01/07/2022		2,100.00
	Total ALAN ARBY							9,000.00
BETTY BOOP									
	Invoice	01/02/2022	2			01/02/2022		1,400.00
	Invoice	01/04/2022	4			01/04/2022		1,680.00
	Invoice	01/06/2022	6			01/06/2022		4,200.00
	Total BETTY BOOP							7,280.00
CANDY CHARLES									
	Invoice	01/08/2022	8			01/08/2022		2,240.00
	Invoice	01/03/2022	3			02/03/2022		3,300.00
	Total CANDY CHARLES							5,540.00
TOTAL								21,820.00

This Open Invoice report zoomed into the section of a customer, in this example, Alan shows that right now these three invoices that we recorded for Alan are currently unpaid. However, after we record receiving payment for the January 1 invoice, the January 1 invoice will not be an Open Invoice and it will simply disappear from the Alan section of the Open Invoice report and that will be the result when we record the transaction.

VAUNDA THE VIDEO VIXEN

Open Invoices

All Transactions

Type	Date	Num	P. O. #	Terms	Due Date	Aging	Open Balance
ALAN ARBY							
Invoice	01/01/2022	1			01/01/2022		3,000.00 ◄
Invoice	01/05/2022	5			01/05/2022		3,900.00
Invoice	01/07/2022	7			01/07/2022		2,100.00

Let's go ahead and put the Open Invoice report up in the icon bar and then we'll record the transaction reports, customers, and receivables open invoice. The rule here is that you always change the report date range to all you want to see the results of all transactions regardless of date.

This is the way the Open Invoice report looks before we record our first payment and if we click **"View"**, **add Open Invoice to the icon bar** and click OK, we now see we can open it directly from the Icon bar and we don't have to go hunting for it in the huge list of main menus choices.

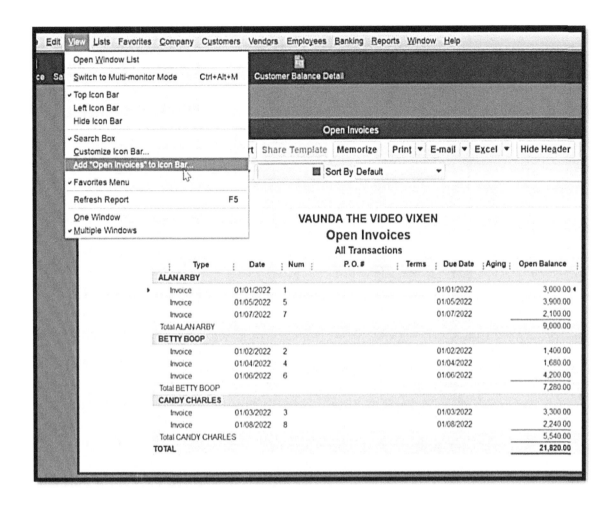

Our payment window is in the icon bar and we can click here to open it, however, you could also open it by clicking "**Customers**", and "**Receive Payment**" and this brings up the window that we need.

126

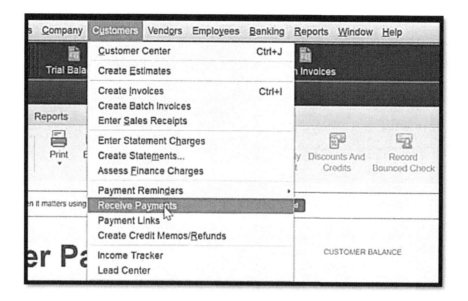

We know that the customer from our example was Alan and you'll notice as soon as you choose Alan his Open Invoices populate the fields down here. We're assuming that he paid us on January 9. If the image below is what shows when you first open up the window, you must change it because the instructions specifically say that the money was deposited directly into a specific bank account and the amount of money is 3000 and you learned in a prior section that to save just this field without saving the whole window you go to the left of the keyboard and hit the tab key.

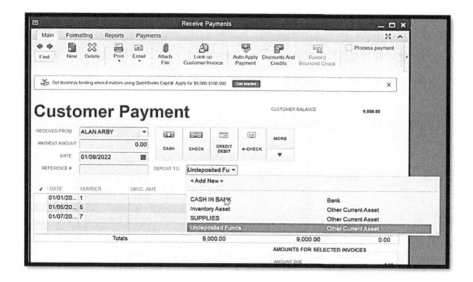

What happens down here is as soon as you hit the tab QuickBooks assumes that you are applying this payment to the top one here and therefore put the checkmark in the left margin; that's the way the computer or QuickBooks saves a payment. It assumes it wants you to apply it to either the oldest one or the one with the numeric match of 3000 here and 3000 there.

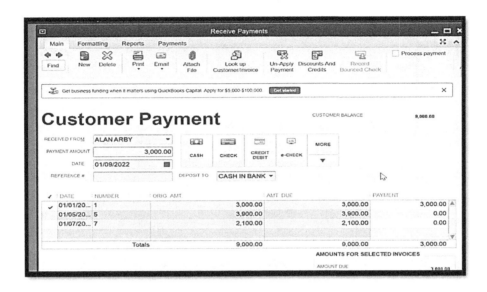

So, in the bottom right of the window, you can now click **"Save & Close"** or hit enter and when you open the reports the results are exactly as what you expected. The trial balance shows that Cash in Bank showed up for the first time as 3000, and Accounts Receivable decreased to exactly the number we expected which is 18,820.

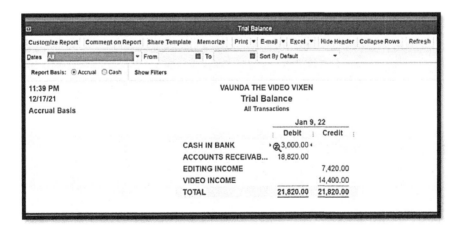

When we open up the Customer Balance Detail and look in the Alan section, we see that this payment happened after the invoices and lowered Allen's balance from 9000 to 6000 but the most important results are in the Open Invoice report. If we click the Open Invoice report, you can see that now Alan only has two open invoices because the January 1 invoice is paid and therefore has disappeared from the Open Invoice report.

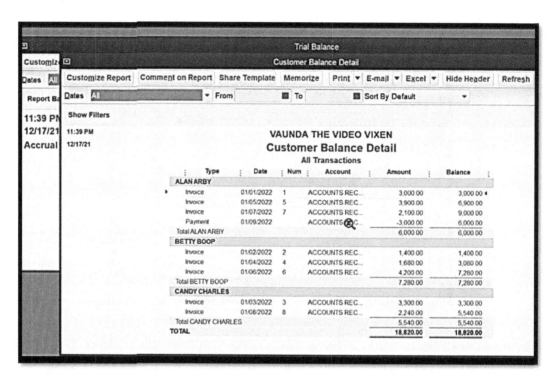

Now let's do a second example. Let's say on January 10 we received 680 dollars from Betty for the January 4th invoice and again let's say that the money was directly deposited into the company bank account at the moment we got paid. So, what will be the result of this 680-dollar payment? We know that Cash in Bank will increase by 680 to become 3680 and we know that if the reason we received the 680 is that the customer owes less then Accounts Receivable will decrease by 680 and become 18,140. We also know that in the customer records, Betty will now have a payment added to her balance at the bottom and that payment of 680 will decrease Betty's specific balance to 6600.

VAUNDA THE VIDEO VIXEN
Trial Balance
All Transactions

	Jan 8, 22	
	Debit	Credit
CASH IN BANK	3,680	
ACCOUNTS RECEIVABLE	18,140	
EDITING INCOME		7,420.00
VIDEO INCOME		14,400.00

If the invoice on January 4th is the one that's being paid you see it's open in the amount of 1680. That means on the Open Invoice, the January 4th invoice will decrease from 1680 and if we apply 680 it will become 1000 dollars even and that's what the report should look like after we record this next payment.

VAUNDA THE VIDEO VIXEN
Open Invoices
All Transactions

Type	Date	Num	P. O. #	Terms	Due Date	Aging	Open Balance
BETTY BOOP							
Invoice	01/02/2022	2			01/02/2022		1,400.00
Invoice	01/04/2022	4			01/04/2022		1,000
Invoice	01/06/2022	6			01/06/2022		4,200.00

So again, we go to the Payment window that we made the shortcut for. We could even collapse the ribbon and make it a little better here. Now, this customer was Betty and as soon as we choose Betty, all of Betty's specific Open Invoices show up in the field in the middle. We know the date that she paid is January 10 and the money is deposited directly into this specific bank account so we choose the bank account. Now the money amount is 680 and you learned many times that to save just the field without closing the window simply go to the left of the keyboard and hit tab and when you do that, QuickBooks assumes that the money will be applied to the oldest invoice but that is not the case.

130

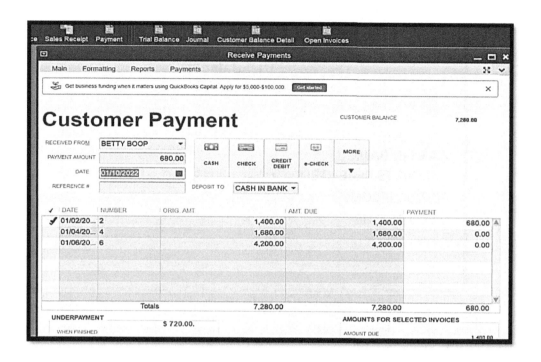

So, if we attempt to move the check mark to the proper invoice, you'll notice something happens. If we leave the check mark alone and just click on the one that we want, we'll get a message asking us to try again.

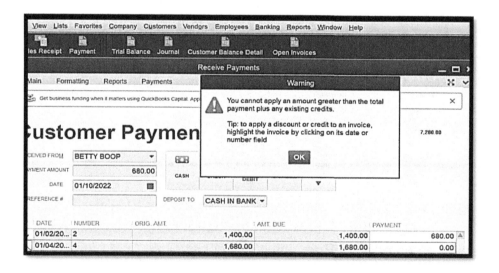

In this case, you don't want the first invoice but you want the second and if you click up, you'll see that you're not able to do it. Why is that? That's because when you use the "**Receive Payment**" window you must first remove the check mark from the wrong one before choosing the correct invoice. So, you have to click on this and remove it because if you don't, you will get that error message since the computer thinks that you have already applied the payment to the oldest invoice. After all, the check mark is still there. What you need to do is remove the check mark and then when you place it on the correct one QuickBooks will apply the payment to the correct invoice. Click to remove the check mark from the wrong one and that one becomes zero now when you click to place it on the right one there is no error message and the 680 shows up in the correct row.

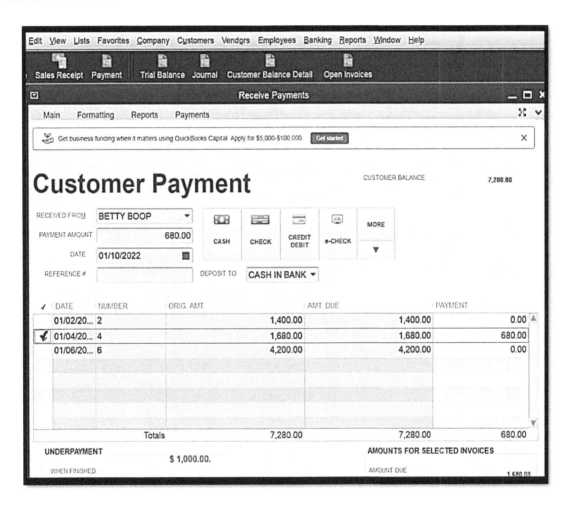

You can click "**Save**" at the bottom or hit enter and now when we open the reports, the results are exactly as we expected. The trial balance shows cash and bank for 3680. The Account Receivable is now down to 18,140.

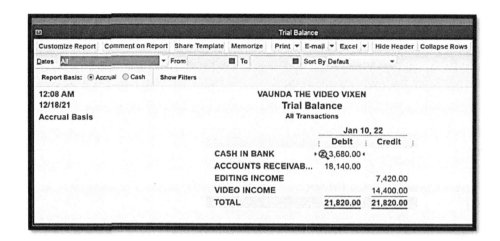

The Customer Balance Detail in the section of Betty shows a payment of 680, decreasing the balance of Betty to 6600.

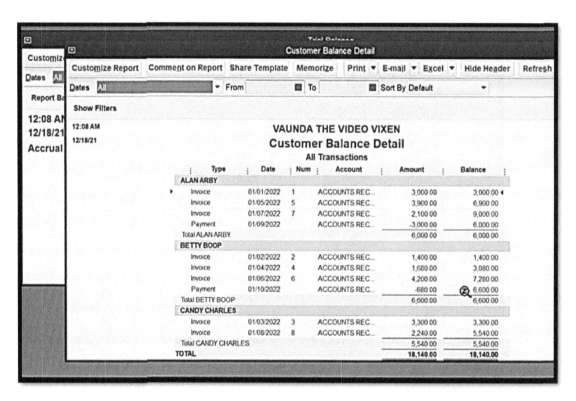

And when you look at the Open Invoice report you see invoice number four is only open in the amount of 1000 and that's because it was 1680 and we applied for the 680 payments.

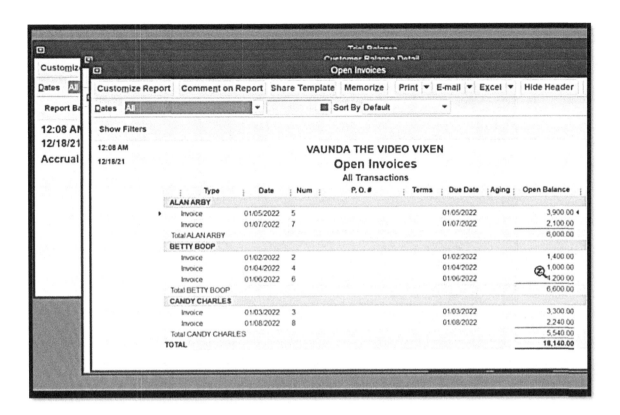

Deleting Transactions

This section is all about learning how to delete transactions and find which transactions were previously deleted. Deleting a transaction is a very simple thing to do but there are some things to remember that go along with it. Sometimes we cannot fix a mistake by editing a transaction therefore we must sometimes fix Mistakes by deleting the transaction and re-entering them. Deleting a transaction permanently removes the effect of the transaction and once it's gone you can never get it back. There is a permanent record of all deleted transactions in the report called "**Voided deleted transaction detail**". Now if you come to QuickBooks and you go to open it up, at first you will see it has nothing because you have not yet deleted anything or you did but you don't remember.

If you go to "**Reports**", then to "**Accountant and taxes**", you'll see "**Voided deleted transaction detail**".

If you click on it, of course, it says "**today**" but if you choose "**for all**," you can see that in the files that you've been using so far, you have not needed to delete any transaction.

You can as well put it up in the icon bar and for that, you simply go to "**View**", then add "**Voided deleted transactions**" to the icon bar and click OK.

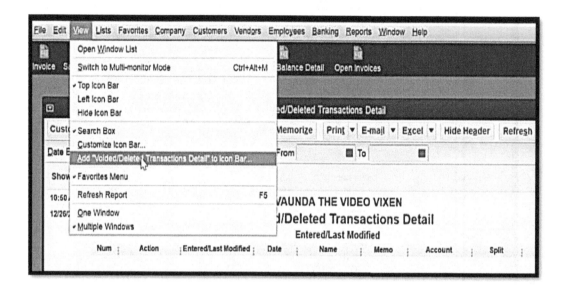

Now you can open it up and it will remember that you like the date range as "for all". Now let's practice deleting a transaction and see what happens. Using our example, we want to delete invoice number eight and the quickest way to find it and open it up would be to click on the Customer Balance Detail. So, we click the Customer Balance Detail and we see invoice number eight and when we double-click, it opens up.

Now how do you delete a transaction? There are two ways to do so: In the ribbon of the very window of the transaction that you're trying to delete there should be a delete button here.

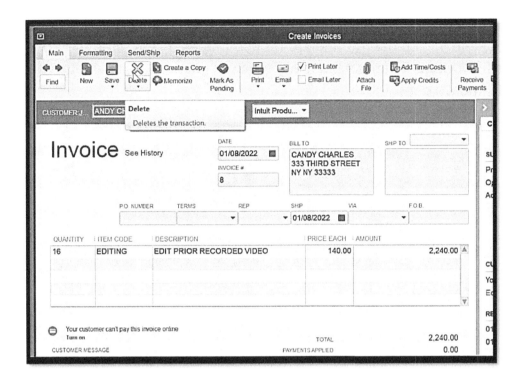

If there's no delete button then you can make the transaction the active window, and click "**Edit**", "**Delete**" and it'll bring up a prompt confirming you want to delete the invoice, delete sales receipt, delete check or whatever you want to have deleted.

The active window will be the name in the Edit drop-down that will give you the option to delete it. You can go ahead and use this as this is often the easy way. When you click to delete, it confirms that you are sure you want to delete this and if you are, click OK and it's gone.

How do you know it's gone? Well, it looks clearly like it disappeared from the report or reports that it's on and when you open the Voided Deleted Transaction Detail report, you can see that on a particular date and time you entered a transaction, and then on a later date, and time you deleted it. So, it gives an entire history of each of the transactions that were deleted and it even tells you the invoice number.

Recovering deleted transactions

Now that you know how to delete transactions let's fix what we just did by re-entering invoice number eight but be careful that when you go to do that you must edit the invoice number and change it back to the invoice number (in this case of our example, number eight). This is because QuickBooks remembers number eight was used and it will automatically open with the number nine; don't worry number nine will automatically be the next auto-generated invoice number after we re-enter number eight. In other words, QuickBooks remembers the pattern of what we do so if we close the reports and we just click the invoice window, QuickBooks suggests that this is invoice number nine because it remembers number eight however, it doesn't know that we're re-entering invoice number eight. So first, we change number nine to eight because we're putting back number eight. We put in the date that we were supposed to put, then the service and amount and for our example, totaling 2240 dollars; this is exactly a replica of the transaction that was deleted, and when we click "Save and close".

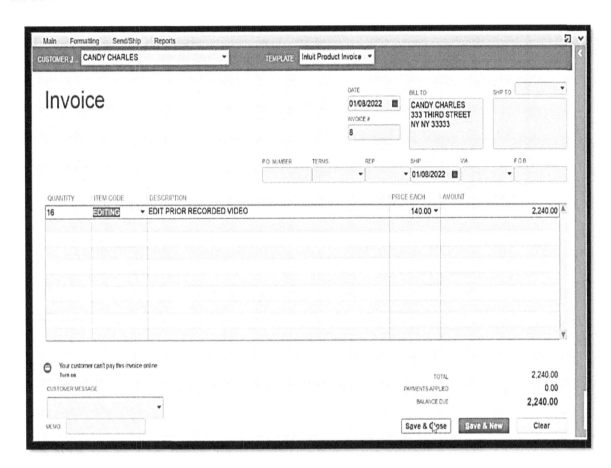

You can see the numbers in the reports go back to exactly what they were. However, the effect can be seen in the journal; the Journal report will also help you track your deleted transactions.

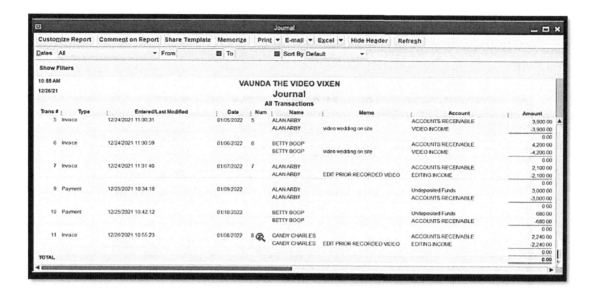

If you look in the leftmost column, you can see between seven and nine there was a transaction that must have been deleted and that was transaction number eight by looking at the date and time of the ones right before and the ones right after and the dates of the transactions of the ones right before and the ones right after, you will have a clear or a clearer picture of exactly what was deleted and what happened. But even more importantly, when you scroll to the bottom of the journal you can see that you just re-entered invoice number eight with the same date but yet transaction number 11.

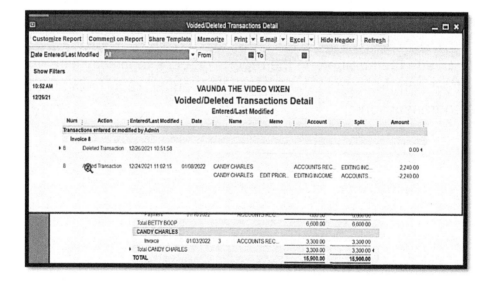

That's the effect of a deleted transaction in the journal and it's the combination of the Voided Deleted report combined with the Journal that helps show what had happened and when it was deleted.

Recording and managing Sales Receipts

In this section, we will look at how to record and manage sales receipts.

It is proper to enter a sales receipt when we receive payment immediately upon delivering our service to our clients. Entering a sales receipt is the same as recording an invoice; all transaction data is the same and the way you physically enter it into the computer is the same.

So, what happens in QuickBooks when you record a sales receipt? Well, you have more money in the bank so logically your cash and bank balance should increase at the moment you record the sale receipt and because you only record a receipt if you earned income, then the specific income account for the service you provided would increase in QuickBooks the moment you record the sale receipt.

For example, let's say on January 11 we did 10 video hours for Alan and we received payment immediately. We know that the money is directly deposited into the bank account in this example and we also know that the money amount will be 3000 dollars because that's 300 for each video hour times the quantity of 10 hours.

Recording your sales receipt

Let's go ahead and record our first sale receipt. From the Icon bar or the main menu, you click "**Sale Receipt**".

You'll see that since this is the first sale receipt it has the number one up here. The first thing you should do is that you have to choose the correct bank account that the money was directly deposited at the moment you provided the service. We'll learn about undeposited funds later if they put a check or cash in your hand but in this example, the money was directly deposited into the bank account and the date that it was deposited was January 11. The customer that gave you the money was customer Allen and the item or service you did was video weddings and the quantity was 10. So, you enter the information into the different fields of data exactly the way you learned previously when we recorded a sale receipt.

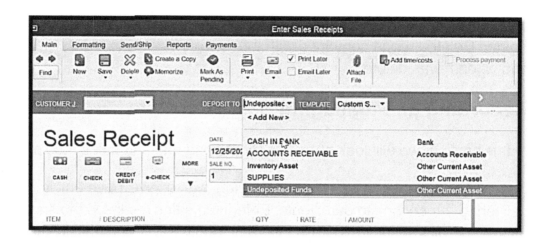

Now when you save this what will be the result? In the Trial Balance, right now Cash in Bank is only 3680. After we save the sale receipt it will increase by 3000 and become 6680. Video income now is only 14,400 as you can see but after you save this sale receipt it will increase by the 3000 dollars that we earned in video income on this receipt and it will become 17,400. When you click "**Save & Close**," notice the numbers are exactly as what we expected (cash and Bank increased to 6680 and video income increased to 17,400).

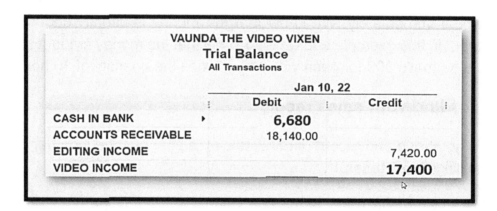

If you double-click video income you can see that the total of 17,400 comes from four previous invoices and one sale receipt and that's the way it looks in this account. However, the big question here is if it will affect `the Customer's Balance. The answer is that it will not.

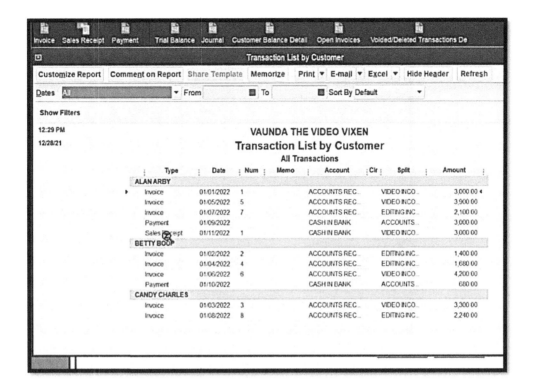

So, what reports will it show up on? Well, it cannot show up on the Customer Balance Detail because as you can see a sale receipt does not change the balance of the individual customer; the customer paid as soon as they got the service so for a sale receipt, they owe neither more nor less. The question now is if you can't see it on the Customer Balance Detail where in the customer records can you find the sales receipts? The answer is a report called "**Transaction List by Customer**".

From the main menu, you can click "**Reports**", and "**Customers and Receivables**" and go down to "**Transaction List by Customer**".

142

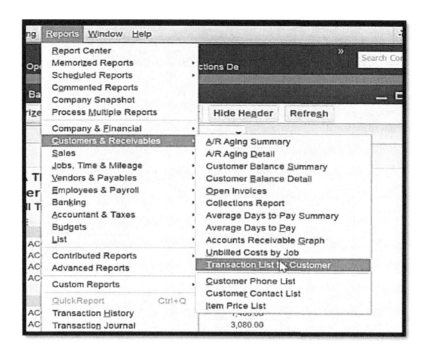

Select "for all" and now you can see that it lists every transaction that you ever recorded for every customer. It will not show you the running balance and it will not be able to tell you which invoices are paid or unpaid; it is simply a list of every event that happened between you and the customer in date order. Now you can see we had a sale receipt with Alan and even though it didn't change his balance it's still part of the history between you and Alan.

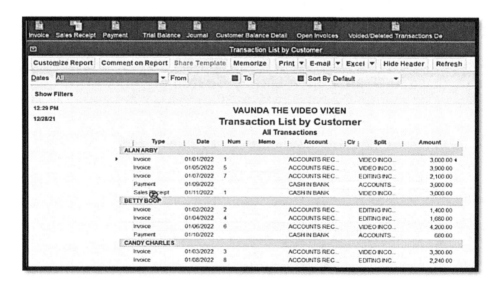

Before we do the second example let's put it up in the icon bar. To do so, go to **"View"**, add **"Transaction List by Customer"** to the icon bar and click OK and you can as well close the windows.

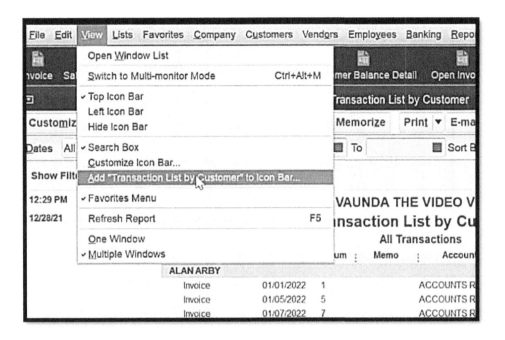

In the second example, on January 12 we did 10 editing hours for Betty and received payment immediately and that money was also directly deposited into the bank account. We know the amount is 1400 because each editing hour is 140 dollars and the quantity is 10. So, what will be the result in the trial balance after recording this second sale receipt? We have 1400 more in cash so cash will increase to 8080. The editing income that we earned will increase by 1400 and become 8820. We'll open the Sales Receipt window and make sure the cash and bank are chosen because that's the account the money went into and the date is the 12th of January. You'll notice QuickBooks automatically suggests Sale Receipt number two. The customer was Betty, the item of service was editing and the quantity was 10. We will enter these fields of data exactly the way we did when we recorded an invoice. Now our Trial Balance accounts change by 1400 and when we click "**Save & Close**" the results in the Trial Balance are exactly as what we expected (cash and Bank increased to 8800 and editing income increased to 8820).

144

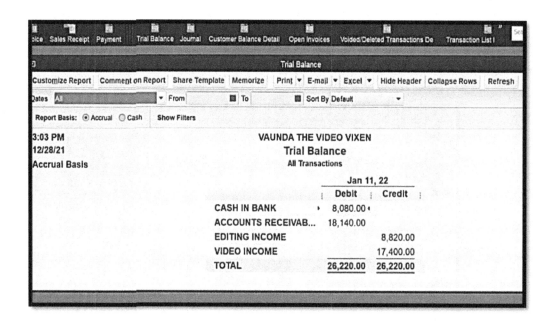

If we also open the Transaction List by Customer and look in the section of Betty, we will see that the Sale Receipt is there and you can see the account is editing income.

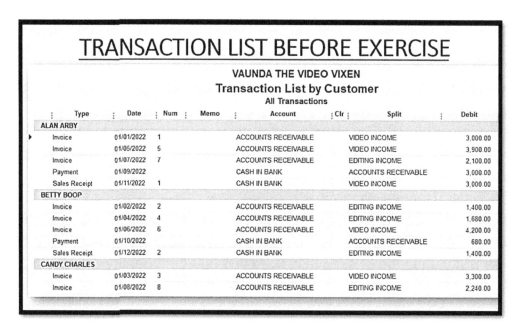

Practice

This section is your first full practice set with all the customer transactions that you just learned. The image below shows what your trial balance should look like.

TRIAL BALANCE BEFORE EXERCISE

VAUNDA THE VIDEO VIXEN
Trial Balance
All Transactions

	Jan 12, 22	
	Debit	Credit
CASH IN BANK	8,080.00	
ACCOUNTS RECEIVAB...	18,140.00	
EDITING INCOME		8,820.00
VIDEO INCOME		17,400.00

Before you begin this exercise, if it doesn't have these same numbers then you have to go back and correct the numbers the way we learned earlier. Make sure your starting numbers are correct before you begin the exercise. The image below is what the Customer Balance Detail should look like the moment you begin your exercise.

CUSTOMER BALANCE DETAIL BEFORE EXERCISE

VAUNDA THE VIDEO VIXEN
Customer Balance Detail
All Transactions

Type	Date	Num	Account	Amount	Balance
ALAN ARBY					
Invoice	01/01/2022	1	ACCOUNTS REC...	3,000.00	3,000.00
Invoice	01/05/2022	5	ACCOUNTS REC...	3,900.00	6,900.00
Invoice	01/07/2022	7	ACCOUNTS REC...	2,100.00	9,000.00
Payment	01/09/2022		ACCOUNTS REC...	-3,000.00	6,000.00
Total ALAN ARBY				6,000.00	6,000.00
BETTY BOOP					
Invoice	01/02/2022	2	ACCOUNTS REC...	1,400.00	1,400.00
Invoice	01/04/2022	4	ACCOUNTS REC...	1,680.00	3,080.00
Invoice	01/06/2022	6	ACCOUNTS REC...	4,200.00	7,280.00
Payment	01/10/2022		ACCOUNTS REC...	-680.00	6,600.00
Total BETTY BOOP				6,600.00	6,600.00
CANDY CHARLES					
Invoice	01/03/2022	3	ACCOUNTS REC...	3,300.00	3,300.00
Invoice	01/08/2022	8	ACCOUNTS REC...	2,240.00	5,540.00
Total CANDY CHARLES				5,540.00	5,540.00
TOTAL				18,140.00	18,140.00

The image below is what the Open Invoice would look like, remember it's still possible that your customer Balance Detail looks correct but your Open Invoice could still have wrong Open balances. One by one, make sure you have applied all previous customer payments to the correct invoice, and then each invoice balance will be correct.

OPEN INVOICE BEFORE EXERCISE

VAUNDA THE VIDEO VIXEN
Open Invoices
All Transactions

Type	Date	Num	P. O. #	Terms	Due Date	Aging	Open Balance
ALAN ARBY							
Invoice	01/05/2022	5			01/05/2022		3,900.00 ◀
Invoice	01/07/2022	7			01/07/2022		2,100.00
Total ALAN ARBY							6,000.00
BETTY BOOP							
Invoice	01/02/2022	2			01/02/2022		1,400.00
Invoice	01/04/2022	4			01/04/2022		1,000.00
Invoice	01/06/2022	6			01/06/2022		4,200.00
Total BETTY BOOP							6,600.00
CANDY CHARLES							
Invoice	01/08/2022	8			01/08/2022		2,240.00
Invoice	01/03/2022	3			02/03/2022		3,300.00
Total CANDY CHARLES							5,540.00
TOTAL							18,140.00

You can also check the Transaction List by Customer to make sure that everything is the same before you start inputting the transactions for the customer.

TRANSACTION LIST BEFORE EXERCISE

VAUNDA THE VIDEO VIXEN
Transaction List by Customer
All Transactions

Type	Date	Num	Memo	Account	Clr	Split	Debit
ALAN ARBY							
Invoice	01/01/2022	1		ACCOUNTS RECEIVABLE		VIDEO INCOME	3,000.00
Invoice	01/05/2022	5		ACCOUNTS RECEIVABLE		VIDEO INCOME	3,900.00
Invoice	01/07/2022	7		ACCOUNTS RECEIVABLE		EDITING INCOME	2,100.00
Payment	01/09/2022			CASH IN BANK		ACCOUNTS RECEIVABLE	3,000.00
Sales Receipt	01/11/2022	1		CASH IN BANK		VIDEO INCOME	3,000.00
BETTY BOOP							
Invoice	01/02/2022	2		ACCOUNTS RECEIVABLE		EDITING INCOME	1,400.00
Invoice	01/04/2022	4		ACCOUNTS RECEIVABLE		EDITING INCOME	1,680.00
Invoice	01/06/2022	6		ACCOUNTS RECEIVABLE		VIDEO INCOME	4,200.00
Payment	01/10/2022			CASH IN BANK		ACCOUNTS RECEIVABLE	680.00
Sales Receipt	01/12/2022	2		CASH IN BANK		EDITING INCOME	1,400.00
CANDY CHARLES							
Invoice	01/03/2022	3		ACCOUNTS RECEIVABLE		VIDEO INCOME	3,300.00
Invoice	01/08/2022	8		ACCOUNTS RECEIVABLE		EDITING INCOME	2,240.00

Below are the transactions in this exercise. You can slowly and carefully read each transaction one by one, this way you can think about each transaction that you're inputting. If you forgot how to put in a particular transaction, then you have to go back and review the chapter or section where we learned how to record that transaction type.

HERE ARE THE TRANSACTIONS

13-Jan	DID 19 EDITING HOURS "ON ACCOUNT" (MAKE INVOICE) FOR CANDY
14-Jan	RECEIVED $1,400 FROM BETTY FRO INVOICE # 2 - JAN 2 - DIRECT DEPOSIT
15-Jan	DID 18 VIDEO HOURS FOR ALAN ARBY - PAID US BY DIRECT DEPSOST
16-Jan	RECEIVED $240 FROM CANDY FOR INVOICE # 8 - JAN 8
17-Jan	DID 17 EDITING HOURS "ON ACCOUNT' (MAKE INVOICE) FOR ALAN
18-Jan	DID 16 VIDEO HOURS FOR BETTY - DIRECT DEPOSIT
19-Jan	RECEIVED $1000 FROM ALAN TO APPLY TO THE OLDEST INVOICE
20-Jan	DID 15 EDITING HOURS FOR CANDY - DIRECT DEPOSIT
21-Jan	DID 14 VIDEO HOURS "ON ACCOUNT" FOR CANDY
22-Jan	RECEIVED $300 FROM CANDY FOR INVOICE # 3

When you finish slowly and carefully recording these transactions in order, the trial balance should look like what you have below. If it does not look exactly like this after finishing these transactions then you have to use the techniques that we learned in one of the chapters to find and fix your mistakes so that when you finish, the Trial Balance numbers are precisely these numbers.

TRIAL BALANCE AFTER EXERCISE

VAUNDA THE VIDEO VIXEN
Trial Balance
All Transactions

	Jan 22, 22	
	Debit	Credit
CASH IN BANK	23,320.00	
ACCOUNTS RECEIVABLE	24,440.00	
EDITING INCOME		15,960.00
VIDEO INCOME		31,800.00
TOTAL	47,760.00	47,760.00

The image below is what the Customer Balance Detail should look like after the exercise. You can compare each transaction one by one to the Customer Balance Detail that you have on your computer to make sure you have the same results.

CUSTOMER BALANCE DETAIL AFTER EXERCISE

VAUNDA THE VIDEO VIXEN
Customer Balance Detail
All Transactions

Type	Date	Num	Account	Amount	Balance
ALAN ARBY					
Invoice	01/01/2022	1	ACCOUNTS REC...	3,000.00	3,000.00 ◄
Invoice	01/05/2022	5	ACCOUNTS REC...	3,900.00	6,900.00
Invoice	01/07/2022	7	ACCOUNTS REC...	2,100.00	9,000.00
Payment	01/09/2022		ACCOUNTS REC...	-3,000.00	6,000.00
Invoice	01/17/2022	10	ACCOUNTS REC...	2,380.00	8,380.00
Payment	01/15/2022		ACCOUNTS REC...	-1,000.00	7,380.00
Total ALAN ARBY				7,380.00	7,380.00
BETTY BOOP					
Invoice	01/02/2022	2	ACCOUNTS REC...	1,400.00	1,400.00
Invoice	01/04/2022	4	ACCOUNTS REC...	1,680.00	3,080.00
Invoice	01/06/2022	6	ACCOUNTS REC...	4,200.00	7,280.00
Payment	01/10/2022		ACCOUNTS REC...	-680.00	6,600.00
Payment	01/14/2022		ACCOUNTS REC...	-1,400.00	5,200.00
Total BETTY BOOP				5,200.00	5,200.00
CANDY CHARLES					
Invoice	01/03/2022	3	ACCOUNTS REC...	3,300.00	3,300.00
Invoice	01/08/2022	8	ACCOUNTS REC...	2,240.00	5,540.00
Invoice	01/13/2022	9	ACCOUNTS REC...	2,660.00	8,200.00
Payment	01/16/2022		ACCOUNTS REC...	-240.00	7,960.00
Invoice	01/21/2022	11	ACCOUNTS REC...	4,200.00	12,160.00
Payment	01/22/2022		ACCOUNTS REC...	-300.00	11,860.00
Total CANDY CHARLES				11,860.00	11,860.00
TOTAL				24,440.00	24,440.00

You also have the Open Invoice after the exercise. Remember the Open Invoice report could still have wrong invoice balances even if the Customer Balance Detail is correct of course this is one of the best reports that will help you find and fix any mistakes you might have made because it simply lists each transaction for each customer in date order.

OPEN INVOICE AFTER EXERCISE

VAUNDA THE VIDEO VIXEN
Open Invoices
All Transactions

Type	Date	Num	P. O. #	Terms	Due Date	Aging	Open Balance
ALAN ARBY							
Invoice	01/05/2022	5			01/05/2022		2,900.00 ◄
Invoice	01/07/2022	7			01/07/2022		2,100.00
Invoice	01/17/2022	10			01/17/2022		2,380.00
Total ALAN ARBY							7,380.00
BETTY BOOP							
Invoice	01/04/2022	4			01/04/2022		1,000.00
Invoice	01/06/2022	6			01/06/2022		4,200.00
Total BETTY BOOP							5,200.00
CANDY CHARLES							
Invoice	01/08/2022	8			01/08/2022		2,000.00
Invoice	01/13/2022	9			01/13/2022		2,660.00
Invoice	01/21/2022	11			01/21/2022		4,200.00
Invoice	01/03/2022	3			02/03/2022		3,000.00
Total CANDY CHARLES							11,860.00
TOTAL							24,440.00

This is to make sure that all your transactions are correct after the exercise but then the question is what if you have some mistakes how do you figure it out? Again, use what you've learned to find and fix your mistakes in bookkeeping. The answer is always there and the answer is always findable.

Some things to consider

Before you even begin the exercise let's look at the three most common mistakes that you might have after the exercise and help you fix them. If your trial balance is correct but the total balance of each customer is wrong what possible mistake could cause that condition? You can take a moment to think about the question and think about what type of mistake would allow all the numbers in your trial balance to be correct but yet some or all of your customers' total balances become wrong. What do you think the answer is? The answer is you chose the wrong customer on an invoice or a payment only. Choosing the wrong customer on an invoice or payment would allow the trial balance to still be correct but the individual customer balances to be wrong. So, if that's the condition, then that's the solution.

This next common mistake is what if your Accounts Receivable balance is too high after the exercise and the Cash in Bank balance is too low after the exercise? This means you have all your income accounts and all your other accounts correct except Accounts Receivable and cash in Bank. The answer is you made an Invoice instead of a Sale Receipt because invoices increase Accounts Receivable when you create them and Sales Receipts increase cash and Bank when you create them. So, if you created an invoice instead of a Sale Receipt, Accounts Receivable was increased instead of cash and bank and that would cause Accounts Receivable to be too high and Cash in Bank to be too low. You would have to delete the wrong one and re-enter the right one because you cannot make a Sale Receipt become an invoice and you cannot make an invoice become a Sale Receipt.

The last common mistake is if the total balance of a customer is correct but the individual invoice balances are wrong. This means that the trial balance is correct, and all the total balances of each customer are correct but the Open Invoice report shows wrong balances on the individual Open Invoices. The answer is you applied a customer's payment to the wrong invoice.

Those are the three puzzles that you might encounter when you finish the exercise and those are the answers to those puzzles. All the other mistakes are easy to fix. If you think you have a date mistake you can use your Journal report to see if the transactions are not put in date order and to see if you're missing any.

150

Review Questions

1. How do you create an invoice?
2. What do we mean by Accounts Receivable?
3. How do you recover deleted transactions?
4. What is a Sales Receipt?

CHAPTER 8

INPUT AND MANAGE SERVICE ITEMS

In this section, you will see how to Input and manage service items on the QuickBooks desktop items list. We will start with explaining the terms involved and proceed to showing you the processes involved in creating an item list.

What is an item?

You may now ask, what is an item? In QuickBooks, an item is a product or service that we buy or sell and of course, if it's a product or service that we buy or sell, therefore, an item is something that we list on a receipt or an invoice and both of these things are true.

For example, if you had a business where you sold oranges, then oranges would be the first item on your items list so that you have the physical ability to place that item on an invoice with all the other information that comes from the item in the items list.

In a company where you give video service, you would have to put video service on the items list with all the other information you see that appears on the invoice.

What items do regarding the magic behind the scenes is that items allow us to track our income so that we know how much money we're making for each of the different services and we can compare how much we made from one compared to how much we made from the other.

The Item List

What do we mean? If you go to your Chart of accounts, you know that if you perform an editing service, the money for the editing service should only be recorded in the editing income account and not the video income account and you know that if you do a video service, the money you earn from that should be recorded and tracked in the video income account and not the editing income account; that's what items on the items list allow us to do so that when we make an invoice we can list the amount of money we earn for editing and that amount would be recorded in editing income and the editing income account would increase and of course, if that same invoice had a line for video Services, then the amount specified for the video service would be tracked and recorded in the video income account. That's what the items list allows us to do.

Below is an example of the list of the two items that a company gives as services. Notice it lists the name, the description, the fact that it's a service, not a product, the hourly rate, and most importantly the column on the right is telling you which account in the Chart of Accounts that item is tracked. That means when we list the video and we put the quantity, it will multiply that times 300 and put that amount here into the video income account but if we put the editing service on the invoice this description would come up 140 comes up and the amount for the editing service would instead be tracked to this account editing income.

NAME	DESCRIPTION	TYPE	RATE $	ACCOUNT
VIDEO	VIDEO WEDDINGS ON SITE	SERVICE	$300 PER HOUR	VIDEO INCOME
EDITING	EDITING PRIOR RECORDED VIDEO	SERVICE	$140 PER HOUR	EDITING INCOME

Opening the Item List

Let's go ahead and record these two items on the items list. From the main menu go to "**List**", then "**Items list**". You can make it a little wider and a little taller.

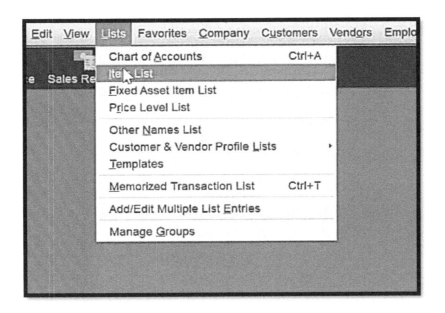

As you learned from the Chart of accounts, the bottom left button of each list window controls the list. Click "**Item**", then "**New**".

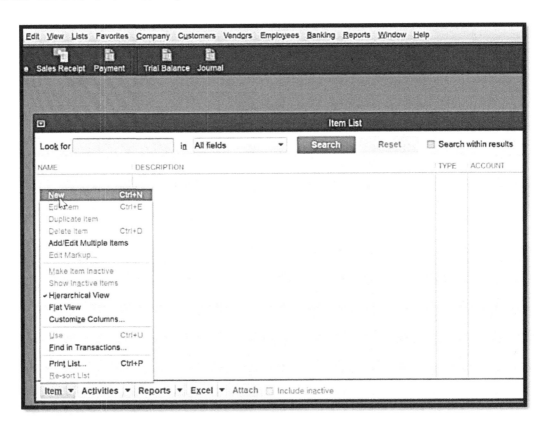

Of course, both of what we are working with are under service. The first one will be a video wedding: the description is "video on-site", and the rate that was charged for videotaping a wedding is 300 but the most important thing is which account this item gets tracked to. Video weddings get tracked to video income so when you click the drop-down, you go down and choose "**video income**". Make sure that's the account chosen and when you click OK you can see from the items list the name, the description, the account that it's tracked to, and the price.

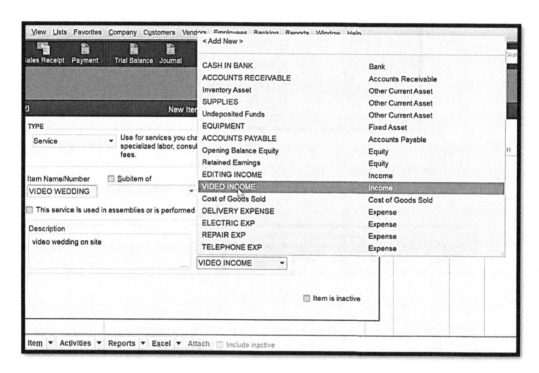

Let's proceed with the second item. Go to "**Item**", and "**New**" and as you saw from the example, the second service is editing. The description is "**Edit prior recorded video**", the company charges 140 an hour for that and the account that that income gets tracked to would not be "video income", you would have to click and choose editing income, and when you click OK you can see the items list is exactly what we need, which is editing for 140 an hour and video weddings for 300 an hour.

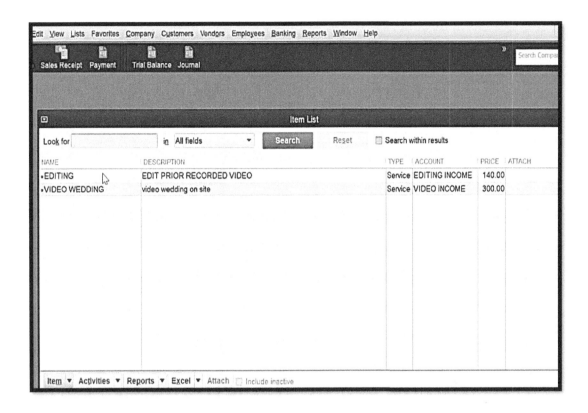

Review Questions

1. What is an item?
2. What is the function of an Item List?
3. How do you record an Item in QuickBooks?

SECTION FOUR

MANAGING EXPENSES & BANKING FEATURES

CHAPTER 9

RECORDING AND MANAGING EXPENSES

Welcome to the section where we shall look at vendors and payable types of transactions. Anything that relates to expenses will be learned in this chapter. We will discuss extensively on how to pay and manage vendors bills, including the accounts involved in these transactions.

Accounts Payable

This section is all about defining Accounts Payable. Account Payable is keeping records of vendors and vendor transactions. It's all about keeping track of what you owe to vendors for products and services that they have given you. Just like total Account Receivable is equal to all the money that every customer together owes us, Accounts Payable is the account, and the Chart of Accounts represents the total money owed to all vendors combined.

For example, let's say that we owe Edison 200. We owe UPS 400 and Staples 600. This means the balance of Accounts Payable in the trial balance should be the total of all three vendors which is 1200 dollars.

Any vendor's balance in Accounts Payable will go up when you enter a bill and receive a service or product and any vendor's balance along with total Accounts Payable will go down whenever you pay a specific vendor for what you owe.

Now just like with customers where we have the Customer Balance Detail, guess what with vendors it's the same thing; there's a report called **Vendor Balance Detail**.

From the main menu go to "**Reports**", "**Vendors & payables**", and **Vendor Balance Detail**.

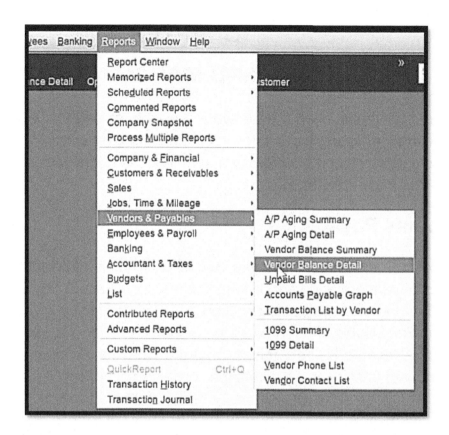

At the moment that this is the active window, click "**View**", **add Vendor Balance Detail to the icon bar** and click OK.

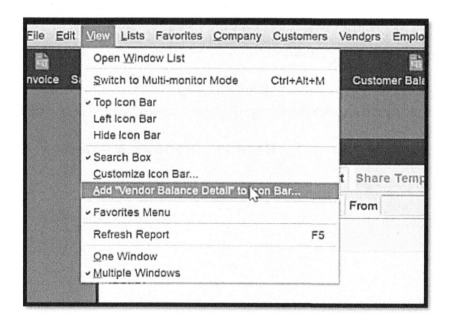

Now you have this shortcut that you can look at right after you record all our vendor transactions.

Entering and managing vendors' bills

In QuickBooks, the word Bill and the word Invoice mostly mean the same thing. QuickBooks calls it an invoice if we are the ones sending it to a customer and QuickBooks calls it a bill if we're the ones receiving it from a vendor, but basically, it's a document asking someone to pay for something that they took or used.

The Bill window is very easy to enter and there's not that much information to put when you enter a bill but the question is what areas of your accounting will be affected?

Entering a bill is a transaction so, of course, your general ledger and Chart of Accounts will be affected and those results will show up on the trial balance but from that very same bill, your vendor records will also be changed.

In our case, we're looking at the vendor records through the Vendor Balance Detail. Let's take a look at our first example: let's say on January 22nd we received the electric bill from Edison, the bill is 1000 dollars and its bill number 6161. What will happen in the trial balance? If we receive an electric bill from Edison on January 22 and we did not pay it, what will be the result in the trial balance?

After recording and entering this first bill, Accounts Payable will show up in the trial balance for the very first time as 1000 dollars because you now owe 1000 dollars to a vendor and electric expense will show up for the first time also as 1000 dollars because you used 1000 dollars' worth of electricity service.

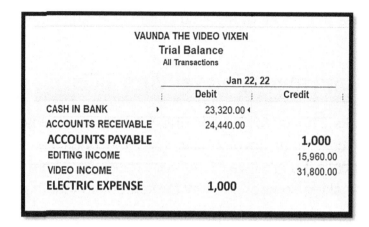

What else will be the result? In the Vendor details subsidiary records, you will see on the Vendor Balance Detail Edison shows up for the first time indicating that we owe this specific vendor 1000 dollars.

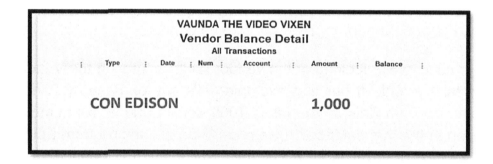

From the main menu we'll go to "**Vendor**", and "**Enter bills**" and this brings up the "Enter Bills" window.

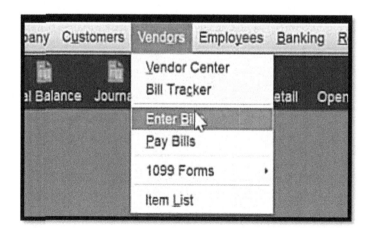

In this window, notice that you have a ribbon that you can collapse just like the other transaction windows that we used and you have a side panel that will show all the transactions from that vendor as soon as you select the specific vendor. In this case, Edison had no prior transactions that we recorded so we won't see anything the moment we choose the vendor Edison.

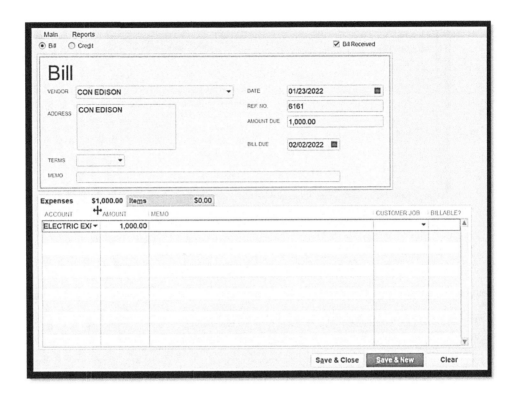

Now we'll put the date January 23rd of 2022, bill number 6161, the amount which is 1000 dollars. If we collapse the side panel you can see that the amount was automatically copied below where you would name the specific expense account that represents the service that you received from the vendor. In this example, it's an electric expense so we have who we have when we have what, how much, and why regarding this transaction, and when we click "Save & Close", we can open the trial balance and you see the results are exactly as what we expected. Accounts Payable showed up for the first time as 1000 dollars and electric expense also showed up for the first time as 1000 dollars.

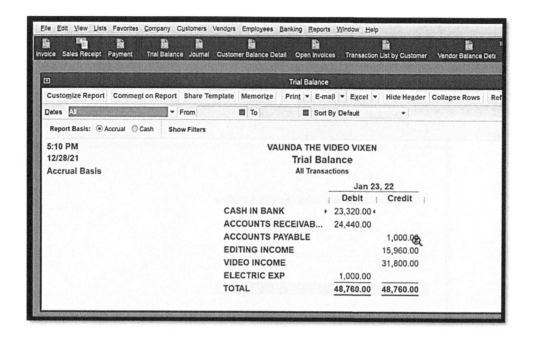

You may also notice that the Vendor Balance Detail right now shows that you owe only Edison 1000 dollars for Bill number 6161.

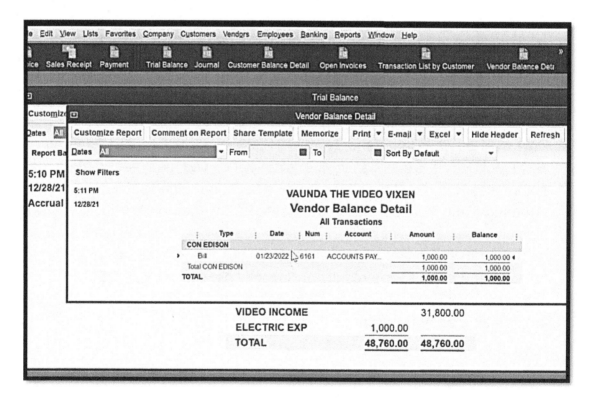

Now let's try a second example: let's say on January 23rd we received a repair bill from Rex repair shop for 2000 dollars with bill number 6262. What will be the result in the trial balance after recording this second vendor's bill?

Repair expenses will show up for the first time as 2000 dollars and because we owe 2000 dollars more to a vendor, we now increase Accounts Payable to 3000 dollars. If you ask why Accounts Payable is 3000 dollars, the vendor balance detail will show you we previously owed Edison 1000 and we also owe Rex repair shop 2000, hence the reason why Accounts Payable in the trial balance is 3000.

	VAUNDA THE VIDEO VIXEN				
	Vendor Balance Detail				
	All Transactions				
Type	Date	Num	Account	Amount	
CON EDISON				**1,000**	
REX REPAIR SHOP				**2,000**	
▶ TOTAL	**NEW TOTAL**			**3,000**	

Let's enter it the way we did, which you are now familiar with. We'll go to "**Vendor**", and Enter "Bills". We'll input the date as January 23rd. Rex repair shop is the vendor, the reference number is Bill number 6262, for 2000 dollars, and the reason why we owe Rex repair shop is for repair expenses. So now we have all the information we need on the bill and then click "Save & Close."

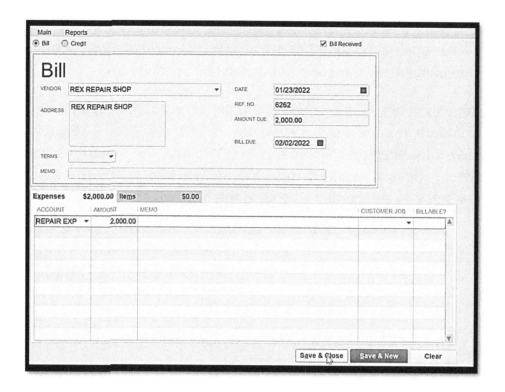

You can see that the results in the trial balance are exactly as we expected. Accounts Payable is 3000 and repair expense is 2000.

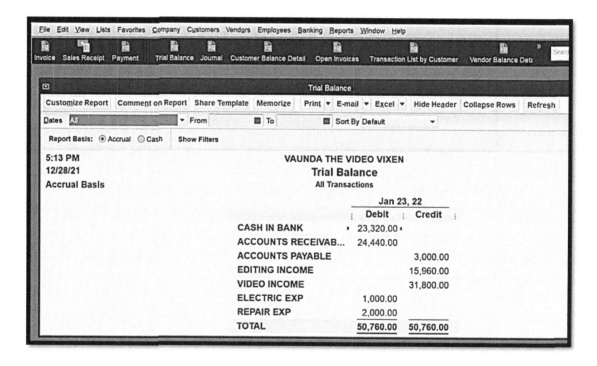

Again, if you want to know why the Accounts Payable is 3000, you can open the Vendor Balance Detail and you can see we owe Edison 1000 for this bill and we also owe Rex repair shop 2000 for this bill that we just entered.

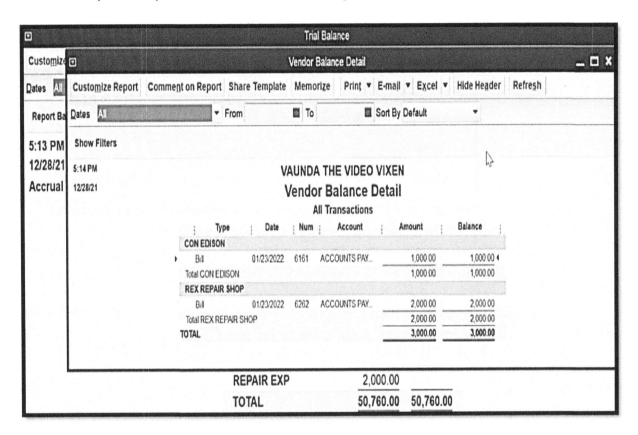

Practice entering bills

Let's look at your first practice exercise with entering bills. You will check your QuickBooks skills in this video by doing an enter Bill exercise entering only the type of transaction that we just recently learned. After that, you will practice your QuickBooks problem-solving skills by answering two logical questions. So you'll have some data entry practice, some QuickBooks practice, and some problem-solving regarding QuickBooks.

For this exercise, the image below is how your trial balance should look before the exercise. Make sure each of the numbers in front of you are the same as the numbers in your trial balance before you start, if not, then you may have to go back to Prior chapters to figure out which one was wrong and use the techniques that you've learned to fix it.

TRIAL BALANCE BEFORE THE EXERCISE

VAUNDA THE VIDEO VIXEN
Trial Balance
All Transactions

	Jan 23, 22	
	Debit	Credit
CASH IN BANK	23,320.00 ◄	
ACCOUNTS RECEIVAB...	24,440.00	
ACCOUNTS PAYABLE		3,000.00
EDITING INCOME		15,960.00
VIDEO INCOME		31,800.00
ELECTRIC EXP	1,000.00	
REPAIR EXP	2,000.00	
TOTAL	50,760.00	50,760.00

The image is what the Vendor Balance Detail should look like at the beginning of this exercise. We only entered two bills and we're not doing bill payments yet.

VENDOR BALANCE DETAIL BEFORE THE EXERCISE

VAUNDA THE VIDEO VIXEN
Vendor Balance Detail
All Transactions

Type	Date	Num	Account	Amount	Balance
CON EDISON					
Bill	01/23/2022	6161	ACCOUNTS PAY...	1,000.00	1,000.00 ◄
Total CON EDISON				1,000.00	1,000.00
REX REPAIR SHOP					
Bill	01/23/2022	6262	ACCOUNTS PAY...	2,000.00	2,000.00
Total REX REPAIR SHOP				2,000.00	2,000.00
TOTAL				3,000.00	3,000.00

The image below shows the bills that you should enter during this exercise. It's very simple eight consecutive bills, clearly marked and you are to record them in the "Enter Bills" window the same way that we did the two prior ones when we first learned.

Here are the bills to enter

24-Jan	RECEIVED THE VERIZON BILL FOR TELEPHONE $1,800 BILL #7171
25-Jan	RECEIVED THE STAPLES BILL FOR SUPPLIES $680 BILL #7272
26-Jan	RECEIVED THE U.P.S BILL FOR DELIVERY $1,600 BILL #7373
27-Jan	RECEIVED THE CON EDISON BILL FOR ELECTRICITY $1,150 BILL #7474
28-Jan	RECEIVED THE REX BILL FOR REPAIR $2,050 BILL #7575
29-Jan	RECEIVED THE STAPLES BILL FOR EQUIPMENT $1,095 BILL #7676
30-Jan	RECEIVED THE VERIZON BILL FOR TELEPHONE $800 BILL #7878
31-Jan	RECEIVED THE U.P.S BILL FOR DELIVERY $1,110 BILL #7979

When you finish, your trial balance after the exercise should look like what you have in the image below. Make sure each of the numbers here matches each of the numbers in your trial balance or you will have to apply the techniques that you learned to find and fix mistakes.

TRIAL BALANCE AFTER THE EXERCISE

VAUNDA THE VIDEO VIXEN
Trial Balance
All Transactions

	Debit	Credit
	Jan 31, 22	
CASH IN BANK	23,320.00	
ACCOUNTS RECEIVAB...	24,440.00	
SUPPLIES	680.00	
EQUIPMENT	1,095.00	
ACCOUNTS PAYABLE		13,285.00
EDITING INCOME		15,960.00
VIDEO INCOME		31,800.00
DELEVERY EXP	2,710.00	
ELECTRIC EXP	2,150.00	
REPAIR EXP	4,050.00	
TELEPHONE EXP	2,600.00	
TOTAL	61,045.00	61,045.00

The image below is what your Vendor Balance detail should look like after the exercise.

168

VENDOR BALANCE DETAIL AFTER THE EXERCISE

VAUNDA THE VIDEO VIXEN
Vendor Balance Detail
All Transactions

Type	Date	Num	Account	Amount	Balance
CON EDISON					
Bill	01/23/2022	6161	ACCOUNTS PAY...	1,000.00	1,000.00 ◄
Bill	01/27/2022	7474	ACCOUNTS PAY...	1,150.00	2,150.00
Total CON EDISON				2,150.00	2,150.00
REX REPAIR SHOP					
Bill	01/23/2022	6262	ACCOUNTS PAY...	2,000.00	2,000.00
Bill	01/28/2022	7575	ACCOUNTS PAY...	2,050.00	4,050.00
Total REX REPAIR SHOP				4,050.00	4,050.00
STAPLES					
Bill	01/25/2022	7272	ACCOUNTS PAY...	680.00	680.00
Bill	01/29/2022	7676	ACCOUNTS PAY...	1,095.00	1,775.00
Total STAPLES				1,775.00	1,775.00
U.P.S.					
Bill	01/26/2022	7373	ACCOUNTS PAY...	1,600.00	1,600.00
Bill	01/31/2022	7979	ACCOUNTS PAY...	1,110.00	2,710.00
Total U.P.S.				2,710.00	2,710.00
VERIZON					
Bill	01/24/2022	7171	ACCOUNTS PAY...	1,800.00	1,800.00
Bill	01/30/2022	7878	ACCOUNTS PAY...	800.00	2,600.00
Total VERIZON				2,600.00	2,600.00
TOTAL				13,285.00	13,285.00

You can pause at this point and check to make sure that all of the bills here match all of the bills in your computer with the same numbers and all the same details. If they don't, you may have one of two common mistakes. Now let's look at a logical question to see if you had one of those mistakes or if you know what went wrong and how to fix it. The first question is, what if your equipment balance is higher than what you saw earlier and the balance of your supplies is lower than what you see in the trial balance, we presented a moment ago? You can pause for a moment and think about what would cause that condition when entering a series of bills. The answer is that you chose the Supplies Account instead of the Equipment account on a bill from Staples when you were entering bills and putting the account in the bottom left part of the window. That would be the type of mistake that would cause that condition. You can go back and fix it if that was your problem. The second logical question is what if your trial balance is correct, which means the total Account Payable is correct but the balance of each vendor or some of your individual vendors' balances is wrong, what would be the only type of mistake that would cause that condition? Well, the answer is you chose the wrong vendor on a bill or bill payment. So, by entering these bills and matching numbers and answering these questions you are improving your QuickBooks skill.

169

Paying vendors bills

When you make a bill payment, obviously that's a transaction and anything that is a transaction will be recorded in the Chart of Accounts in the general ledger and the results will always immediately change the trial balance. When you pay a specific vendor's Bill, the vendor records will change at that moment, and as you remember the report that we're using to reflect the vendor records is the **Vendor Balance Detail**. So, from that same bill payment, both the trial balance and the Vendor Balance Detail will change. For example, let's say on February 1st we paid Edison 1000 dollars specifically for Bill number 6161 and we paid with check number one which is a handwritten check. As we proceed, we'll explain more about checks but for now, let's just concentrate on how to record this bill payment. So, what will be the results after we record this first bill payment? Cash in Bank should go down because we just paid money and because we owe less to a vendor as a result of this transaction, Accounts Payable will also decrease by the same 1000-dollar bill payment. Therefore, what will be the result in the trial balance after we record the February 1st bill payment? Cash in Bank decreases by 1000 to become 22,320 and Accounts Payable also decreases by 1000 to become 12,285.

VAUNDA THE VIDEO VIXEN
Trial Balance
All Transactions

	Jan 31, 22	
	Debit	Credit
CASH IN BANK	22,320	
ACCOUNTS RECEIVAB...	24,440.00	
SUPPLIES	680.00	
EQUIPMENT	1,095.00	
ACCOUNTS PAYABLE		12,285
EDITING INCOME		15,960.00
VIDEO INCOME		31,800.00
DELEVERY EXP	2,710.00	
ELECTRIC EXP	2,150.00	
REPAIR EXP	4,050.00	
TELEPHONE EXP	2,600.00	

We know that the changes are also in the vendor records in the **Vendor Balance Detail**.

WHAT WILL HAPPEN IN THE VENDOR BALANCE DETAIL?

VAUNDA THE VIDEO VIXEN
Vendor Balance Detail
All Transactions

	Type	Date	Num	Account	Amount	Balance
CON EDISON						
▶	Bill	01/23/2022	6161	ACCOUNTS PAY...	1,000.00	1,000.00 ◀
	Bill	01/27/2022	7474	ACCOUNTS PAY...	1,150.00	2,150.00
BILL PAYMENT		02/01/2022			**-1,000**	**1,150**

The image above shows what Edison's detail looks like before this bill payment but this bill payment will lower the balance of this particular vendor and it will be listed separately. So, on the Vendor Balance Detail, each bill will be listed with each payment in date-order to give you the running balance of 1150.

However, you will notice that in this case the Vendor Balance Detail is not enough and that's because it's difficult when you look at the Vendor Balance Detail to know what bills were paid and what bills were not paid. In other words, you don't know how the bill payments were applied so we need another report. We need to see what bills were paid and what bills remain unpaid. The name of the report that shows the unpaid bills is called the **Unpaid Bills Detail** report.

From the main menu, go to "**Reports**", "**Vendors & Payables**" and then "**Unpaid Bills Detail**" and this opens up the window for that.

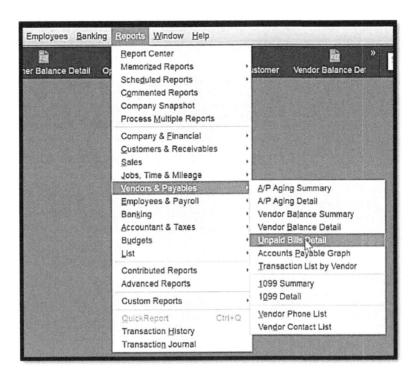

The image below shows what the Unpaid Bills Detail report looks like.

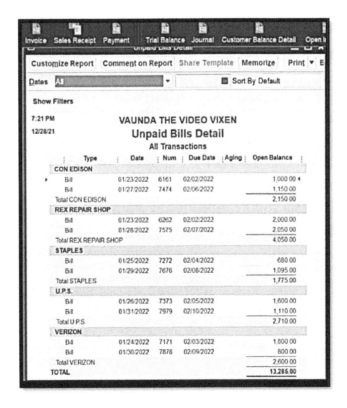

You'll see it says today but if we click the drop-down and select "All", you can see that at this moment the Unpaid Bills report looks very similar to the Vendor Balance Detail.

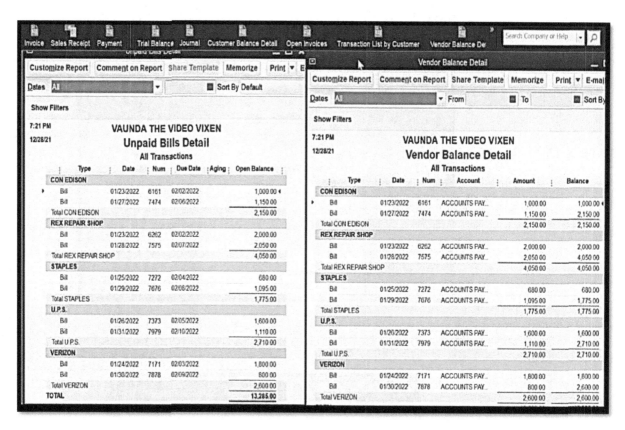

If we put them side by side you can see that if you only have bills and you don't have any bill payments these two reports are exactly alike, however, what's going to happen after the bill is paid is that in the Vendor Balance Detail, you will see what we saw a moment ago; a minus here for the bill payment and the balance going down but in the Unpaid Bills report for the same bill payment you will see this bill simply disappear from the Unpaid Bill report and then it would start to look different from the Vendor Balance Detail even though it will have the same balance.

Let's go ahead and put the unpaid bills into the icon bar. From the top left click **"View,"** then **add Unpaid Bills to the icon bar** and click OK.

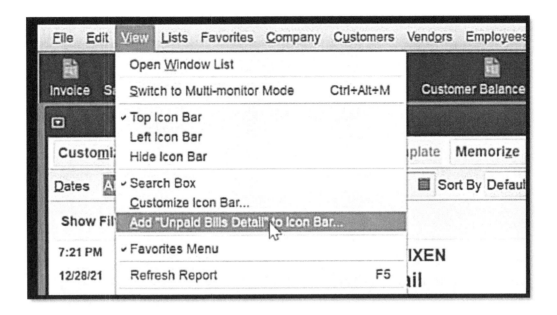

Now when you open it, it will already say "all" transactions. From the main menu click "**Vendors**", and "**Pay Bills**" and it opens up the "**Pay Bills**" window.

Notice it has every unpaid bill listed on the left and the best thing you can do is click the filter drop-down and choose the vendor whose bills you're paying. This way it will isolate those bills and it will be easy to see.

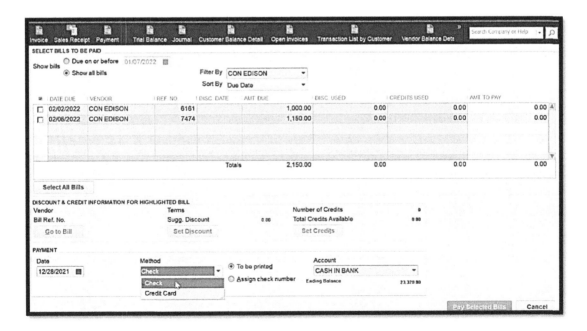

174

Then of course you have to be very careful down here; don't let this trip you up. You'll see that in the method of payment, by default they put schedule online payment so that they can sell you their online bill payment services but if you're just writing a handwritten check, choose check and that gives you the ability to put in the date that you're paying the bill which in this case is February 1 (be careful here as this frustrates a lot of people) and now that you're able to put the date and you chose which vendor, all you have to do is go to the middle section here and if this is the bill you're paying all you have to do is click the check box in the left column and by clicking to put the check mark there QuickBooks will indicate that the amount you're paying is the amount of the whole bill.

Now you have to make sure that you choose the correct bank account you're paying from and you have to put this assigned check number. We're going to talk more later about checks in general and specifically printing checks but these should be the options to give you a smooth bill payment without a problem.

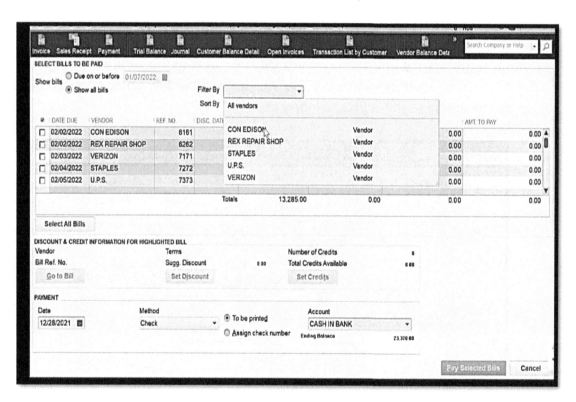

Now when you click "Pay Selected Bill," another window pops up and you have to put number one (we're imagining that we paid with check number one, and of course, a full discussion of checks is coming in another chapter but this is the way that you would put it), click OK, now click "Done" and now let's check our results.

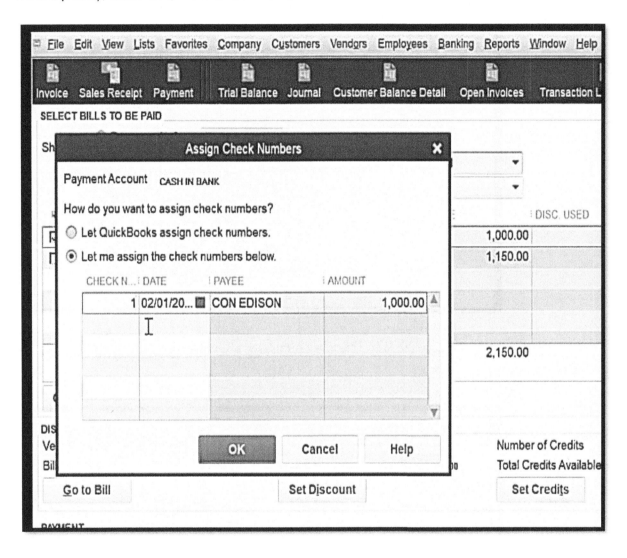

When we open the Trial Balance, you can see that the numbers are exactly as we expected: Cash in Bank went down by 1000 to 22320, and Accounts Payable went down by a thousand to 12285.

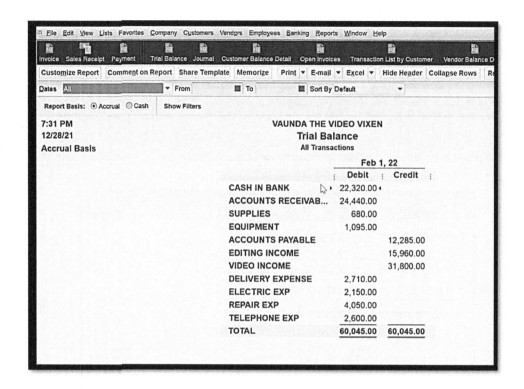

We can look at the Vendor Balance Detail and for Edison, you can see that the balance decreased by a thousand to 1150.

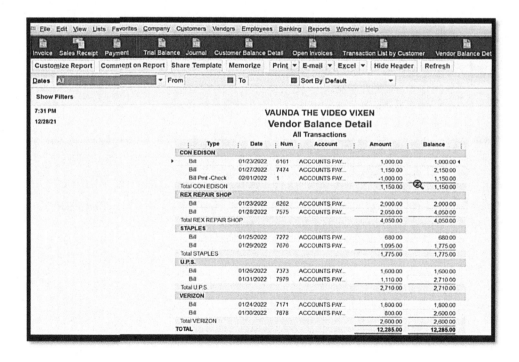

Most importantly when we look at the Unpaid Bills Detail, we see for Edison there's only one unpaid Bill left (the one we didn't pay) and the balance here is the same as in the Vendor Balance Detail.

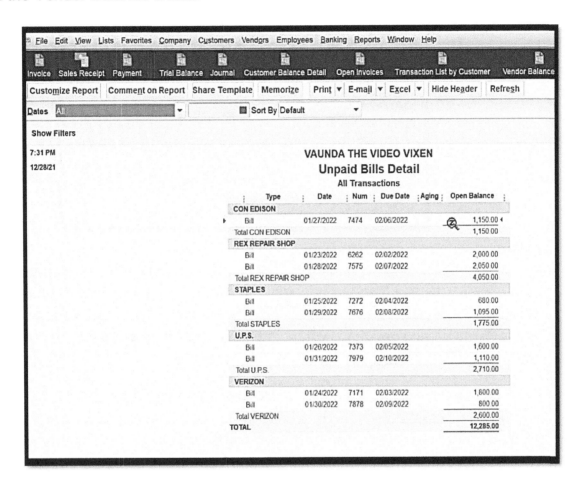

Now let's bring this home with a second example. Let's say on February 2nd we paid only 550 dollars to Rex repair shop for Bill number 7575 and we paid with check number two; now what will be the results in the trial balance? If we paid cash of 550 then cash should decrease by 550 and become 21770 and if we're paying a past bill of 550 that means Accounts Payable should also decrease by 550 and become 11735.

VAUNDA THE VIDEO VIXEN		
Trial Balance		
All Transactions		
	Jan 31, 22	
	Debit	Credit
CASH IN BANK	21,770	
ACCOUNTS RECEIVAB...	24,440.00	
SUPPLIES	680.00	
EQUIPMENT	1,095.00	
ACCOUNTS PAYABLE		11,735
EDITING INCOME		15,960.00
VIDEO INCOME		31,800.00
DELEVERY EXP	2,710.00	
ELECTRIC EXP	2,150.00	
REPAIR EXP	4,050.00	
TELEPHONE EXP	2,600.00	

In the Unpaid Bill Report, however, for this bill number 7575, you can see it is more than 550. So, what's going to happen? The bill is still going to be on the Unpaid Bill report because you did not completely pay it but it's going to decrease to the amount that remains unpaid and that's what the Unpaid Bill Detail will continue to show for the rest of the bill until it is paid.

From the main menu, we'll go over to "**Vendor**," and then "**Pay Bills**." Again, we want to choose the correct vendor (Rex repair shop), and now notice we only have two bills here. We'll proceed to put the date and not forget to put the check as the method, then assign the check number or you will have error messages that are not yet explained. You have to be very careful up here. If you click the check box in the left margin QuickBooks will assume that you're paying the whole amount but if you're only paying a partial amount of the bill you are required to highlight the money amount over type with the amount that you're paying and then hit the Tab Key. So, you can see the amount was 2050 but you're only paying 550 with this particular check. Click "**Pay Selected Bill**" and in the second field, check number two is the number of the handwritten check which we will discuss more in another chapter. Click OK and then just click "Done".

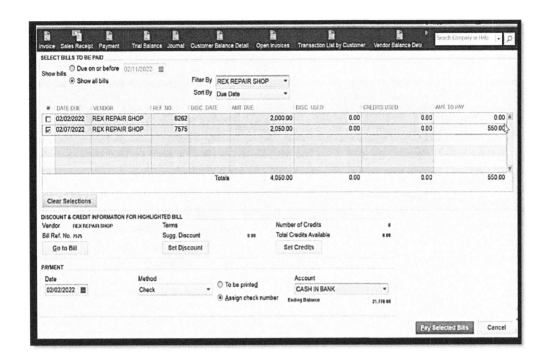

Now when you open the Trial Balance you can see the numbers are exactly as what we expected: Cash in Bank is 21770 and Accounts Payable is 11735.

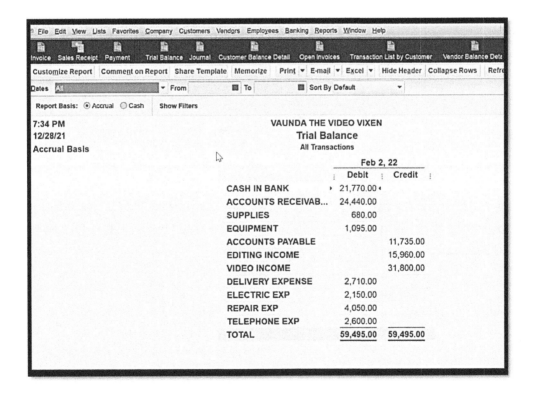

The Vendor Balance Detail for Rex repair shows a minus to the balance in general bringing it down to 3500.

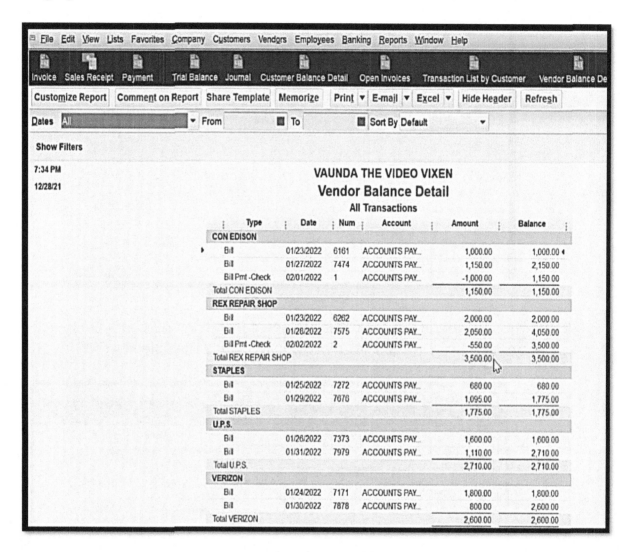

But most importantly when you open the Unpaid Bills Report you can see for Rex repair that this bill number 7575 remains on the Unpaid Bills Detail for the amount of 1500 dollars.

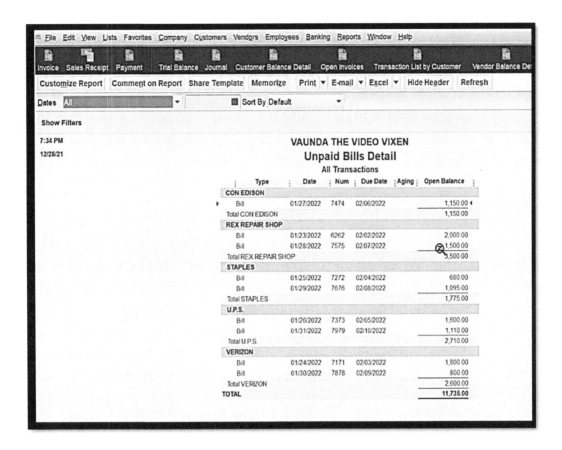

Review Questions

1. Define Accounts Payable.
2. What is a Bill?
3. What are the accounts involved when entering a bill?
4. When paying a vendor's bill, what report reflects this?

CHAPTER 10

MANAGING CASH AND BANK ACCOUNTS

Every business deal with cash and the bank account is where they store their cash. Managing your cash and bank accounts is one essential function of QuickBooks and this chapter is solely focused on that.

Writing checks

You may well ask when you should use the "**Write checks**" window and the answer is we use the "**Write checks**" window when we pay immediately upon receiving a service or product from a vendor. We will not use the "**Write checks**" window to pay a previously entered bill. In a previous chapter, when we got the bill, we recorded only the bill and then we waited a while until we paid it by using the "**Pay Bills**" window; that is not what we're talking about here so you have to make sure to keep the ideas from the previous chapter separate from what we're learning.

We use the "**Write checks**" window for any transaction that reduces the bank account except for paying a previously entered bill because then we would use the "**Pay Bills**" window as we learned in the previous chapter.

So, when do we use "**Write checks**"? Well, if we physically have a handwritten check that we're sending out for something we just received and we did not enter the bill as we did before, then we would use the right checks window. But of course, we can also record a transaction in the "**Write checks**" window if we paid an online direct deposit from our bank account directly to the vendor for a product or service we received. Just like a debit card transaction, any transaction that reduces the bank account can be recorded and should be recorded in the "Write checks" window; even an ATM withdrawal and you will learn later the difference between withdrawing cash for business and withdrawing cash for personal but regardless of which one, if you withdrew cash from the company bank account and an ATM you would record that in one way or another from the "Write checks" window. You can even record a transfer if you're transferring money out of the account during that transaction. That transaction could be recorded in the "Write checks" window even though there's a separate very simple window for transfers between bank accounts.

For example, let's say on February 3rd we paid 500 to Staples for supplies and we gave them handwritten check number three. What will happen if we pay money from the bank account to buy more supplies? Well, at the moment we pay, Cash in Bank will go down because we just paid money and of course, if we have more supplies as a result of the transaction, supplies go up. Now, what will happen in the Trial Balance the moment we record this check? We will have 500 dollars Less in the bank so Cash in Bank will decrease to 21270 and because we purchased 500 dollars more of supplies, supplies will increase by 500 and become 1180.

VAUNDA THE VIDEO VIXEN
Trial Balance
All Transactions

	Feb 2, 22	
	Debit	Credit
CASH IN BANK	**21,270**	
ACCOUNTS RECEIVAB...	24,440.00	
SUPPLIES	**1,180**	
EQUIPMENT	1,095.00	
ACCOUNTS PAYABLE		11,735.00
EDITING INCOME		15,960.00
VIDEO INCOME		31,800.00
DELEVERY EXP	2,710.00	
ELECTRIC EXP	2,150.00	
REPAIR EXP	4,050.00	
TELEPHONE EXP	2,600.00	

You may well be wondering, for this check what will happen to the Vendor's Balance? The answer is that nothing will happen. There is no change to the vendor's balance if you pay immediately upon receiving a product or service because you paid immediately and you owe neither more nor less to the vendor.

What report can you use if you can't see this transaction on the Unpaid Bill Report and you cannot see this transaction in the Vendor Balance Detail? The answer is several reports list these types of checks but the best one is the Transaction List by Vendor.

From the main menu, we'll go to **"Reports**," **"Vendors & Payable"** then to **"Transaction List by Vendor"** and of course, we can make it nice and tall and select "All" under the date category.

184

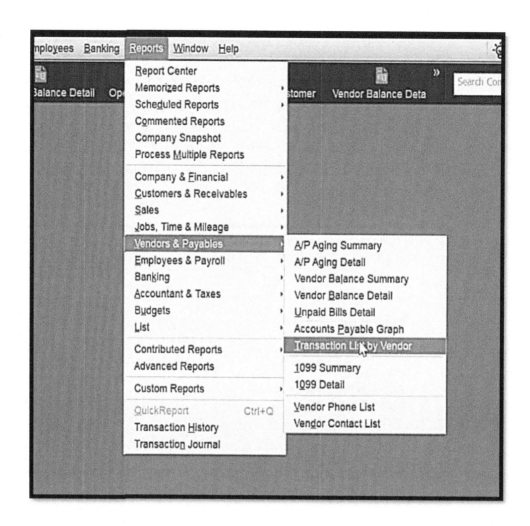

Now that it looks the way we want, we'll go to "**View**", **add "Transaction List by Vendor" to the icon bar** and click OK.

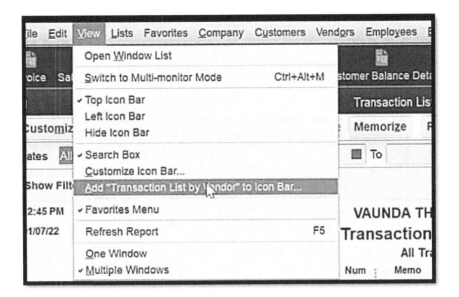

Keep in mind that if you run out of space in your icon bar you have an extra drop-down arrow that will open it up.

Now let's record our first check. From the main menu go to "**Banking**", then "**Write checks**."

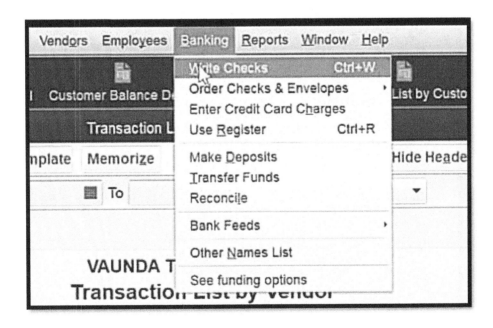

Before we proceed let's bring your attention to the section of the top ribbon. It is very important that as soon as you open the "Checks" window, you click the little check mark box to remove the option for printing later. You must do that so that QuickBooks will allow you to enter the check number or transaction number yourself and we will learn why this is so in a later section when we learn about printing checks but for now just remember to ensure this option is unchecked so that you can enter the check number.

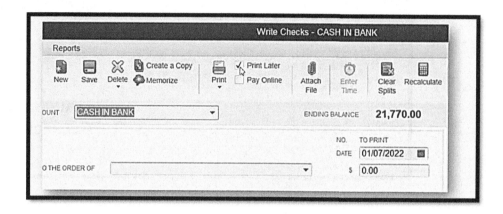

If you remove the check mark, you'll see that the check number appears, QuickBooks remembers where we left off and that the next consecutive number is the number three according to our example.

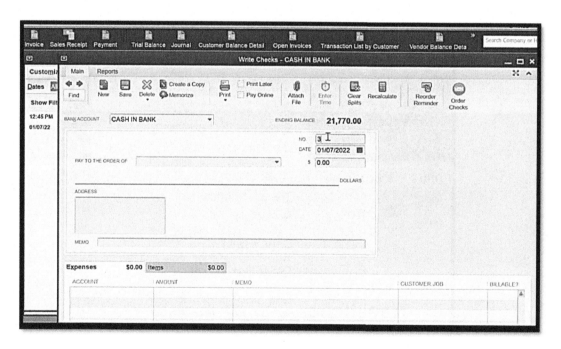

Now let's carefully put in the rest of the data such as the date which was February 3rd and the Vendor was Staples. You'll notice that when you choose a vendor that already has an unpaid bill from the Accounts Payable section, a window pops up and this message is there to help you so that you don't make a mistake. Note that this pops up every time you choose a vendor in the checks window that has an unpaid bill. QuickBooks is trying to help you make sure that you are not paying a previous bill by using the wrong window.

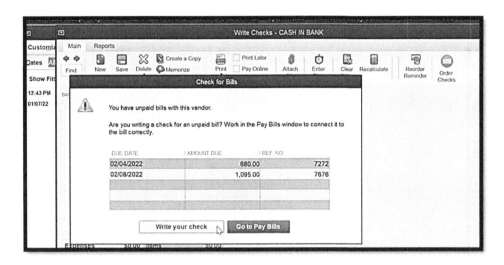

If you want to pay a previous bill that was entered from the "Enter Bills" window, you use the window that we used in the previous chapter which is the "Pay Bills" window. This window is for payments immediately upon receiving the service or product even if you had a past unpaid bill so since we know what we're doing we click "**Write your check**," we put in the specific asset or expense that we're purchasing with this check and we put in the correct money amount, hit tab and from the bottom right you can click Save & Close" and now let's check that the results are exactly as what we expected.

If we open the Trial Balance, you can see the numbers are what they are supposed to be: Cash in Bank has decreased by 500 dollars and became 21270 and supplies increased by 500 dollars and became 1180.

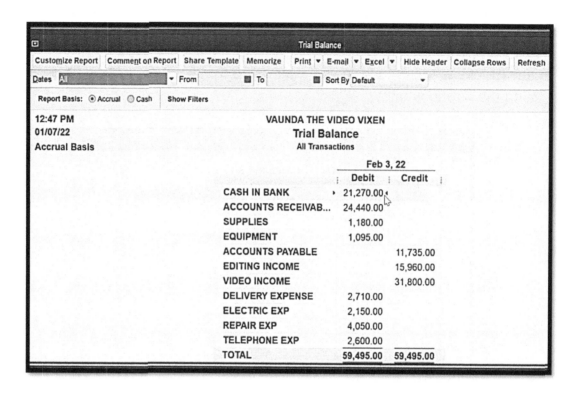

If you look at the Transaction List by Vendor you can see this check shows up at the bottom of the Staples section as the last transaction for Staples and we can double-click to open it, fix it and do whatever we like.

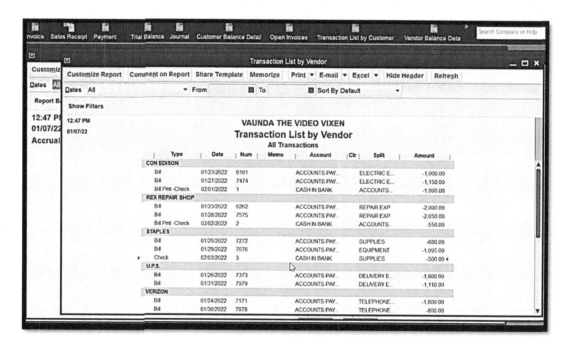

189

Now let's do a second example. Let's say on February 4th we paid Rex repair for a repair job done and the amount is 1000 dollars. Now let's say this one was an online payment and they gave you a confirmation number on February 4th. Now when we record this in the "Checks" window what will happen in the trial balance?

We have 1000 dollars less in the bank because we just paid a check for 1000 so Cash in Bank should decrease to 20270 since what we paid for was Repair Expenses, we have 1000 dollars more in Repair Expenses and Repair Expenses will increase to 5050 dollars.

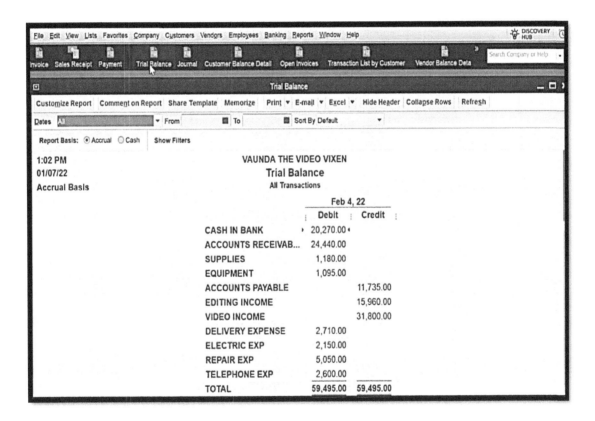

Now we'll go to "Banking" then "Write checks" and of course, we make sure the "Print later" button is not selected. Then fast forwarding to February 4th, we make sure the money is coming from the bank account and pay to the order of Rex repair shop. QuickBooks remembers we have unpaid bills with Rex repair but this transaction has nothing to do with the previous unpaid bills so when we click "Write your check" QuickBooks remembers Rex repair goes with Repair Expense. Now you just put in the money amount and it will copy.

Remember this was an online payment (it was not a check) so even though it was not a check we still record it in the "Checks" window and we put in the confirmation number that the bank gives for the online payment because any reduction in the bank account at all is something that we would record in the "Write checks" window. When we click "**Save & Close**" the results in the trial balance are exactly as we expected: Cash in Bank went down to 20270 and Repair Expense increased to 5050.

You can double-click Repair Expense and see that the other two transactions with Repair Expense were for entered bills but this transaction was with this check and you can see this very same check in the Transaction List by Vendor.

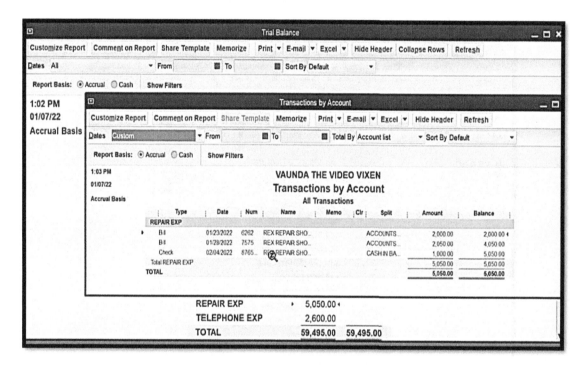

If you look in the section of Rex repair you can see these were bills comprising the bill payment and this is the check we just recorded.

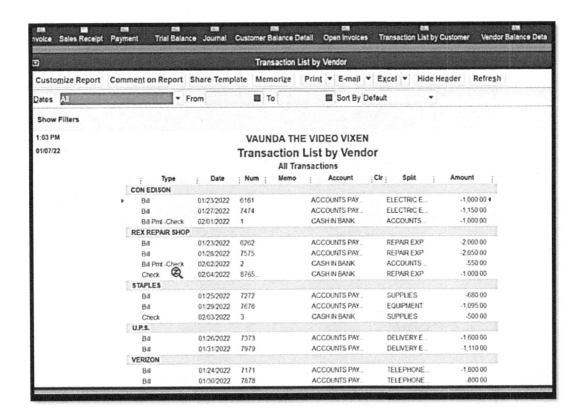

Managing your Cash on Hand/Petty Cash

Petty cash physically can be kept in a physical lock box that someone has the key to and the cash is inside but petty cash could also be a separate section of the owner's wallet. It doesn't matter as long as you physically have a place to deposit the cash and physically can take from that place to spend for business expenses then you have a petty cash fund.

Now think about that description: a place where you can deposit to and spend from. That description is the same as a typical bank account, therefore keeping records of a petty cash fund is the same as keeping records of a bank account and petty cash in your QuickBooks records should be a bank type of account.

So, we go from the top left list to the Chart of Accounts and in the bottom left corner we go to "**Account**," then "**New**" and you can see that this is a bank type of account.

If you click "**Bank**" you can see that one of the things that QuickBooks designates for a bank type of account is Petty Cash. We click "**Continue**" and type in "**Petty Cash**"

192

then "**Cash on Hand**". After that, save and close, click no for the pop-up and now you have an account to record your cash transactions with.

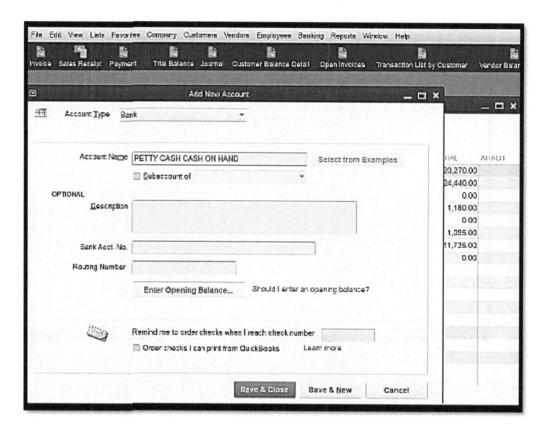

So, what exactly happens with Petty Cash or Cash on Hand? When you have these types of cash transactions, first, you establish the fund by writing a check or withdrawing the money from an ATM then you spend from the petty cash fund for business reasons and after you finish spending from petty cash you will record each cash payment with a physical receipt. The physical receipt you get for the cash payment should be placed back in the lockbox or back in the same place where the cash is physically stored so you can compare what was spent with what was put in and then when the petty cash fund gets too low, you have to replenish the fund with a check or an ATM withdrawal again.

Recording petty cash transaction

Let's do our first petty cash transaction. On February 5th we wrote check number four to cash for 500 dollars to establish the petty cash fund.

193

What will change in the trial balance the moment we record check number four? If we paid 500 dollars from this bank account, the bank account will decrease by 500 and become 19770 and because we just established the fund, Petty Cash will show up in the trial balance for the first time as 500 dollars and none of the other numbers will change.

FEBRUARY 5, WROTE CHECK #4 TO "CASH" FOR $500 TO ESTABLISH THE FUND

VAUNDA THE VIDEO VIXEN
Trial Balance
All Transactions

	Feb 4, 22	
	Debit	Credit
CASH IN BANK	19,770	
PETTY CASH	500	
ACCOUNTS RECEIVAB...	24,440.00	
SUPPLIES	1,180.00	
EQUIPMENT	1,095.00	
ACCOUNTS PAYABLE		11,735.00
EDITING INCOME		15,960.00
VIDEO INCOME		31,800.00
DELEVERY EXP	2,710.00	
ELECTRIC EXP	2,150.00	
REPAIR EXP	5,050.00	
TELEPHONE EXP	2,600.00	

From the main menu, we go to "Banking," and then "Write a check." We know the date is February 5th, this is check number four that we're writing, the money is coming from the bank account to the petty cash fund and we know that the amount is 500 dollars. You could leave the payee blank or you could add a new payee called other and just call it cash so that you have a record of checks made out to cash but now that the check to establish the fund looks the way we need it to look we click "Save & Close."

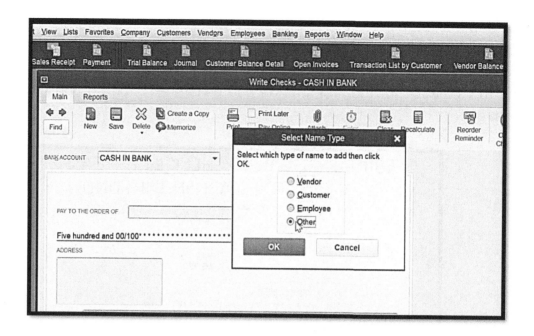

You can see the Trial Balance has the numbers that we expected: Cash in Bank is 19770 and Petty Cash or Cash on Hand is 500 dollars.

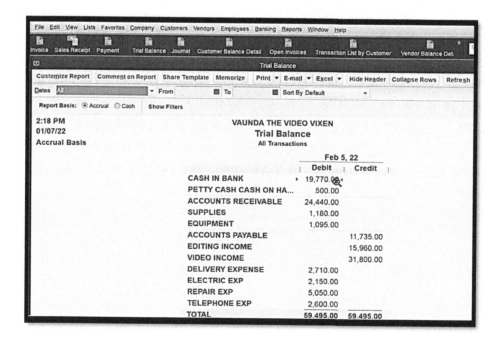

Now let's try spending from the petty cash fund. Let's say on February 6th we paid 80 dollars to Verizon for a prepaid phone card and got receipt number 1234. What would change?

If we're spending 80 dollars from Petty Cash, then the petty cash will decrease by 80 dollars and 500 becomes 420. But we spent it on the telephone for a prepaid card so the Telephone Expense increases by 80 dollars and becomes 2680.

FEBRUARY 6, PAID $80 TO VERIZON FOR A PRE-PAID PHONE CARD AND GOT RCPT #12345

VAUNDA THE VIDEO VIXEN
Trial Balance
All Transactions

	Feb 5, 22	
	Debit	Credit
CASH IN BANK	19,770.00	
PETTY CASH / CASH ON HAND	420	
ACCOUNTS RECEIVABLE	24,440.00	
SUPPLIES	1,180.00	
EQUIPMENT	1,095.00	
ACCOUNTS PAYABLE		11,735.00
EDITING INCOME		15,960.00
VIDEO INCOME		31,800.00
DELEVERY EXP	2,710.00	
ELECTRIC EXP	2,150.00	
REPAIR EXP	5,050.00	
TELEPHONE EXP	2,680	

From the main menu, we'll go over to "Banking" and Write a Check (now be careful as this money is coming from the petty cash fund), click OK for the pop-up, and ensure that the date is correct.

Now we're paying Verizon, remember when we used the "Write a Check" window for a vendor that has a previously open Bill? We have to make sure we're not paying one of the previous bills which we are not using so we click "Continue", and "Write the Check".

196

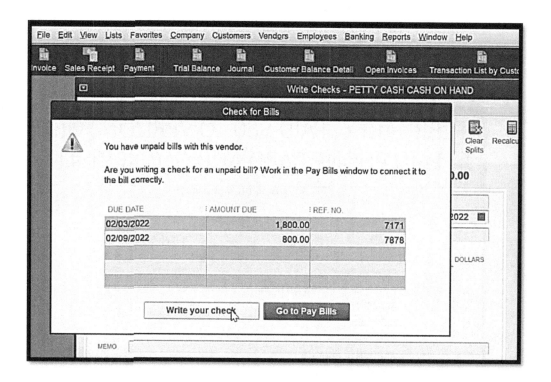

Now the amount that we're spending from cash is 80 dollars, so we make sure it goes on the top and the bottom of the window and the receipt number you believe was 1234 so instead of a check number, if it's cash, you put the physical receipt number, take a picture of the receipt and save it as your proof then put the hard copy of the receipt with the physical cache in the lock box or the wallet or wherever it belongs. Then when you click "Save & Close" you can see from the Trial Balance the numbers are exactly as what we expected: Petty cash is down to 420 and Telephone Expense is 2680.

Now let's try another transaction. Let's say on February 7 we paid Staples 120 dollars cash for equipment and they gave us receipt number 8472. Well, if we spend another 120 dollars in petty cash that means petty cash decreases by 120 dollars and becomes 300 dollars and because we purchased equipment with it Equipment goes up by 120 dollars and becomes 1215 dollars; these are the numbers after spending our second petty cash transaction.

Replacing the petty cash

Finally, let's replenish the petty cash fund and bring it back to what it was. Let's imagine on February 8th we withdrew from the ATM to replenish the petty cash fund. How much do we need to replenish it? We need to withdraw 200 dollars from the ATM and if we do that and we put it in petty cash, petty cash will increase to 500 but remember the 200 came out of the Cash in Bank so Cash in Bank will decrease by 200 and become 19570.

FEBRUARY 8, WITHDREW FROM THE A.T.M TO REPLENISH THE PETTY CASH FUND $200

VAUNDA THE VIDEO VIXEN
Trial Balance
All Transactions

	Feb 7, 22	
	Debit	Credit
CASH IN BANK	19,570	
PETTY CASH / CASH ON HA...	500	
ACCOUNTS RECEIVABLE	24,440.00	
SUPPLIES	1,180.00	
EQUIPMENT	1,215.00	
ACCOUNTS PAYABLE		11,735.00
EDITING INCOME		15,960.00
VIDEO INCOME		31,800.00
DELEVERY EXP	2,710.00	
ELECTRIC EXP	2,150.00	
REPAIR EXP	5,050.00	
TELEPHONE EXP	2,680.00	

So, you'll go to "Banking," "Write a Check" and you would put the ATM slip number (whatever that number was that's what you would put) but remember in this case the money is coming from the bank account and it's going to the Petty Cash fund on February 8 for 200.

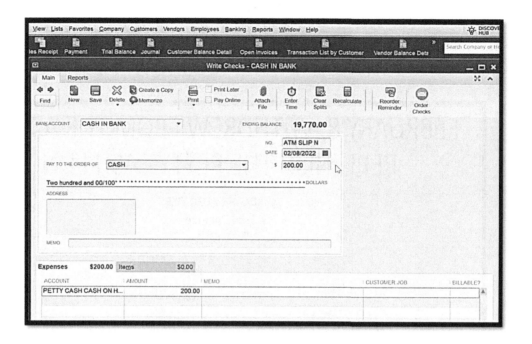

Some people like to keep their records straight by making the check out to cash and recording the payee so when we click "Save & Close" our Trial Balance should look exactly as what we expect: Cash in Bank is 19570 and Petty cash went up to 500 dollars.

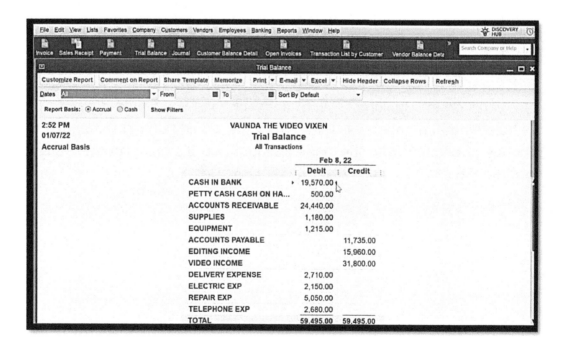

Review questions

Let's finish part three with an account payable exercise to practice everything we've learned in this section. Below is an illustration of what your trial balance should look like before you begin the exercise. Make sure each number you see is the same as each number in your trial balance in your QuickBooks file. If you get stuck along the line, you can use the techniques and methods that we learned to correct your numbers before you start.

Below is an illustration of what your Vendor Balance Detail should look like before you begin the exercise.

Below is an illustration of what your Unpaid Bills Detail should look like before you begin the exercise. Make sure that you not only have the right balances but the right individual amounts to be paid.

You also have a list of every transaction that we have ever had with any vendor since the beginning of this section. If it all checks out then you can start recording the transactions.

The image below shows the transactions for this exercise.

You can pause at this point to read each line of the transaction set and then slowly and carefully record each transaction. If you forgot how to enter a particular transaction you need to go back to the chapter where we learned about that transaction and review it then you should remember how to put in each of these transactions.

As part of the exercise, go slowly and carefully, think about each one and when you finish the image below shows what your trial balance should look like after you record each of the transactions in the exercise set. Again, if it doesn't match you have to go through everything one by one. Pay careful attention to the Vendor Balance Detail after the exercise as well as the Unpaid Bills because there are some important things about the remaining unpaid bills that you need to know as part of a logical set of questions to make sure you understood everything in the context of this exercise.

Now you have some questions to answer to see if you can figure out what mistake you might have made:

What if your Cash in Bank account is too high and your Cash on Hand or Petty Cash is too low? You can pause at this moment while you think about the answer.

The answer is that you chose the wrong bank account when you wrote a check or paid an expense or Bill. This happens all the time. QuickBooks tries to remember the previous bank account for each transaction window but it's not always the same and you have to check it carefully. Of course, the opposite is also true if your Cash in Bank was too low and your Cash on Hand or Petty Cash was too high. That means you recorded a Petty Cash expenditure from the Cash in Bank account and that's a mistake that you would have to go and fix using the techniques that you've learned. Secondly, what if each vendor's total balance is correct but the individual Bill balances are wrong? Think about that for a second and try to figure out on your own what would cause that condition. If you thought well, you would agree that the answer is that you applied a bill payment to the wrong bill. You got the right vendor and you got the right amount. That's why the vendor's balance is correct but you applied it to the wrong bill.

If you find yourself in this situation, use what you've learned so far to find and fix your mistakes. Keep fixing until your numbers are the same as what we have.

Review Questions

1. How do you manage your cash?
2. When should you use the "Write checks?"
3. What is Petty Cash?
4. How do you manage your cash on hand?

CHAPTER 11

FINDING TRANSACTIONS IN QUICKBOOKS

This chapter is all about learning how to find anything you're looking for using the Find window. The Find window makes QuickBooks one of the easiest software that you could use. You can find any transaction just by describing it to the find window. You can find several transactions that fit a specific description and then you can open and check them as soon as you find them. You can even make a report from the results of the Find window and the transactions listed there will be subject to all the different customization of reports that you can use when you use reports in QuickBooks desktop.

The Find Window

For example, let's find all the invoices from Alan between January 1 and January 15th. This is a very simple task. From the top left go to "**Edit**", and then "**Find**".

The Find window has a simple tab and an advanced tab. If you click the simple tab, you can start by simply choosing to find every single one of a specific transaction type.

Finding transactions and reports

For example, if you say "**Invoice**" and you click "**Find**", you'll get a list of every single invoice that has ever been entered into the file. You can double-click to open up and examine or even fix any of these invoices.

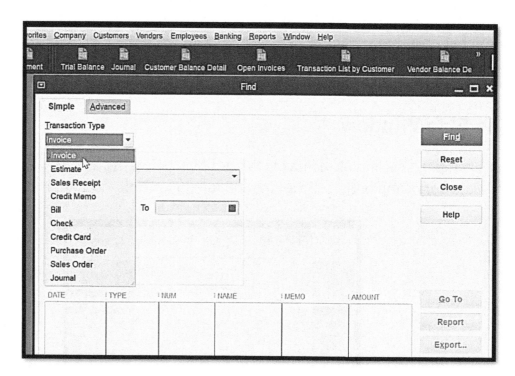

If you click "**Receipt**" you can find every sale receipt ever entered into the file and so on. For our example, we want to find invoices specifically for this customer Alan and we want to find all invoices between January 1 and January 15. Now that we've described it appropriately, we click "find" and you can see that there are only three invoices in the entire file that fit that description.

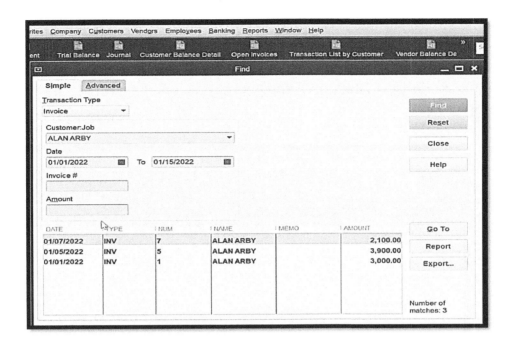

If we want to show this to someone we can click "**Report**" and now these search results have been listed in a typical QuickBooks report that we can use the customization for and make it look nicer and export it or do anything we want, the same way we could with any of the other QuickBooks reports. If we are not saving it, we simply close it out and we'll click "reset.

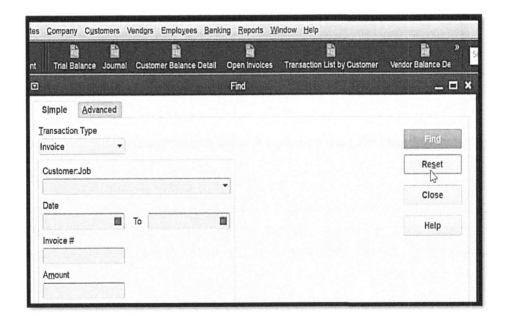

204

What else can we find? We can also find all of the sales receipts in the entire file which equals 3000 in our example. So based on our examples so far in this book, we want to find a sale receipt with an amount of 3000. After we type in the criteria we click "find" and you see in the entire film there's only one sale receipt for exactly the amount of 3000 dollars.

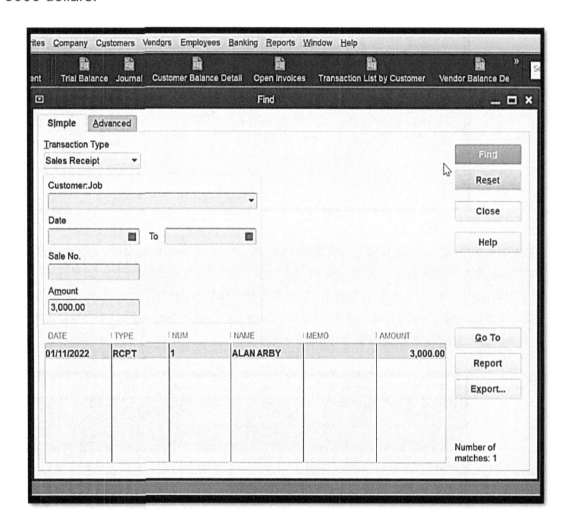

What else can we find? How about we just check a number such as 3? If you have thousands of checks and you have to call up a specific check it would be so easy to click **"Edit"**, then **"Find Check"** and in the Check number field type 3, click "find" and you'll find that in there. From here you can double-click to open it up and you can do whatever you want.

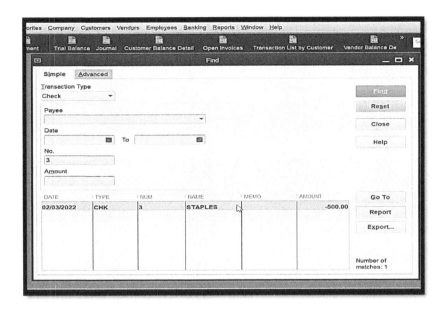

How about all checks to the Rex repair shop? First, let's completely reset the window then we go to "Invoice," "All checks" and the payee is Rex repair shop. Now when we click "find," we see that there are two check payments to Rex repair shop and if we look a little bit closer, we can see that one of them is the check that we wrote in the previous chapter and the other is a bill payment check (a bill payment is the only transaction that looks different when you reopen it).

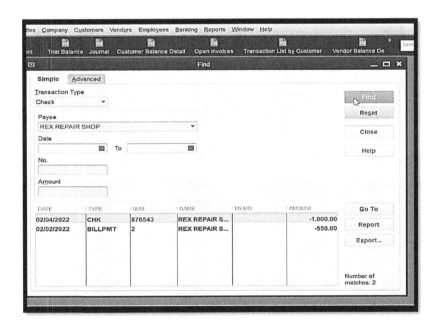

If you double-click you see that this was more than just a check; it was specifically paying bill number 7575 a partial payment that we did before in a previous chapter but this is the way it looks when you reopen it.

When you first go to "Vendor," and then "Pay Bills" you can see the way the window looked when we recorded it (as illustrated in the image below).

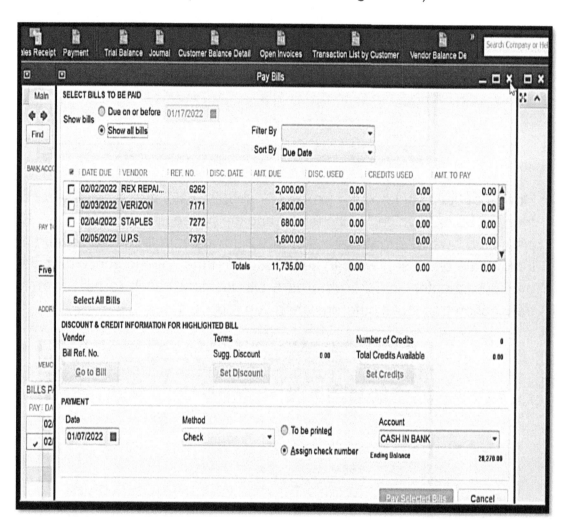

But a bill payment looks like what you have below when you reopen it, so that's just something that will help you later.

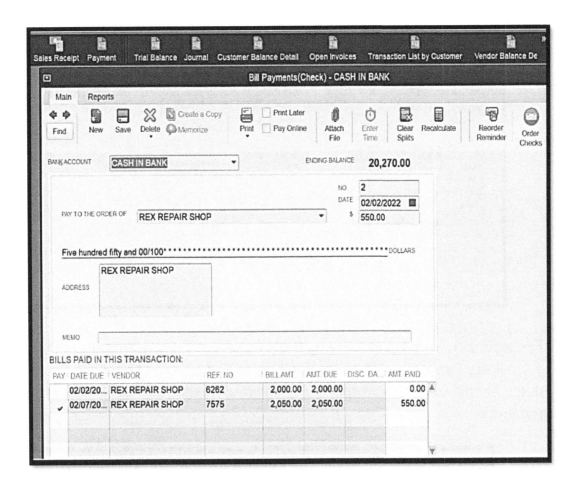

Using advanced find

What if you want to use the "advanced find"? That's something that takes practice, patience, and quite frankly imagination because you have to think of how you would search for something to benefit you depending on what you're looking for.

For example, let's find all transactions with Alan greater than 3000 dollars. First, we go to "Edit", and "Find", now when we click the "**Advanced**" tab you'll notice there are three sections at the top of the "**Advanced Find**" window on the left. Here, you will see the box where you choose the criteria that you're filtering on and you can choose more than one but notice when you click different criteria, the middle section here changes. That's because it's the middle section that clarifies what you're looking for.

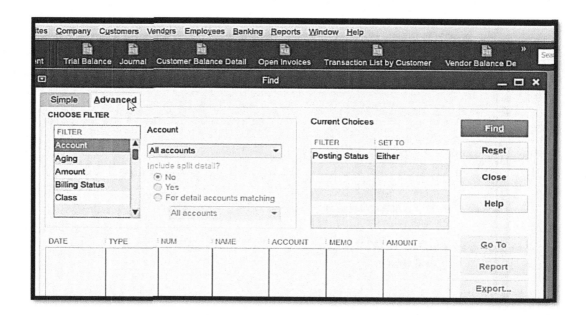

For example, we want to find any transaction, let's say greater than 3000. Now when you hit the tab key, you'll notice the box on the side is showing the rules or the filter that's already on and you can click here and delete any of the other filters that were put there.

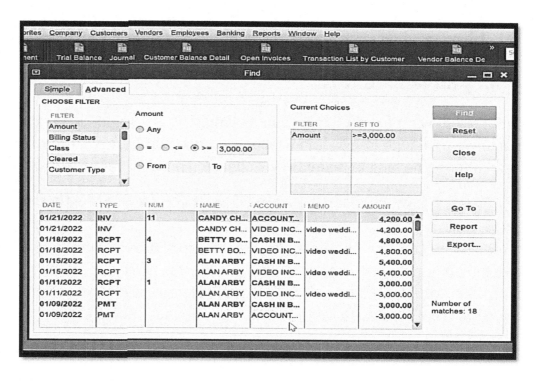

So right now, an amount greater than 3000 is the only criterion and if you click "find" you get a list of every transaction in the file that's greater than 3000 after which you click to reset.

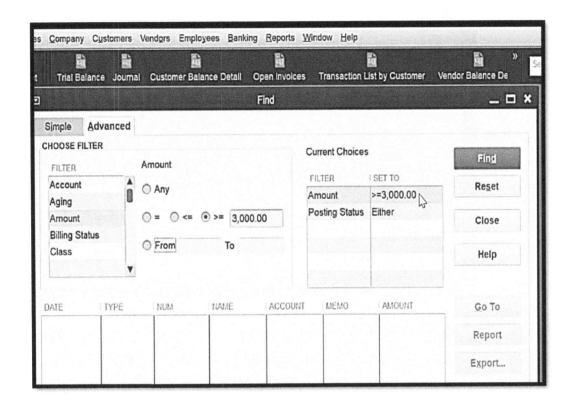

To remove this, you can push delete but if you want to put two criteria you have to put both and make sure they're both here before you click the "Find" window. So, if you click the filter box and hit the letter N you get the option to choose by name and now the drop-down arrow allows us to choose just Alan.

We don't want to click "**Find**" yet because we don't need every transaction for Alan. Instead, we come back to the filter box and push the letter A to get the filter for the amount and recall that we want the amount to be greater than 3000 so we indicate that we want to see all of Alan's transactions that are greater than 3000. When we click "Find" you can see a list of all the transactions that fit into our description; 10 of the transactions we had with Alan were greater than 3000.

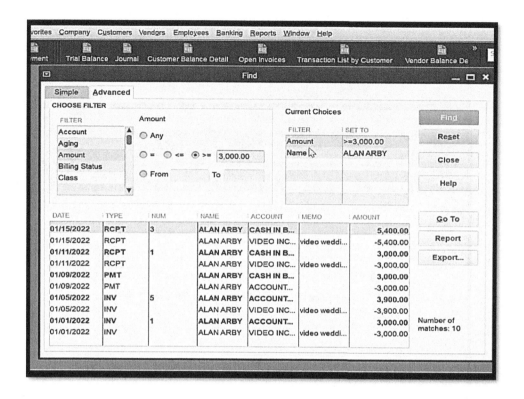

Now if we reverse this to go for transactions for Alan that were less than 3000 and click "Find," you can see that we now have 12 transactions less than 3000 dollars from Alan.

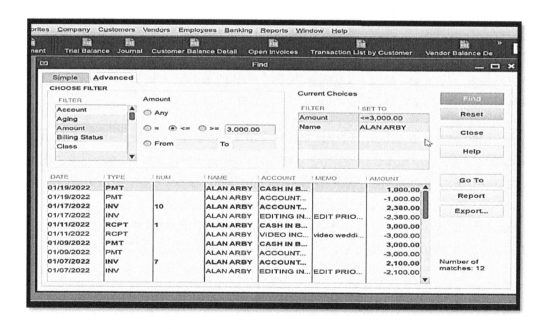

Notice the three sections of the advanced find. You can always explore and experiment using this window. It's one of the most powerful tools that gets you to be an expert in QuickBooks desktop 2023.

Review Questions

1. How do you locate a transaction?
2. Where can you locate the "Find" option?
3. Mention 2 functions of the "Advanced Find" feature?

CHAPTER 12

BASIC DEPOSITS AND UNDEPOSITED FUNDS

In this chapter, we will be dealing with all the transactions relating to basic deposits and undeposited funds. You'll learn how to record basic deposits, petty cash transactions and managing undeposited funds.

Basic deposits

You may well be wondering what we mean by a **Basic deposit**. Well, it's when the payment we receive from the customer for a service goes directly into the bank account and we do not need to track the quantity of the service item that we gave the customer nor do we need the deposit to affect the customer's records or the Customer Detail Reports.

Recording Basic Deposits

Looking at an example, let's say on February 20th we received 2000 in cash from Candy for an editing service and it was directly deposited into the bank account with confirmation number 09876. If we record this then what should be the result in the trial balance?

We have 2000 more in the bank account so Cash in Bank should increase to 16770, and the reason we have more money is that we did an editing service and earned 2000 more in editing income. So, after we record this basic deposit, editing income increases by 2000 and becomes 17960.

From the main menu, you go to "**Banking**" then "**Make Deposit**" and this brings up that window.

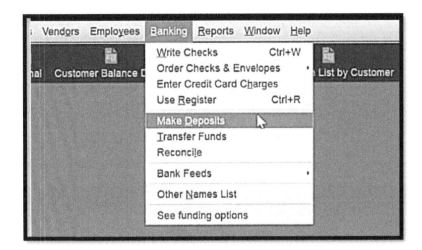

The "**Make Deposit**" window is very simple but the purpose of learning basic deposits is to get accustomed to how this window works. First, you'll choose the specific bank account that you deposited the money into then of course you put the date of the physical deposit. Now even though you are going to put the name of the customer here, this transaction will still not show up in Candy's records and you'll see it's warning you that this customer has outstanding invoices.

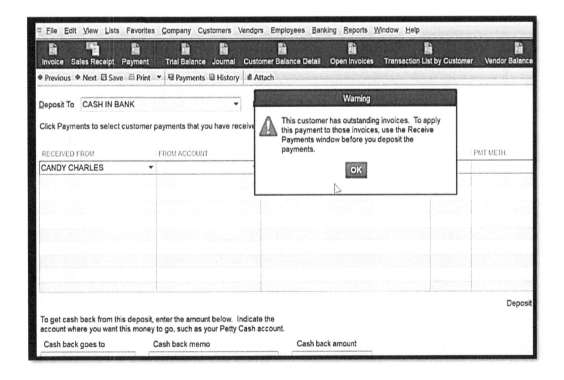

If you want to apply this payment to those invoices, you do what you've learned in previous chapters and you use the receive payment window but right now we're just learning an example of a basic deposit that would not affect the customer's records if we had a simple company that did not need to keep customer records. So, we just click OK and we put in the Income account that represents what we earned for this particular 2000 dollars.

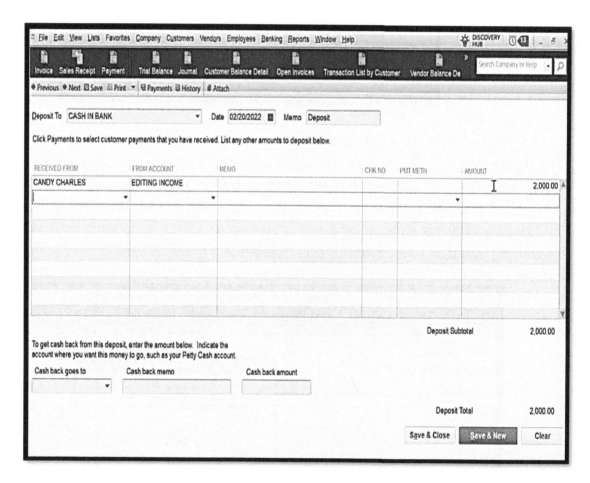

So, if we had a company that didn't have to track items and didn't have to keep customers' balances, this would be the simple way to record getting paid from the customer. This way when we click "Save & Close" we can open the trial balance and you can see the results are exactly as what you expected: Cash in Bank decreased to 16770 and Editing income increased to 17960.

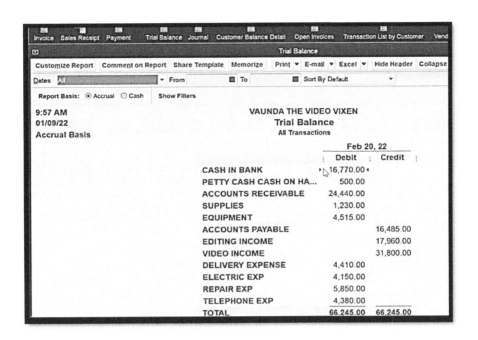

Now here's a question: where will this deposit transaction not show up? It won't show up on any customer report, it won't show up in the Customer Center and it won't show up on any Sales reports because there was no item associated.

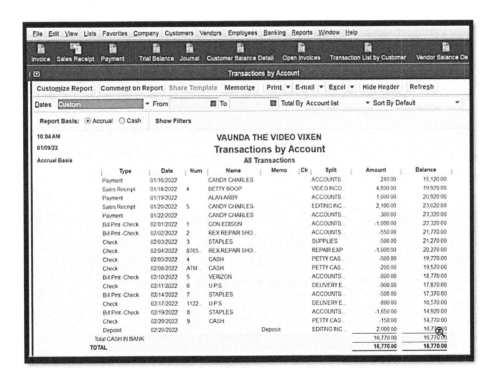

If you double-click Cash in Bank and go to the bottom you can see that this deposit was the last transaction that increased cash in Bank and the same thing applies to the Editing income.

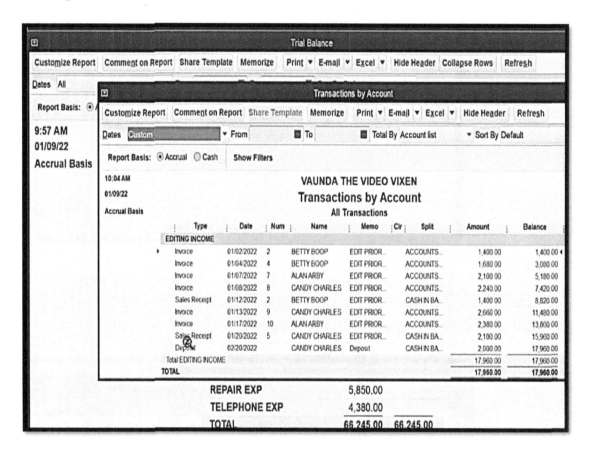

You can double-click the account in the Chart of Accounts and see the transaction deposit that we just recorded increasing the balance of the account but if you click Customer Balance Detail it's nowhere to be found in Candy's records.

If you click Transaction List by Customer, it's nowhere to be found in Candy's records, and if you open the Customer Center and choose Candy, if you look at the transactions for all times you will see every receipt payment or invoice but you will not see the deposit because it's a basic deposit meant for simple companies.

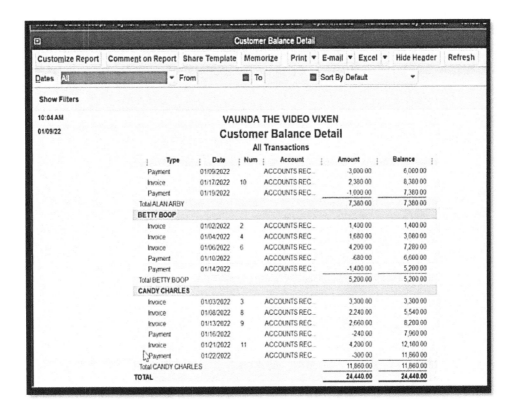

Moving to example two, on February 21 we received 3000 cash from Alan for a video service. It was directly deposited into the bank account with confirmation number 543210. Now, what will be the result in the trial balance if we have 3000 more in cash because we just earned 3000 more in video income?

As you may already know, cash increases by 3000 to become 19770, and video income increases by 3000 to become 34800.

Entering this is very simple. Go to "**Banking**" then "**Make Deposit**."

Enter the date which is February 21, and the bank account the money went into of course you should probably put the confirmation number in the memo field but anyway make sure you choose the customer even though it won't show up in the customer's records. So, let's choose Alan and again we'll get a message (that if we have open invoices for this customer the only way to apply this payment to an Open Invoice is to do it the right way that we learned before and use the Receive Payment window) but right now we're just learning the basic way so since we know what we're doing we click OK.

218

Now when we click "**Save & Close**" the results and the Trial Balance are exactly as we expected: Cash in Bank went up to 19770 and video income went up to 34800 and none of the customer reports for Alan will show this transaction because we recorded it in the most basic way.

	Debit	Credit
VAUNDA THE VIDEO VIXEN		
Trial Balance		
All Transactions		
Feb 20, 22		
CASH IN BANK	**19,770**	
PETTY CASH / CASH ON HA...	500.00	
ACCOUNTS RECEIVABLE	24,440.00	
SUPPLIES	1,230.00	
EQUIPMENT	4,515.00	
ACCOUNTS PAYABLE		16,485.00
EDITING INCOME		17,960.00
VIDEO INCOME		**34,800**
DELEVERY EXP	4,410.00	
ELECTRIC EXP	4,150.00	
REPAIR EXP	5,850.00	
TELEPHONE EXP	4,380.00	

What type of company would record deposits this way? Many small businesses don't need to keep customer records and they have very simple bookkeeping needs so if the company does not need to track Customers' balances or apply payments to invoices, they could just record deposits this way and that would still be fine. Also, if you don't need to know how many hours of video or editing you did, you could get away with recording deposits this very simple way in the Deposits window.

Now, what would be a better way of recording these deposits? Of course, you would use a Sale Receipt as you've learned. You learned that you can record a sale receipt that is directly deposited into the bank and it will also show up in the Customer records. If you use a Sale Receipt instead, it also obviously gives you the ability to track the number of items. But for what we just did in this section, even though this company which we used as our example has a more complex situation, needs customer balances, and needs to track items, we still wanted to show you this way because it's perfect for learning how the Deposit window works. As we go further, we will look at more complex deposit situations and it's better to learn how the Deposit window Works before we proceed.

219

Recording deposits with Cash Back

What circumstance would cause you to take cash back from depositing a customer's money? We're talking about a situation where we first collect the cash from the customer for a service before we record collecting the cash, we spend some of the cash on business-related expenses.

The way to handle this is to record receiving the cash and the expenses at the moment we make the deposit. Usually, this method would apply to a situation where all the transactions happen on the same day.

For example, let's say on February 22nd we collected 900 dollars for three Video hours for Betty. Now on the way to the bank we paid 100 dollars out of the 900 that we got from Betty to Staples specifically for supplies, then we walked up the street and stopped off at the UPS store and paid 200 out of the 900 for delivery and when we finally got to the bank, we deposited the remaining 600 and got a deposit slip with the slip number 616161.

Before we look at how to record this let's just think about what the results should be in your trial balance. If these were the four transactions that you wish to record all at once, we originally earned 900 more in video income (that's what started the set of transactions from the beginning) so even though the net deposit that went into the bank account was only 600 we still have to indicate that we earned 900 as that was originally put in our hand. So, video income will increase by 900 and become 35700. We also bought 100 dollars more in supplies so after we got the 900 from video income, we spent 100 dollars more in supplies; so, supplies should increase by 100 and become 1330. Then we paid 200 dollars more for delivery so our delivery expense then increased by 200 and became 4610 and then the remaining 600 that we did not spend on expenses got deposited into the bank account which means the bank account increased by 600 and became 20370. These are the four numbers that will change and the image below shows the results that should be in our trial balance when we finish recording the deposit with cash back.

So, from the main menu, we go to "**Banking**" and then "**Make Deposit**".

The date was February 22nd and originally, we received it from Candy. You'll see again that we have a warning telling us that we have Open Invoices for candy and if we want to apply this payment to those invoices, we use a different window but this is a different example situation so we click OK. Since we earned video income, we put video income, for the amount that we earned we click over there in the amount field type 900 (because that's what we initially earned), and hit the tab key. Now deducted from what we earned was supplies so from Staples we bought supplies and we bought 100 dollars' worth of supplies but you have to put a minus in front of the 100 dollars and then hit the tab Key.

Now if you put minus on one of the lines of the deposit, QuickBooks will subtract; it'll put the positive and negative numbers together and the subtotal down here comes down to the amount that you're physically depositing.

We also gave money to UPS for delivery and that was 200 so again, we put a minus because we deducted that 200 from the deposit. Now we're done, you can see that we earned 900 but deducted from that 100 that we spent on supplies and 200 that we spent on delivery and it's this 600 which is the final amount that will increase the Cash in Bank. This is the way to do it when you earned money that you're ready to deposit but deducted and paid expenses from that cash; you can record them all in one shot. After ensuring we have correctly entered the right amount, we click "Save & Close" and take a look at the trial balance.

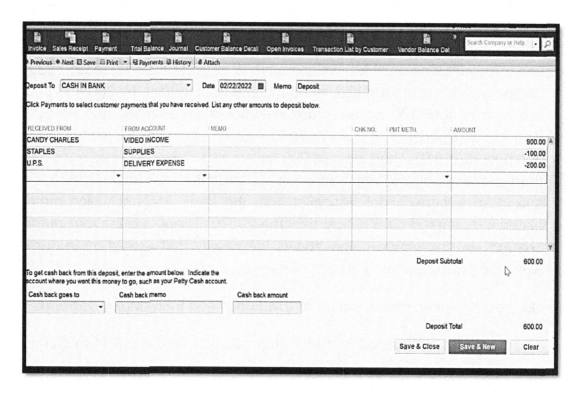

In the trial balance, you can see the numbers are exactly as what we expected: video income increased to 35700, the supplies increased to 1330, the delivery expense increased to 4610, and Cash in Bank increased to 20370.

VAUNDA THE VIDEO VIXEN
Trial Balance
All Transactions

	Feb 21, 22	
	Debit	Credit
CASH IN BANK	19,770.00	
PETTY CASH / CASH ON HA...	500.00	
ACCOUNTS RECEIVABLE	24,440.00	
SUPPLIES	**1,330**	
EQUIPMENT	4,515.00	
ACCOUNTS PAYABLE		16,485.00
EDITING INCOME		17,960.00
VIDEO INCOME		**35,700**
DELEVERY EXP	**4,610**	
ELECTRIC EXP	4,150.00	
REPAIR EXP	5,850.00	
TELEPHONE EXP	4,380.00	

To dig further into this, you can open up each of the four accounts and see how it looks. If you double-click Cash in Bank and you go to the bottom you see the last transaction was a deposit of 600 but if you double click you can see the whole deposit when it comes up. It is the same thing with any of the other accounts. You can go to supplies and when you double-click, you'll see the deposit that increases supplies for 100 and when you double-click you get the whole picture about that deposit and so on.

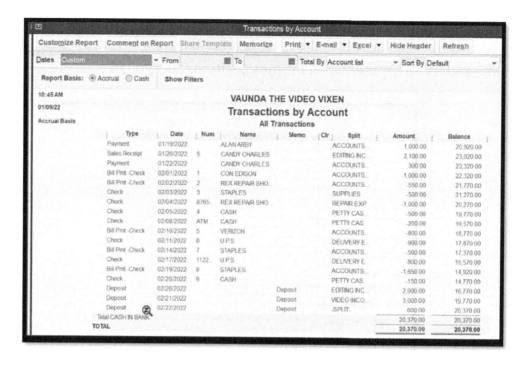

Managing Undeposited funds

One of the most important features of QuickBooks desktop is learning how to use and manage the undeposited funds' account. We all know that sometimes we get paid by check and of course there's usually a big-time difference between the day we get paid by check and the day that we physically deposit the money into the bank. Up until now, we have been recording transactions that get directly deposited into the bank but if we get it paid by check on one day and we don't deposit the money for two weeks, what do we reflect in our accounting records during those two weeks? Remember our records have to show the fact that the customer does not owe the money during those two weeks.

During those two weeks, our records should reflect the fact that we physically have the money but we can't record it in the way that we recorded it in earlier chapters because the money was not put directly into the bank so what do we do?

What happens if we get money from a customer who previously owed us money? Both Accounts Receivable in the Chart of Accounts and that particular customer's balance goes down, and in previous chapters, you saw how we recorded the money into Cash in Bank because that's what happened in that example but if the money did not go into Cash in Bank at the moment, we physically were handed a check which

223

account do we record where the money is going into? Well, that's the reason why we have this special account called Undeposited Funds.

Undeposited Funds is an account in the Chart of Accounts that allows us to keep track of each check, a bit of collected cash and credit card swipes that we received from customers but have not yet been deposited into the bank account. Anything currently undeposited can be seen in the payments section of the "Deposit" window.

Let's quickly review receiving money and we will distinguish between money that goes into the bank account and money that gets held in Undeposited Funds.

Let's say on February 23rd we did 10 editing hours for Candy. She gave us check number 1717 and we did not yet deposit the check but we will later in the week. If that's the transaction what will happen when we receive money that we intend to deposit later? The editing income must increase because we did earn editing income and since we're holding the money to deposit later and did not deposit it into the bank account that means that the account that will show up for the first time in the trial balance that represents the money, we are holding is called **Undeposited Funds**.

What will be the result in the trial balance after recording this Sale Receipt into Undeposited Funds? Well, we did earn 1400 more in editing income so editing income will increase by 1400 and become 19360, and because the money is not in the bank account but is in our hand, Undeposited Funds will show up for the first time in the trial balance for 1400 dollars.

```
                    VAUNDA THE VIDEO VIXEN
                        Trial Balance
                        All Transactions

                                    Feb 22, 22
                              Debit    :        Credit      :
CASH IN BANK             ▸    20,370.00 ◂
PETTY CASH / CASH ON HA...        500.00
 Undeposited Funds             1,400
ACCOUNTS RECEIVABLE          24,440.00
SUPPLIES                      1,330.00
EQUIPMENT                     4,515.00
ACCOUNTS PAYABLE                             16,485.00
EDITING INCOME                                 19,360
VIDEO INCOME                                 35,700.00
DELEVERY EXP                  4,610.00
ELECTRIC EXP                  4,150.00
REPAIR EXP                    5,850.00
TELEPHONE EXP                 4,380.00
```

Let's take a look at how to record it. We will open the Sales Receipt window and we go forward to February 23rd. We would make sure we choose the correct customer and also ensure we put the right item which in this case is editing and 10. Now we have to make sure that we put in the correct check number but the most important part of this transaction is choosing the right place to record where the money went to; in this case, it did not go into Cash in Bank, instead, it went into Undeposited Funds. Now that everything is correct, when we click "**Save & Close**," we can open the trial balance and you can see the results are exactly as we expected.

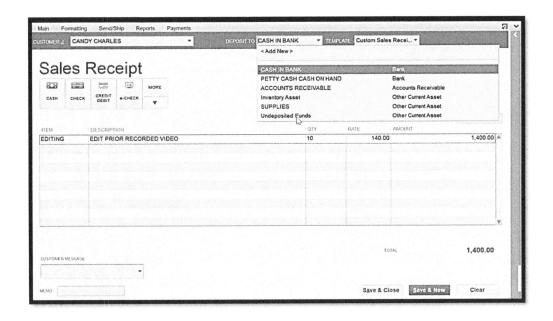

Editing income increased to 19360, and an Undeposited Funds increase showed up for the first time as 1400 dollars.

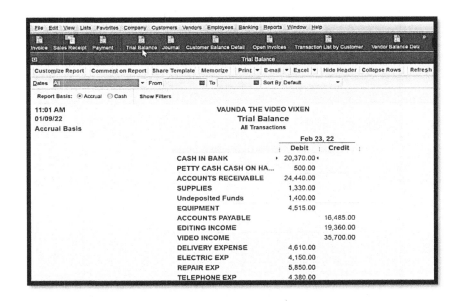

Let's try a second example and for this let's remember how to record receiving payments for past invoices. Let's say on February 24th we received 1000 dollars cash from Betty for payment of the oldest invoice. What will happen when we receive this money? We know that Undeposited Funds will go up because we're holding the money to deposit later and that will increase by 1000. Accounts Receivable this time is the account that goes down. If a customer is paying, if your bank account or your

Undeposited Funds went up because someone was paying off a past invoice that means their customers' Balance decreased because they paid you what they owe you; and that means the account that will decrease is the Accounts Receivable. What will be the result in the trial balance after recording this transaction? The customer owes us 1000 dollars less as a result of paying us now so Accounts Receivable will decrease by 1000 and become 23440 but because we have 1000 dollars more that we're holding and waiting to deposit in the future, Undeposited Funds increases by 1000 and becomes 2400.

To record this, we go to "Payment" and we advance the date to the 24th. The customer is Betty, the amount we got was 1000 dollars and you'll notice QuickBooks automatically applies the 1000 dollars to the oldest one. Now that we're almost finished, we have to make sure that this money (that we intend on holding for several days before we make a separate deposit transaction) gets recorded into Undeposited Funds.

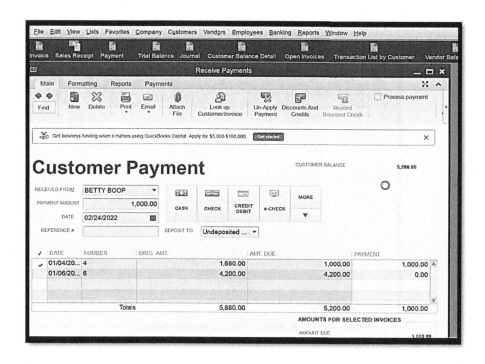

Now when we hit Enter and close the window you can open the trial balance and you can see the numbers are exactly as what we expected. Accounts receivable decreased to 23440 and Undeposited Funds increased to 2400.

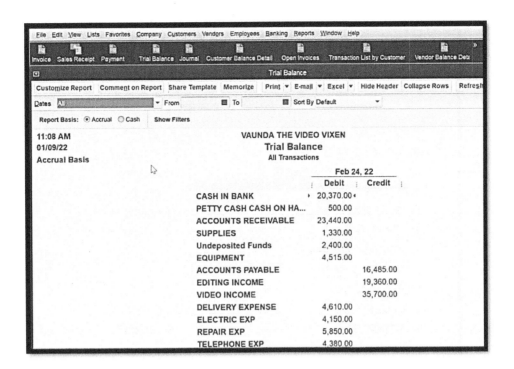

Now you should practice entering the two questions as displayed in the image below without anyone's help.

> • FEBRUARY 25TH, RECEIVED $2,000 CASH FROM CANDY FOR PAYMENT OF INVOICE #8
>
> • FEBRUARY 26, DID 20 VIDEO HOURS FOR ALAN AND HE GAVE US CHECK #1818

See if you can remember how to record payments and receipts; the only difference is now you have to make sure that each of these transactions gets recorded into Undeposited Funds. You can pause at this point, go ahead and record these two transactions and if you recorded them correctly then the results in your Trial Balance should be similar to what we have here. You should have 10400 dollars in Undeposited Funds, and 21440 in Accounts Receivable, and these should be the numbers for video income and editing income respectively.

VAUNDA THE VIDEO VIXEN
Trial Balance
All Transactions

	Feb 26, 22	
	Debit	Credit
CASH IN BANK	▸ 20,370.00 ◂	
PETTY CASH / CASH ON HA...	500.00	
ACCOUNTS RECEIVABLE	21,440.00	
SUPPLIES	1,330.00	
Undeposited Funds	10,000.00	
EQUIPMENT	4,515.00	
ACCOUNTS PAYABLE		16,485.00
EDITING INCOME		19,360.00
VIDEO INCOME		41,700.00
DELEVERY EXP	4,610.00	
ELECTRIC EXP	4,150.00	
REPAIR EXP	5,850.00	
TELEPHONE EXP	4,380.00	

Depositing from Undeposited Funds

Now that you've mastered recording money into Undeposited Funds, let's talk about what happens when we finally deposit the money. When we go to deposit the money, we must use the Special Payments window which is a subsection of the Deposit window.

When you first open the Deposit window you won't see anything but if you click the little button here that says "Payments," you will see a special sub window will open up. That window is called the "**Payments to Deposit**" window and it will list every single item in Undeposited Funds. This is a special window that places items after you make a transaction only. If you chose the Undeposited Funds account and at any given moment, the balance of Undeposited Funds at any given moment will equal the total of the items that are sitting and waiting to be deposited from Undeposited Funds. Now let's deposit two items from Undeposited Funds and see what happens. Let's say on February 27 we deposited check number 1717 from candy that we got on the 23rd and on February 24th we deposited cash of 1000 dollars that we got from Betty. That'll be a total of 2400 dollars leaving Undeposited Funds and being deposited into the bank account.

What happens when we deposit from Undeposited Funds? Undeposited Funds will decrease by the amount of the items we deposit because the money is now in the bank and the bank account will increase for the same reason the money is now in the bank. Let's take a look at what the results should be in the trial balance when we finish making the deposit. We first deposited 2400 into the bank so Cash in Bank should increase by 2400 and become 22700. Undeposited Funds just gave up 2400 so Undeposited Funds should decrease to 8000.

VAUNDA THE VIDEO VIXEN		
Trial Balance		
All Transactions		
	Feb 26, 22	
	Debit	Credit
CASH IN BANK	22,770	
PETTY CASH / CASH ON HA...	500.00	
ACCOUNTS RECEIVABLE	21,440.00	
SUPPLIES	1,330.00	
Undeposited Funds	8,000	
EQUIPMENT	4,515.00	
ACCOUNTS PAYABLE		16,485.00
EDITING INCOME		19,360.00
VIDEO INCOME		41,700.00
DELEVERY EXP	4,610.00	
ELECTRIC EXP	4,150.00	
REPAIR EXP	5,850.00	
TELEPHONE EXP	4,380.00	

Let's take a look at how to record this deposit. Take notice of what happens when we go to "Banking" and then "Make Deposit". You can see both windows open up now that there are payments to deposit and Undeposited Funds. As soon as the Deposit window opens up the Payment window opens up too.

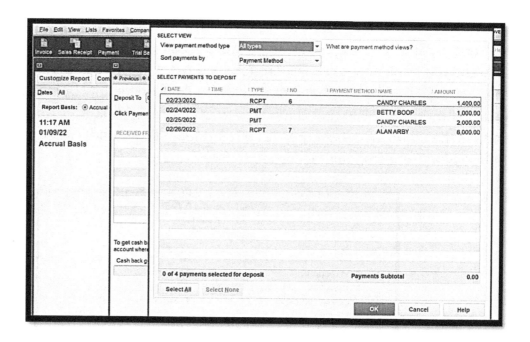

Don't worry if you accidentally close the Payments window because you can always reopen it by clicking the "Payments" button in the main deposit window, but you don't have to because if there are payments available it means as soon as you open the Deposit window the Payments window will open as well.

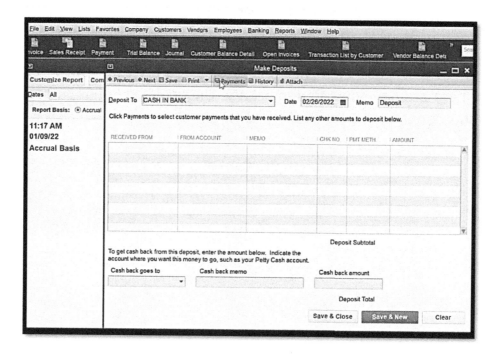

Now the specific items that we are depositing are the 1400 dollars here and the 1000 dollars here. These are the two specific items that were listed in the transaction and notice when we click on one of them the Payment subtotal changes. Click on each item that was deposited on that same day from that one deposit then click OK and you will see the two items listed right here in the Deposit window for a total of 2400. Then we click "Save & Close" and you can see in the Trial Balance the results are exactly as what we expected. Cash in Bank is 22700 and Undeposited Funds decreased to 8000 dollars.

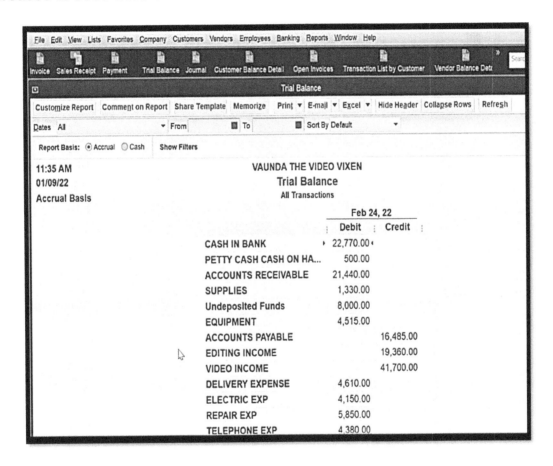

If we look a little closer, we can double-click on Deposited Funds to determine why it says 8000. When we double-click, you can see that the remaining balance of 8000 is a result of having this item deposited but other items have not yet been deposited; when you double-click that account it's clearer.

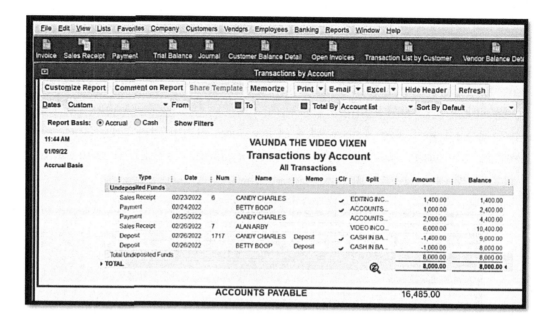

If you now go to "**Banking**," then "**Make Deposit**," you can see that these two items that are left in the Payments to Deposit window total 8000 dollars and that explains why the balance of Undeposited Funds is 8000. Again, if you open it up, you'll be able to see that these were put into Undeposited Funds individually but this one big deposit of 2400 lowered the balance to 8000 and you can always double-click, come right back to the Deposit window to see exactly what happened.

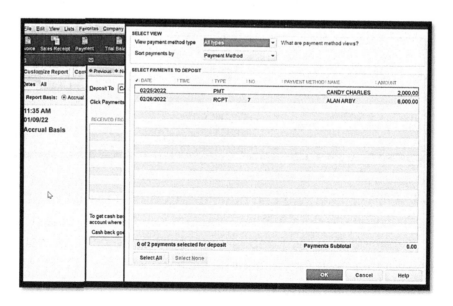

Now let's finish up by depositing the rest of the money. Let's say on February 28th we deposited the remaining items from Undeposited Funds. If there's nothing left in

233

Undeposited Funds that should become zero but if all 8000 dollars that remained went into the bank account, then the bank account should increase by 8000 and become 30770.

VAUNDA THE VIDEO VIXEN
Trial Balance
All Transactions

	Feb 26, 22	
	Debit	Credit
CASH IN BANK	30,770	
PETTY CASH / CASH ON HA...	500.00	
ACCOUNTS RECEIVABLE	21,440.00	
SUPPLIES	1,330.00	
Undeposited Funds	-0-	
EQUIPMENT	4,515.00	
ACCOUNTS PAYABLE		16,485.00
EDITING INCOME		19,360.00
VIDEO INCOME		41,700.00
DELEVERY EXP	4,610.00	
ELECTRIC EXP	4,150.00	
REPAIR EXP	5,850.00	
TELEPHONE EXP	4,380.00	

So, we will go to "**Banking**," "**Make Deposit**" and of course, we put a checkmark on each item that we're depositing in the pay from the Payments window where the subtotal is 8000. Click OK at the bottom and confirm the actual date that we brought the money to the bank. When we click "Save & Close," the Trial Balance shows nothing in Undeposited Funds and 30770 in the bank.

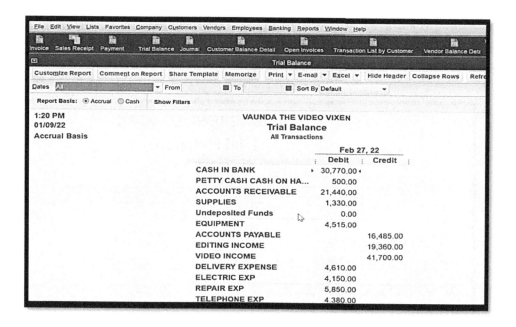

When you open up Undeposited Funds again the individual items were received as payments or Sales Receipts but the summary amounts are the ones that get recorded as coming out as one big fat deposit and that's how the undeposited funds feature Works in QuickBooks desktop.

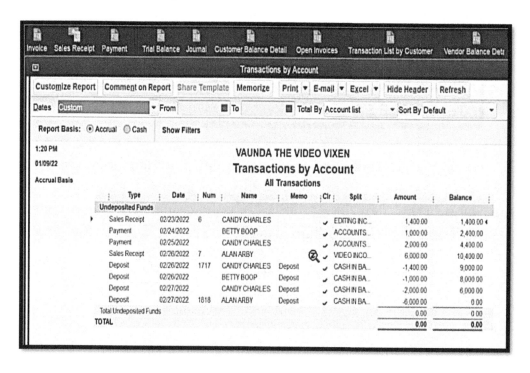

235

Review Questions

1. What do we mean by Basic Deposit?
2. What do we mean by Undeposited funds?
3. How do you record Undeposited funds?
4. What accounts and reports are involved after depositing Undeposited funds?

CHAPTER 13

THE AUDIT TRAIL

This chapter is all about using the Audit Trail to have total control over everything in your QuickBooks desktop file.

Now you may be wondering what the audit Trail is. Well, it's the most powerful report in all of QuickBooks. It shows everything that happened to any transaction from the moment the file was created and it shows when, who and how every transaction was ever recorded or changed in the file since the file was created.

Now let's go ahead and put it up in the icon bar and then we'll talk more about it. From the main menu, we go to "Reports," "**Accountant & Taxes**" and go down to "**Audit Trail**".

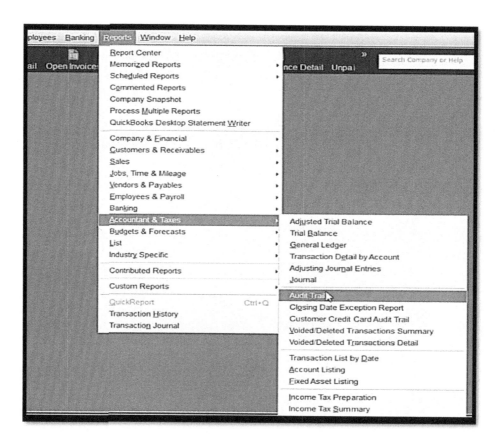

You may well notice that the drop-down date caption here does not say the date of the transaction, it says the date entered or last modified and as a general rule in the book, we click the drop-down and select "All". We want this to show the results of all transactions regardless of the date and the fact that this says the date entered or last modified rather than the date of the transaction, makes the Audit Trail different from any other report in QuickBooks.

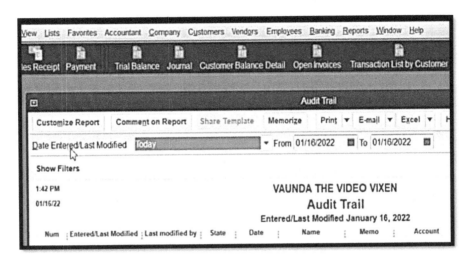

Opening the Audit Trail

Now that it's in front of us, we go to "**View**" and then we click to **add "Audit Trail" to the icon bar**, and then click OK.

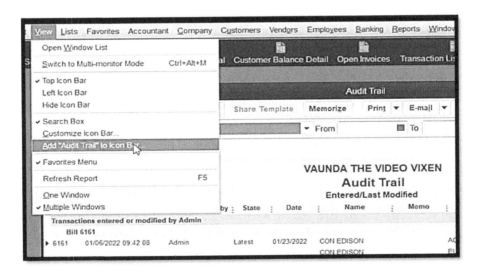

Because we have so many items open in the icon bar, you might not see the Audit Trail listed but you can click the drop-down here and there it is. When you open it up, you can see It also remembers we wanted the report for all transactions.

238

How the Audit Trail works

Now you may also be wondering how the Audit Trail works. To answer that, it lists every transaction-by-transaction type. That means that for example, all checks get listed together, all deposits get listed with other deposits and invoices are listed with invoices, and so on. So, the transaction types are in the categories and the categories themselves are displayed in alphabetical order.

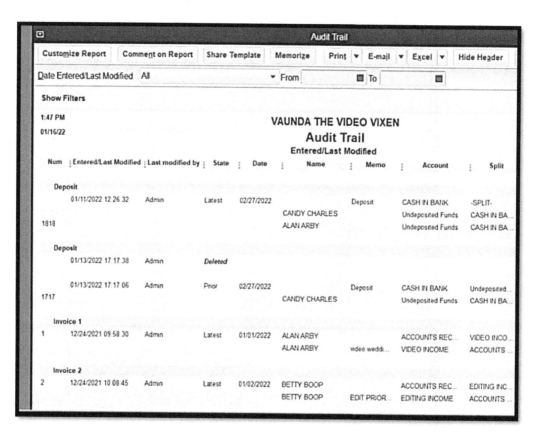

For example, B is the letter of the alphabet that represents the name of one of the transactions type "Bills" so bills are displayed first. C comes after B so all of the checks in the file are listed in the Audit Trail after all the bills, D comes after C so all of the deposits are listed in the audit Trail after all the checks and I come after D so all of the invoices ever recorded in the file will be listed together after all of the deposits and so on.

However, within each transaction type, transactions can be listed by the date of the transaction or the date the transaction was entered and that's what makes the Audit Trail such a powerful forensic tool.

239

Auditing transactions

From all our examples so far, let's find something in the Audit Trail that we changed and see what it looks like. Remember the invoice from January 3rd; it was invoice number three, it was to Candy, and earlier in the book we opened it up, changed it to millions of dollars, and then changed it back. Let's see what that would look like in the Audit Trail.

Since you already listed it in the icon bar, you can easily find it in the icon bar. If you run out of room, click the double-arrow and there it is; it also remembers that we had set it to "All" transactions.

If we go to the bill section and scroll down slowly, we will not find this transaction here. The same thing happens if we go to the checks section and even the deposit section of the audit Trail where all the deposits are listed. Now if we go to the invoice section, notice that invoice number one is one line because it was never changed, invoice number two is one line in the Audit Trail because it was never changed but invoice number three has several lines. If you come down to the bottom of the section of invoice number three, you can see the first transaction we did was on December 24th. Imagining a scene here, on this day we were entering transactions and we screwed up and put the date as February 3rd but we had put in the right amount. 20 seconds later we reopened this and changed the date to January 3rd from February 3rd so it lists the first time we recorded it and it lists the first change. Then what happened was a little while after that, probably a couple of two or three hours after that, we reopened the same transaction and changed the money amount from 3300 to 333300 and that was the change from here to there. Then of course you can see some minutes later, we reopened this very same transaction and changed the money amount back to 3300. So, all the details of any one transaction and all of its changes are listed right here.

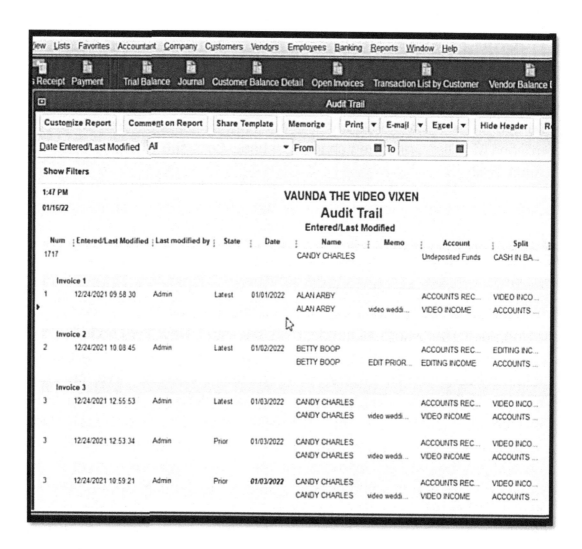

One of the most helpful things about the Audit Trail is that it's best for fixing the most difficult type of mistake which is to find a date mistake that's because date mistakes are always misleading when you search for them and in most cases, you may not even know that the mistake is a mistake on the date.

241

Customer Balance Detail

All Transactions

	Date	Num	Account	Amou
...LACE				
	07/29/2016	14	ACCOUNTS R...	9
	07/29/2016	15	ACCOUNTS R...	5
	01/03/2017	1	ACCOUNTS R...	1,3
	01/06/2017	2	ACCOUNTS R...	1,3
	04/14/2017	20	ACCOUNTS R...	3
...ON PLACE				4,6
...IRD LANE				
	01/09/2017	3	ACCOUNTS R...	1,3
	01/14/2017		ACCOUNTS R...	2,7
	01/17/2017	5	ACCOUN...	
	01/20/2017	61	ACCOUNTS R...	-1,0
	01/23/2017	66	ACCOUNTS R...	-1,0
	03/14/2017	16	ACCOUNTS R...	1,1
	03/22/2017	17	ACCOUNTS R...	1,7
	04/05/2017	18	ACCOUNTS R...	2,5
...NGBIRD LANE				8,8

Let's show you what we mean. If the image we have below is a typical QuickBooks report, you can see that the report lists the details of the transactions in date order, specifically the date that you recorded as the date of the transaction.

Customer Balance Detail

All Transactions

Type	Date	Num	Account	Amount	Balance
BROWN CO					
HANSON PLACE					
Invoice	07/29/2016	14	ACCOUNTS R...	975.00	975.00
Invoice	07/29/2016	15	ACCOUNTS R...	537.50	1,512.50
Invoice	01/03/2017	1	ACCOUNTS R...	1,350.00	2,862.50
Invoice	01/06/2017	2	ACCOUNTS R...	1,350.00	4,212.50
Invoice	04/14/2017	20	ACCOUNTS R...	396.00	4,608.50
Total HANSON PLACE				4,608.50	4,608.50
MOCKINGBIRD LANE					
Invoice	01/09/2017	3	ACCOUNTS R...	1,350.00	1,350.00
Invoice	01/14/2017	4	ACCOUNTS R...	2,700.00	4,050.00
Invoice	01/17/2017	5	ACCOUNTS R...	1,350.00	5,400.00
Payment	01/20/2017	61	ACCOUNTS R...	-1,000.00	4,400.00
Payment	01/23/2017	66	ACCOUNTS R...	-1,000.00	3,400.00
Invoice	03/14/2017	16	ACCOUNTS R...	1,175.00	4,575.00
Invoice	03/22/2017	17	ACCOUNTS R...	1,775.00	6,350.00
Invoice	04/05/2017	18	ACCOUNTS R...	2,500.00	8,850.00
Total MOCKINGBIRD LANE				8,850.00	8,850.00

So, if you accidentally put in the wrong month, what's going to happen is you're going to be looking up in the section of the month that you thought you recorded it in when in fact the transaction you're looking for is in a completely different place because you didn't realize you put in the wrong month. So, a report that lists the transactions in date order would make it almost impossible for you to find that specific type of mistake but you see, the Audit Trail can be sorted by date entered not just the date of the transaction itself, of course, the date entered within a category of transactions. That means if you can remember approximately When you entered the transaction you can find it in the Audit Trail and fix it.

For example, let's find all the transactions that are dated between January 1 and January 15th. Also, since those same transactions were physically entered between January 1 and January 15th it would have to fit both criteria to show up on the Audit Trail after we asked for this. So, we'll open our good friend the Audit Trail. Notice you only have in the display bar entered "last modified". What you have to do is Click "**Customize Report**" and you get the "**Modify Report**" window.

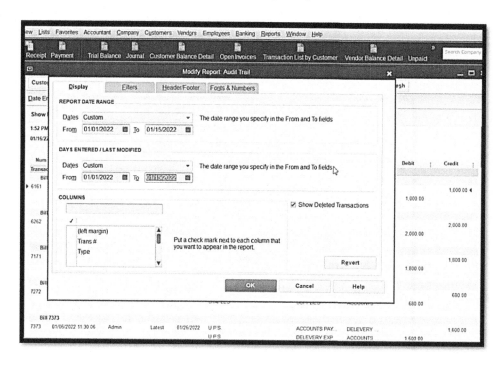

Now within the four tabs if you click "Display," you'll notice the Audit Trail allows you a date range of the date of the transaction and it's the only report in QuickBooks that allows you to enter a date range based on the date it was either entered or last modified. So, all we have to do is set both and it will filter out everything except for

243

what fits the criteria of both. So, regarding the date of the transaction, we want it to be between January 1 and January 15th and regarding the date entered and modified the same date range, and of course, we rarely enter transactions on the day that they happen so if it fits both of these criteria, we'll then click OK.

In the case of our example, you can see that it's only one transaction with Bill number 8181 that falls under the criteria. You can see that it's showing that it was physically entered on the 9th and then what happened was about some minutes later the date was corrected. As you now know, this is the only one transaction that's both dated as a transaction between those two dates as well as entered or modified within those two dates.

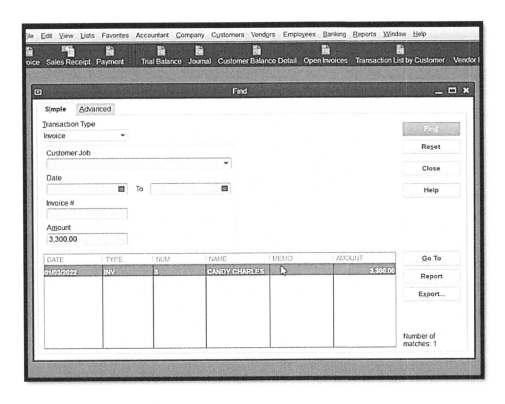

So, by knowing both of them you can find mistakes where you put the wrong date on a transaction and if you're advanced, you can use it in conjunction with the "Find" window to find everything that ever happened to anything. As long as you know something about the transaction you're looking for, you can find it in the "Find" window first, that'll help you identify it in the Audit Trail, and then you can see everything about it.

For our second example, let's say that somewhere in the file there was an invoice in the amount of 3300 that somebody opened up, made several changes to, and then changed back to the original amounts and you want to know who did it, when it was changed and what it was changed to before it was changed back. What do you have to do?

First, you have to use the "Find" window to find the transaction that fits that description, then use the Audit Trail to find it by transaction type and date, and then once you identify it in the Audit Trail you can see everything else about that transaction.

Let's use the original transaction we were working with as our example. We will go to "Edit" then go to "Find" and "Invoice" because that's the transaction type exactly in the amount of 3300 dollars and if we click "Find", we can see that there's only one that fits that description; if there were several, we would have to know a little more about it to narrow our search but we can see that that's invoice number three, dated January 3rd.

Now January 3rd is the date of the transaction. We need to find the date entered and everything else so we open the Audit Trail and for this purpose, we want to customize the report. Since we don't know what date, it was entered we leave this as all but we do know the date that the transaction was recorded and you saw that this transaction was recorded on January 3rd, so we want to see everything on January 3rd in the section of invoices that we will scroll to and then we'll find out what date it was entered, after which we click OK.

You can see that this was the only transaction entered on January 3rd (in a real situation you might have more) but at least if you scroll to the Invoice section for the invoices that were created for that date you can see here's the one in the amount of 3300. After you have confirmed that this is the one, you're looking for, you can see every change to that transaction since it was entered.

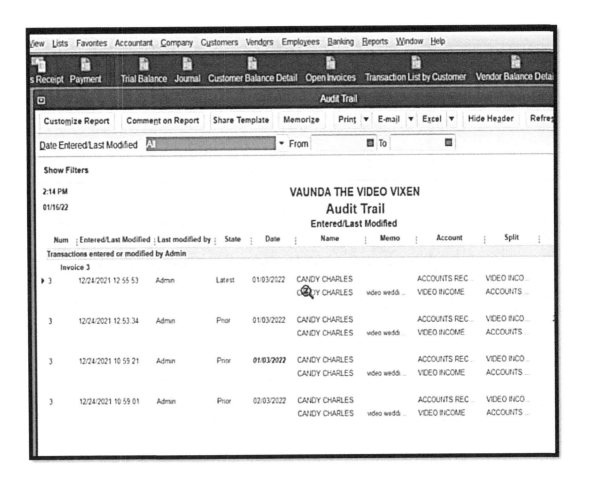

Review Questions

The image below is what the trial balance should look like before you start this exercise. And before you start you have to go through your numbers and make sure that you're starting with the same numbers because the only way to finish with the same numbers is, to begin with, the same numbers.

TRIAL BALANCE BEFORE EXERCISE

VAUNDA THE VIDEO VIXEN
Trial Balance
All Transactions

	Feb 27, 22	
	Debit	Credit
CASH IN BANK	29,370.00	
PETTY CASH / CASH ON HA...	500.00	
ACCOUNTS RECEIVABLE	21,440.00	
SUPPLIES	1,330.00	
Undeposited Funds	1,400.00	
EQUIPMENT	4,515.00	
ACCOUNTS PAYABLE		16,485.00
EDITING INCOME		19,360.00
VIDEO INCOME		41,700.00
DELEVERY EXP	4,610.00	
ELECTRIC EXP	4,150.00	
REPAIR EXP	5,850.00	
TELEPHONE EXP	4,380.00	

Also, here in the image below is the Customer Balance Detail. Before the exercise make sure that the total balance of each customer is equal to the total balance of each of your customers.

CUSTOMER BALANCE DETAIL BEFORE EXERCISE

VAUNDA THE VIDEO VIXEN
Customer Balance Detail
All Transactions

Type	Date	Num	Account	Amount	Balance
ALAN ARBY					
Invoice	01/01/2022	1	ACCOUNTS REC...	3,000.00	3,000.00
Invoice	01/05/2022	5	ACCOUNTS REC...	3,900.00	6,900.00
Invoice	01/07/2022	7	ACCOUNTS REC...	2,100.00	9,000.00
Payment	01/09/2022		ACCOUNTS REC...	-3,000.00	6,000.00
Invoice	01/17/2022	13	ACCOUNTS REC...	2,380.00	8,380.00
Payment	01/19/2022		ACCOUNTS REC...	-1,000.00	7,380.00
Total ALAN ARBY				7,380.00	7,380.00
BETTY BOOP					
Invoice	01/02/2022	2	ACCOUNTS REC...	1,400.00	1,400.00
Invoice	01/04/2022	4	ACCOUNTS REC...	1,680.00	3,080.00
Invoice	01/06/2022	6	ACCOUNTS REC...	4,200.00	7,280.00
Payment	01/10/2022		ACCOUNTS REC...	-680.00	6,600.00
Payment	01/14/2022		ACCOUNTS REC...	-1,400.00	5,200.00
Payment	02/24/2022		ACCOUNTS REC...	-1,000.00	4,200.00
Total BETTY BOOP				4,200.00	4,200.00
CANDY CHARLES					
Invoice	01/23/2022	3	ACCOUNTS REC...	3,300.00	3,300.00
Invoice	01/08/2022	8	ACCOUNTS REC...	2,240.00	5,540.00
Invoice	01/13/2022	11	ACCOUNTS REC...	2,660.00	8,200.00
Payment	01/16/2022		ACCOUNTS REC...	-240.00	7,960.00
Invoice	01/21/2022	16	ACCOUNTS REC...	4,200.00	12,160.00
Payment	01/22/2022		ACCOUNTS REC...	-300.00	11,860.00
Payment	02/25/2022		ACCOUNTS REC...	-2,000.00	9,860.00
Total CANDY CHARLES				9,860.00	9,860.00
TOTAL				21,440.00	21,440.00

And before you start the exercise take great care in going through the Open Invoice report for each Open Balance one by one. Remember, it's not enough to start with the same total balance of the customer; you have to start with each Open Invoice Balance being the same to complete the exercise.

OPEN INVOICE BEFORE EXERCISE

VAUNDA THE VIDEO VIXEN
Open Invoices
All Transactions

Type	Date	Num	P. O. #	Terms	Due Date	Aging	Open Balance
ALAN ARBY							
Invoice	01/05/2022	5			01/05/2022	12	2,900.00
Invoice	01/07/2022	7			01/07/2022	10	2,100.00
Invoice	01/17/2022	13			01/17/2022		2,380.00
Total ALAN ARBY							7,380.00
BETTY BOOP							
Invoice	01/06/2022	6			01/06/2022	11	4,200.00
Total BETTY BOOP							4,200.00
CANDY CHARLES							
Invoice	01/13/2022	11			01/13/2022	4	2,660.00
Invoice	01/21/2022	16			01/21/2022		4,200.00 ◄
Invoice	01/03/2022	3			02/03/2022		3,000.00
Total CANDY CHARLES							9,860.00
TOTAL							21,440.00

The image below is what the Vendor Balance Detail should look like before you start the exercise. Of course, you can pause for a moment and go through it one by one to make sure that it matches before you start putting in any of the transactions.

VENDOR BALANCE DETAIL BEFORE EXERCISE

VAUNDA THE VIDEO VIXEN
Vendor Balance Detail
All Transactions

Type	Date	Num	Account	Amount	Balance
CON EDISON					
Bill	01/23/2022	6161	ACCOUNTS PAY...	1,000.00	1,000.00
Bill	01/27/2022	7474	ACCOUNTS PAY...	1,150.00	2,150.00
Bill Pmt -Check	02/01/2022	1	ACCOUNTS PAY...	-1,000.00	1,150.00
Bill	02/09/2022	8181	ACCOUNTS PAY...	2,000.00	3,150.00
Total CON EDISON				3,150.00	3,150.00
REX REPAIR SHOP					
Bill	01/23/2022	6262	ACCOUNTS PAY...	2,000.00	2,000.00
Bill	01/28/2022	7575	ACCOUNTS PAY...	2,050.00	4,050.00
Bill Pmt -Check	02/02/2022	2	ACCOUNTS PAY...	-550.00	3,500.00
Bill	02/13/2022	8282	ACCOUNTS PAY...	700.00	4,200.00
Total REX REPAIR SHOP				4,200.00	4,200.00
STAPLES					
Bill	01/25/2022	7272	ACCOUNTS PAY...	680.00	680.00
Bill	01/29/2022	7676	ACCOUNTS PAY...	1,095.00	1,775.00
Bill Pmt -Check	02/14/2022	7	ACCOUNTS PAY...	-500.00	1,275.00
Bill	02/18/2022	8484	ACCOUNTS PAY...	3,300.00	4,575.00
Bill Pmt -Check	02/19/2022	8	ACCOUNTS PAY...	-1,650.00	2,925.00
Total STAPLES				2,925.00	2,925.00
U.P.S.					
Bill	01/26/2022	7373	ACCOUNTS PAY...	1,600.00	1,600.00
Bill	01/31/2022	7979	ACCOUNTS PAY...	1,110.00	2,710.00
Total U.P.S.				2,710.00	2,710.00
VERIZON					
Bill	01/24/2022	7171	ACCOUNTS PAY...	1,800.00	1,800.00
Bill	01/30/2022	7878	ACCOUNTS PAY...	800.00	2,600.00
Bill Pmt -Check	02/19/2022	5	ACCOUNTS PAY...	-800.00	1,800.00

If you go through the Unpaid Bills report you have to make sure that the Open Balance of each bill that's listed here is the same as the Open Balance on your report before you start the final exercise.

UNPAID BILLS BEFORE EXERCISE

VAUNDA THE VIDEO VIXEN
Unpaid Bills Detail
All Transactions

	Type	Date	Num	Due Date	Aging	Open Balance
CON EDISON						
▶	Bill	01/27/2022	7474	02/06/2022		1,150.00 ◀
	Bill	02/09/2022	8181	02/19/2022		2,000.00
Total CON EDISON						3,150.00
REX REPAIR SHOP						
	Bill	01/23/2022	6262	02/02/2022		2,000.00
	Bill	01/28/2022	7575	02/07/2022		1,500.00
	Bill	02/13/2022	8282	02/23/2022		700.00
Total REX REPAIR SHOP						4,200.00
STAPLES						
	Bill	01/25/2022	7272	02/04/2022		180.00
	Bill	01/29/2022	7676	02/08/2022		1,095.00
	Bill	02/18/2022	8484	02/28/2022		1,650.00
Total STAPLES						2,925.00
U.P.S.						
	Bill	01/26/2022	7373	02/05/2022		1,600.00
	Bill	01/31/2022	7979	02/10/2022		1,110.00
Total U.P.S.						2,710.00
VERIZON						
	Bill	01/24/2022	7171	02/03/2022		1,000.00
	Bill	01/30/2022	7878	02/09/2022		800.00
	Bill	02/16/2022	8383	02/26/2022		1,700.00
Total VERIZON						3,500.00
TOTAL						16,485.00

Below is an image displaying the first half of the transaction set. You can pause now and slowly and carefully record each of the different transactions one by one. If you forget how to record a particular transaction, feel free to go back to the chapter where you learned about that transaction and review how to record it then come back here and try entering it.

1-Mar	Did 11 video hours for Candy - on account
2-Mar	Received the electric bill from Con Edison $900 #9191
3-Mar	Paid $50 cash for supplies - Staples gave us receipt #441166
4-Mar	Paid Verizon $1,700 for #8383 Check #10
5-Mar	Did 18 editing hours and received all cash from Alan
6-Mar	Receivd $2,660 from Candy for invoice #1011 - paid with check $ 5678
7-Mar	Wrote check #11 to u.p.s for delivery done today (March 7) $450
8-Mar	Paid Rex Repair via electronic transfer from our bank account - $1,000 for repairs #919123
9-Mar	Depsited check # 5678 from Candy received on March 6

Below is an image of the second half of the transaction list and again you could pause at this point, and record them slowly.

10-Mar	Did 16 editing hours on account for Betty
11-Mar	Received the telephone bill from Verizon $880, # 3210
12-Mar	Paid $30 cash for a prepaid phone card fromVerizon rcpt # 292198
13-Mar	Paid check #12 for $595 to Staples for bill #7676
14-Mar	Did 14 video for Candy, she gave us check #40961
15-Mar	Received $380 from Alan for invoice #1013 - he gave us cash
16-Mar	Paid check #13 to Staples forEquipment received today (March 16) $725
17-Mar	Paid an online trnasfer $700 to u.p.s for delivery done today (March 17) #44332211
18-Mar	Took $50 from undeposited funds for supplies from Staples
	and $100 from undeposited funds for a repair from rex and deposited the rest of the cash

Now after you finish recording all given transactions, the image below is a display of what your Trial Balance should look like when you finish the entire practice set.

TRIAL BALANCE AFTER EXERCISE

VAUNDA THE VIDEO VIXEN
Trial Balance
All Transactions

	Mar 18, 22	
	Debit	Credit
CASH IN BANK	31,010.00	
PETTY CASH / CASH ON HA...	420.00	
ACCOUNTS RECEIVABLE	23,940.00	
SUPPLIES	1,430.00	
Undeposited Funds	4,200.00	
EQUIPMENT	5,240.00	
ACCOUNTS PAYABLE		15,970.00
EDITING INCOME		24,120.00
VIDEO INCOME		49,200.00
DELEVERY EXP	5,760.00	
ELECTRIC EXP	5,050.00	
REPAIR EXP	6,950.00	
TELEPHONE EXP	5,290.00	

Remember: if you have any different numbers you have to go back and do the techniques that you learned to find and fix mistakes so that when you finish your trial balance looks exactly like what you see above. The image below is a display of what the Customer Balance Detail should look like after the exercise.

CUSTOMER BALANCE DETAIL AFTER EXERCISE

VAUNDA THE VIDEO VIXEN
Customer Balance Detail
All Transactions

Type	Date	Num	Account	Amount	Balance
ALAN ARBY					
Invoice	01/01/2022	1	ACCOUNTS REC...	3,000.00	3,000.00
Invoice	01/05/2022	5	ACCOUNTS REC...	3,900.00	6,900.00
Invoice	01/07/2022	7	ACCOUNTS REC...	2,100.00	9,000.00
Payment	01/09/2022		ACCOUNTS REC...	-3,000.00	6,000.00
Invoice	01/17/2022	13	ACCOUNTS REC...	2,380.00	8,380.00
Payment	01/19/2022		ACCOUNTS REC...	-1,000.00	7,380.00
Payment	03/15/2022		ACCOUNTS REC...	-380.00	7,000.00
Total ALAN ARBY				7,000.00	7,000.00
BETTY BOOP					
Invoice	01/02/2022	2	ACCOUNTS REC...	1,400.00	1,400.00
Invoice	01/04/2022	4	ACCOUNTS REC...	1,680.00	3,080.00
Invoice	01/06/2022	6	ACCOUNTS REC...	4,200.00	7,280.00
Payment	01/10/2022		ACCOUNTS REC...	-680.00	6,600.00
Payment	01/14/2022		ACCOUNTS REC...	-1,400.00	5,200.00
Payment	02/24/2022		ACCOUNTS REC...	-1,000.00	4,200.00
Invoice	03/10/2022	13	ACCOUNTS REC...	2,240.00	6,440.00
Total BETTY BOOP				6,440.00	6,440.00
CANDY CHARLES					
Invoice	01/03/2022	3	ACCOUNTS REC...	3,300.00	3,300.00
Invoice	01/08/2022	8	ACCOUNTS REC...	2,240.00	5,540.00
Invoice	01/13/2022	11	ACCOUNTS REC...	2,660.00	8,200.00
Payment	01/16/2022		ACCOUNTS REC...	-240.00	7,960.00
Invoice	01/21/2022	16	ACCOUNTS REC...	4,200.00	12,160.00
Payment	01/22/2022		ACCOUNTS REC...	-300.00	11,860.00
Payment	02/25/2022		ACCOUNTS REC...	-2,000.00	9,860.00
Invoice	03/01/2022	12	ACCOUNTS REC...	3,300.00	13,160.00
Payment	03/06/2022	5678	ACCOUNTS REC...	-2,660.00	10,500.00

You can compare the total balance of each customer to each of the customers in your file to make sure they have the same ending balance, of course, if you go through the Open Invoice report again, make sure you applied for Invoice Payments properly by comparing each invoices' open balance to the open balance of the invoices in your file.

OPEN INVOICE AFTER EXERCISE

VAUNDA THE VIDEO VIXEN
Open Invoices
All Transactions

Type	Date	Num	P. O. #	Terms	Due Date	Aging	Open Balance
ALAN ARBY							
Invoice	01/05/2022	5			01/05/2022	12	2,900.00
Invoice	01/07/2022	7			01/07/2022	10	2,100.00
Invoice	01/17/2022	13			01/17/2022		2,000.00
Total ALAN ARBY							7,000.00
BETTY BOOP							
Invoice	01/06/2022	6			01/06/2022	11	4,200.00
Invoice	03/10/2022	13			03/10/2022		2,240.00
Total BETTY BOOP							6,440.00
CANDY CHARLES							
Invoice	01/21/2022	16			01/21/2022		4,200.00
Invoice	01/03/2022	3			02/03/2022		3,000.00
Invoice	03/01/2022	12			03/01/2022		3,300.00
Total CANDY CHARLES							10,500.00
TOTAL							23,940.00

251

The image below displays what the Vendor Balance Detail should look like after the exercise. While these are quite a lot of transactions, you can pause and go through them one by one so you can compare the Unpaid Bills report.

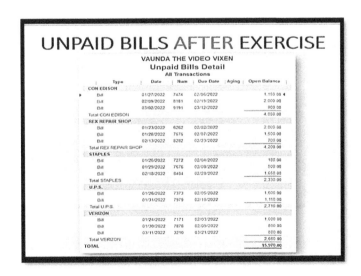

After the exercise, you have to make sure that each Open Balance and Unpaid Bill that you see here on the screen matches each Open Balance in your Unpaid Bills in your file.

CHAPTER 14

BUDGETING

One of the popular subjects right now is budgeting. To succeed in any kind of business you need to plan and that's what we're going to cover in this chapter. Would you like to know if your jobs are under or over budget? Well, then you need to know how to make a **Budget by Job**.

The **Budget by Job** feature in QuickBooks desktop is one of the most simple but helpful tools in QuickBooks. It is simply a data sheet that remembers the amounts of each expense or other account that you input into the data sheet as the budgeted amounts.

After putting in budget amounts simply run the report called "**Budget versus Actual**" and you will see all the differences between the budgeted amounts and the actual transactions. That's all it does and that's all it needs to do.

You can change any budgeted amount or any actual transaction and the "**Budget versus Actual**" report will reflect the change immediately. If you rerun the report, you'll get the updated numbers. For example, if you reopen the budget and you change the amount of delivery expense that's budgeted, as soon as you open the Budget versus Actual report you will see the new difference reflected in the report including the change that you just made to the budget.

EVEN IF YOU CHANGE TRANSACTIONS

	BUDGETED	ACTUAL	DIFFERENCE
COST OF WALLPAPER SOLD	$800.00	$600	$200
DELIVERY EXPENSE	$600	$500.00	$100
DEMOLITION EXPENSE	$600.00	$500.00	$100.00
REAIR EXPENSE	$500.00	$500.00	$0.00
SUPPLIES EXPENSE	$400.00	$500.00	-$100.00

STILL THE REPORT CHANGES IMMEDIATELY

The same thing is true if you change the actual transactions; as soon as you save the changes to a transaction the reports will immediately open with the new difference between the actual transactions that you changed and the budgeted amounts. So that report changes immediately no matter which one you change so that you can see whatever the currently updated difference is. You may now ask, how are budgets saved in QuickBooks desktop? Each budget is simply a data sheet that you can reopen and change. You can have two separate budgets for each fiscal year where one of the budgets is a general budget based on the account balances and the second budget can be your Budget by Job. You can set up the budget for any period you like, the budget can be monthly budget, weekly budget, quarterly, daily, annual, or whatever you like.

Creating a budget

Let's say that we're making a budget for the job expenses for January 2022. Now that means that it's the fiscal year 2022, job by month just for the company name. Let's say these are the budgeted amounts for these five expenses: 8,7,6,5,4. From the main menu go to "**Company**", "**Planning & Budgeting**" then "**Set up budgets**".

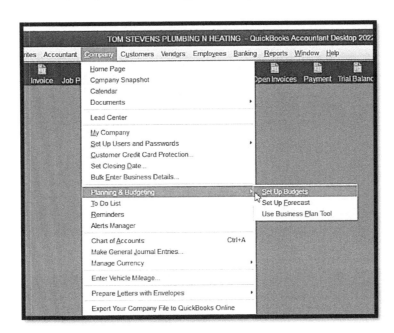

Now we want the fiscal year 2022 and "**Profit & Loss by Job**" is a Profit & Loss type of budget if you're doing it by Job. Click "Next" to proceed.

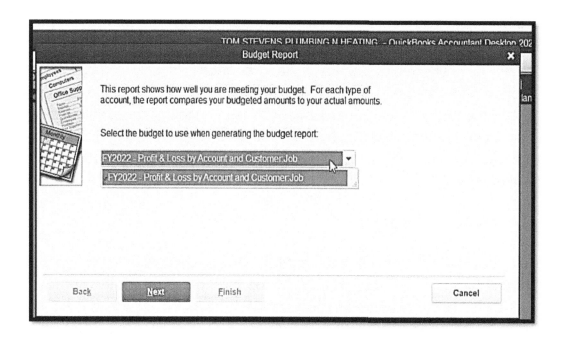

We want it by Customer job because we're contractors and we need to see if the job is under or over budget.

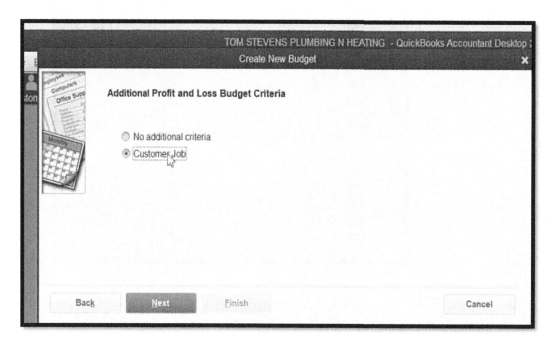

Now in this example, we're creating the numbers from scratch (we're not using the previous year's actual data to assume what the budgeted numbers will be) so click "**Create Budget from scratch**" and click "**Finish**".

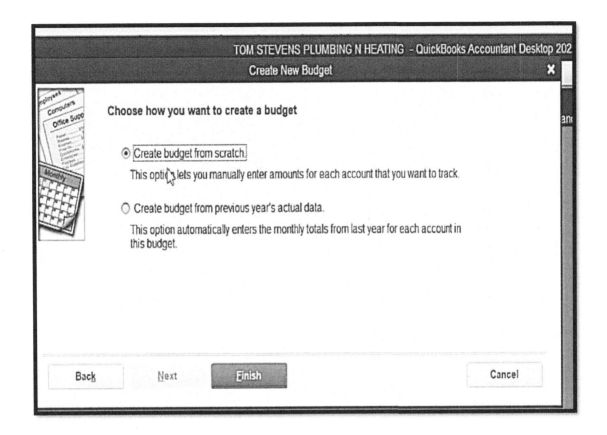

The first thing you must do is make sure that you choose the right job before you start putting in the numbers. Notice the numbers that we want are down here, if we come here, these are the budgeted amounts that we're going to put in to see what happens. So, we start with the cost of goods sold specifically for January of 2022, type in the budgeted amount, and hit the tab key to save the field. Next, we enter the delivery expense hit tab, and enter demolition expense, repair expense, and supplies expense for January specifically for the job; please note that these can change based on the company you're working with. So, these are the budgeted amounts (for our example) that we've just input. Now we click OK and QuickBooks will remember that these are the budgeted amounts.

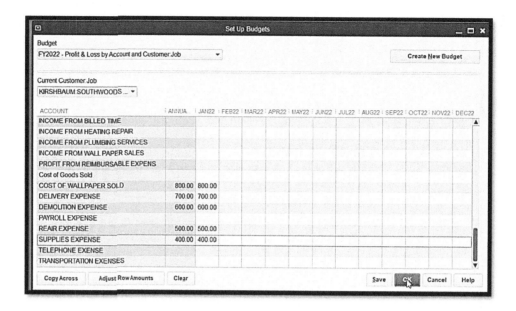

Budget versus Actual report

Before we start recording any actual transactions for January of 2022 for the job let's open the "**Budget versus Actual**" report. From the main menu, we go to "**Reports**", "**Budgets & Forecasts**" and then "**Budget versus Actual**". The other choices here are not nearly as helpful as Budget versus Actual.

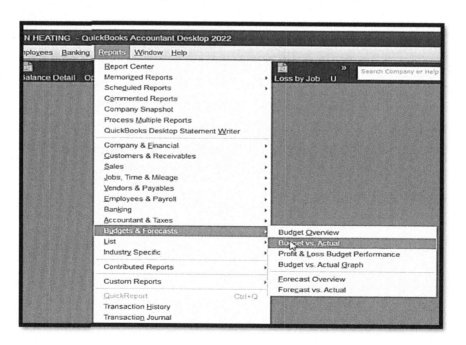

We want it for the 2022-year account and Customer Job and since that's the only budget we made, that's the only budget we will see on the list. Click "**Next**".

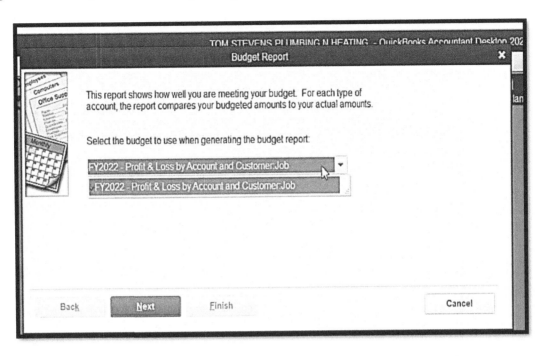

We don't want "Account by month" when it comes to this choice; you must choose "**Account by Customer Job**" as that's the only format of this report that is helpful.

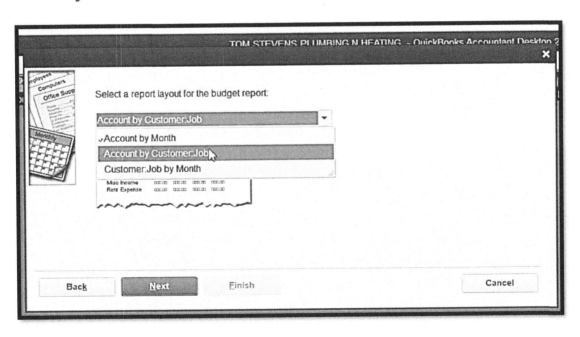

We'll click "**Next**" and "**Finish**" now.

Modifying your budget

Sometimes the report opens in a big mess so we have to filter it down for the two things we need; we have to filter it specifically for our job and we have to filter it specifically for the date range that we're looking for. So, we click "**Customize report**", go to "**Filter**" then enter the letter N for the name and choose the name of the job.

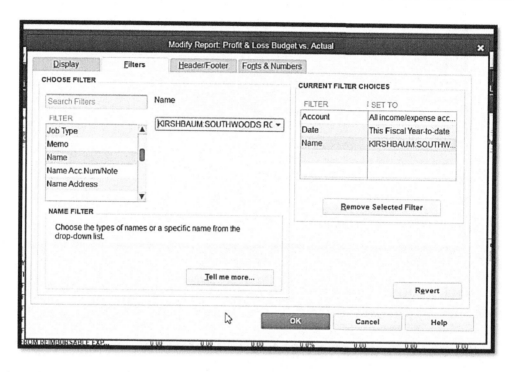

If we don't choose only the job we're working on, we're going to get every single job in this file as we scroll from left to right so the first thing we want to do is go to Customize, filter by n for name, click the drop-down and choose our job then click Ok.

Now that it only has our job, we have to isolate the date range and click "refresh" and you can see that it looks like something that can help us. You'll notice in the format that the first four columns are just our current job then the next four columns are everything for another job in total so if there were other jobs besides our current job those budgeted amounts would show up here and then the total is the total of all jobs together. Unfortunately, there's no way to filter out the total and you can make it a little clearer by moving the mouse to one of the three dots when you get the cross to click and drag to the right and if you want all columns to be big you can adjust accordingly so you can see it nice and clear.

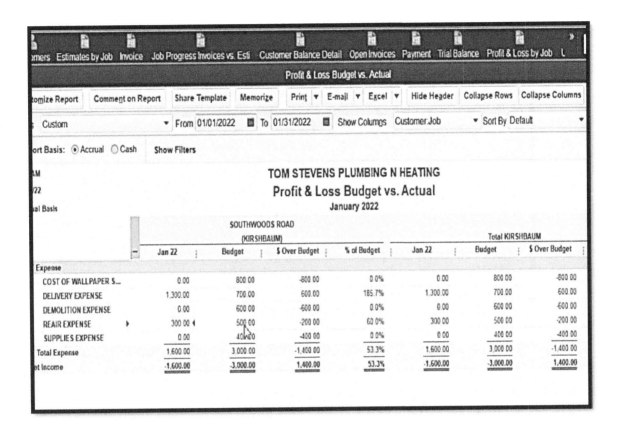

You can see the budgeted amount and the actual transactions in the left column. The budgeted amounts are in one column, then the amount under or over budget is shown in the next column, and the percent under or over budget shows in the last column. So, there are only four columns to the budget, the rest are totals.

Let's enter some actual transactions and see what happens to the Budget versus the Actual report. On January 5th we paid UPS 1300 dollars for a delivery related to a south wood's road.

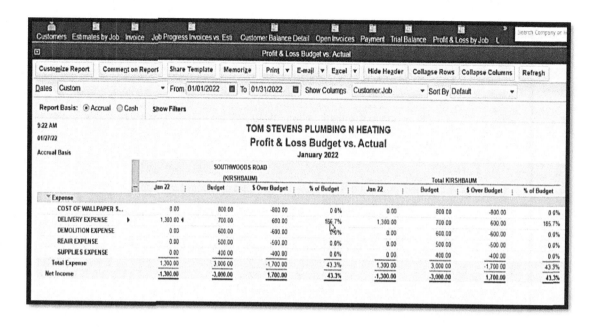

We'll go to "**Banking**" then "**Write a Check**". This is January 5th of 2022 and it is a delivery to UPS. QuickBooks knows they have bills, click "Write a Check" now. The amount is 1300 and the most important field is this: if you forget to put Customer Jobs in the bottom right then you will not see the difference in that Jobs Budget. So, you have to go down and click your customer, in this case, it's not billable just hit Enter to save it and when you come back and refresh the report you can see the amount that was recorded, the amount that was budgeted, whether you're under or over budget and your budget percent.

Moving to January 10th, we paid 300 to Rex repair for repairs that relate to our previous job.

To record this, we'll go to "Banking" and then "**Write a Check**".

This one on the 10th is to the Rex repair shop. Go to Write your Check and enter the amount. When we hit enter to save it, the most important thing is to choose the job or it won't know to include it in that Jobs budget, and when you come back and refresh the report you can see the amount that was recorded, the amount that was budgeted, whether you're under or over budget and your budget percent.

Modifying a budget is very easy. You can reopen the budget by going to "**Company**," "**Planning & Budgeting**" then "**Set up budgets**". Now you can make changes to the

261

Budget and click Ok. When you refresh the report, you can see whether you are now under budget or over budget.

Creating a Budget in QuickBooks Online

If you go to QuickBooks online, in the left-hand side gear menu on the third row under "**Tools**", you'll see "**Budgeting**".

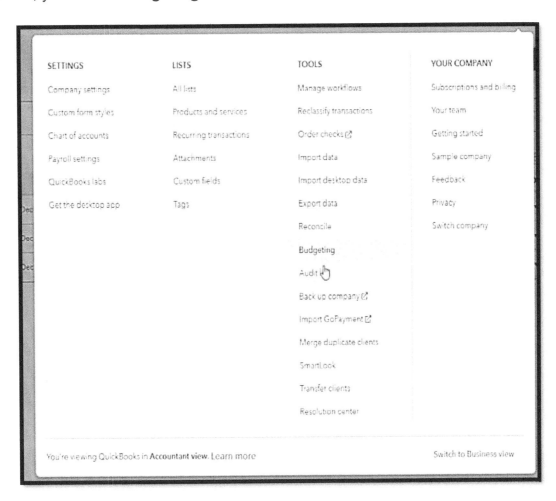

To add a new budget, you're just going to go ahead and click on the green button over here and you can give that whatever name you want.

You may have the fiscal year already selected here and that could be January through December but you can change it if yours is different. We're going to keep it monthly but you can do it quarterly or yearly, you can pre-fill the data or you can just leave it without refilling. You can subdivide it by Customer or you can just leave it without subdividing. After entering your criteria, you can choose to preview or not. You're going to go ahead and click on **"Next"** and there you have it.

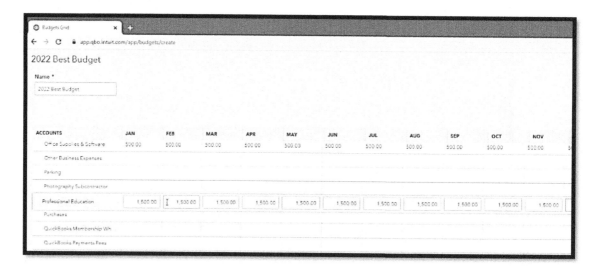

To fill out those bills we're going to start with sales here and we're going to add up a number, and if you want to fill the rest of the column you can click on the blue arrow right at the end and it will fill out the rest of the row.

You can do this pretty much with everything. You can do this for a service fee. We'll go ahead and add the expense as well, click on the arrow, and if your business is seasonal, you can go and update the information for the specific months you want to update.

Now we can fill out all the information including legal, professional, shipping, software, taxes, and license. So, if you're satisfied you can go ahead and save it.

Modifying your budget

Once you save this it is now in Budgeting and if you want to make changes to this budget you can go to the blue button at the end of the row and it's going to bring it back. You can modify this budget anytime you want.

You can also click on the gear menu on the top right-hand side and you can change it the way you want to view it, be it quarterly, yearly, or whatever works for you.

Comparing your budget and report

If you click on the arrow right next to "**Edit**" you can run the budget versus the actual report.

That's going to give you an idea of how far you are from your target or how close you are to your target.

Review Questions

1. What do we mean by "Budget by Job?"
2. How do you create a budget?
3. Explain the term "Budget vs Actual."
4. What are the steps involved in modifying a budget?

CHAPTER 15

JOB COSTING

In this chapter, we'll go over customer and job setup in QuickBooks desktop and you can follow along either with your company or a sample company.

QuickBooks desktop doesn't have a module that's like projects within QuickBooks online. The QuickBooks Online Job costing has some project management features that we haven't seen get pushed into the Desktop version. We're not sure if they are going to offer that within the Desktop version however, with the Desktop version there's the advantage that you have a lot more reports available to you and your desktop product can hold a lot more information. Up here is where you have your customer Center and so with setting up your customers there are a couple of options that you can do. You can have your parent customers, you can have your sub-customers (as you can see there are Customers and Jobs), so anything that is underneath a parent customer is a job.

For example, there are beemer homes and then there are some jobs under beemer homes if you want to, you can change the view setting and switch it to hierarchical view and this will indent all of your jobs. That way it's easier for you to identify which ones are your parent customers and which ones are your jobs.

Creating a customer Job

To create a new customer or job you can either come up here to the "**New Customer Job**," and if you so wish, you can add in multiple customers and jobs. Looking at your screen, this works a lot like an Excel template. If you have an Excel spreadsheet that has all of your customers and all of your job information you can copy from that Excel file that you have just make sure that the columns up at the top match the company name, job name, and job description, and then that way you can just copy-paste all that. As you make and save changes it'll tell you how many customer records have been updated.

Adding Columns

If you want to add any columns you'd go to "**Customize columns**" and then you can add in different pieces of information such as if you want to bulk add, credit limits, new account numbers, or job statuses; there are a lot of different pieces of information that you can capture within your customer center. You can also move the columns as well and you can right-click and just add new customers. So, the first screen will have your address information and your customer's name. Generally, we recommend that you don't use the Open Balance because if you want to enter some of the details about that customer you may not be able to do that in an Open Balance. It just drops that information into the Open Balance equity. Then you have payment settings; if you have a merchant services account you can add their information here, for example, this connects with intuit payments and you can process credit cards and bank transfers through here. If they need sales tax, you can track their resale exemption, and their exemption certificate, as well as add in tax codes and tax items. If you have additional information on sales tax that needs to be collected you could add in a customer type and you can add in a rep.

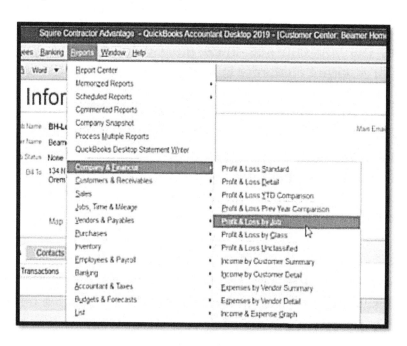

Define fields are where you can add other types of information that you want to have as a customer. This is a little bit limited on Premiere. Enterprise has a lot more options for custom fields and then you can also mark whether it's just for the customer, if you want to add it to the vendor or if you want to add it to the employee as well. For job information, if there is a specific job type that you're doing such as if you want to change orders, or if you want to look at commercial versus residential, you can add those types of details here. You can choose a job status but unfortunately, these can't be altered. It's either one of these statuses you find here. If you decide to do that, you can add a start date and projected end date as well as a finalized end date.

Adding Jobs and sub-jobs

You can add another job in a very similar screen and at the top, you would tell it which customer you want to add that to, and if you want to add it as a job that's underneath the customer or if you want to add it as a sub-job.

We do recommend that you be careful with the number of sub-jobs that you use because of the way that QuickBooks structures your reports. It gets more difficult to read them with the increased number of sub-jobs underneath each other that is why we generally recommend you keep it to about two or no more than three. Similarly, you can add in details regarding that particular job such as if it has different contact details if it has a different address that you need to be concerned with (such as if you're working for a customer who says they have one job that's in one location and another job in another location). At the job level, you can go ahead and have different addresses for those. Then again it has payment settings; if you decide to bill your job separately from the customer again with the additional info you can add that in as well and then you can also add in job information as well.

How do you enter this information within QuickBooks desktop? There are Customer fields that pop up in various forms within your QuickBooks file. For example, if you are entering in a bill and say you have to purchase some materials, if you have problems seeing information that's on the right-hand side of the screen (which is the part where you can link it to customers), if you go over to the three little dots there you can just hover over it until that shows up and then you can add in here your different jobs. If you enter the drop-down again you have your customer and your jobs and they're all clearly labeled on the right side for you so you can add them here.

If you track something as billable what that means is that you want to track this expense as something separate that you want to be able to pull into an invoice when you're invoicing that customer.

There are a couple of different ways you can invoice: either from customers, create invoices, new transactions invoices or you can even do Ctrl-I and which will pull up the invoice.

Another thing to keep in mind too is as you're entering the information into QuickBooks and using all that customer information if you go into Reports and you want to look at your Profit and Loss by Job, you will see you have a lot more information about that job. Let's say you have the customer in a job, if you have a sub-job underneath that there are going to be two tiers that are summed. This makes it more confusing if you have multiple layers of customer jobs and sub-jobs so that's why we generally recommend that you don't do more than two or three at the most because again it will go ahead and total that at the end.

As you can see, we have our income, our cost of goods sold, and any job costs incurred, and then if you need to see any details you could go ahead and click here and find out more information about those.

There is the ability to look at income by customer summary or detail as well if you'd like to see how much income you've received per customer.

Review Questions

1. How do you create a customer, Job?
2. What is a customer Job?
3. What is the difference between Jobs and Sub-jobs?

SECTION FIVE
MAINTAINING QUICKBOOKS

CHAPTER 16
KEEPING YOUR DATA CONFIDENTIAL

QuickBooks has great security features but they can all be undermined if you don't properly prepare for things that you need to do before you even get to QuickBooks. In this chapter, we will explore some security measures to keep your data files secure in QuickBooks.

QuickBooks Security procedures

Before you get to QuickBooks you have to manage three additional things or all the security features and QuickBooks will be undermined:

- You have to manage the people whom you're hiring to work with your QuickBooks
- You have to manage your office and this means what must be there physically regarding equipment and regarding the time of things that happen in your office
- You have to manage your computer

We're going to touch on some of the main points just to get you ready to be able to start putting security features into QuickBooks. Before you hire people to start working on your QuickBooks, there are some easy and very affordable things that you can do to make sure that the people whom you hire behave properly and that you will not have any kind of security issues with them. Now, these are all common-sense things but they're things that most people don't think about within the context of hiring a bookkeeper or an assistant who will help them with QuickBooks.

First, you should do a background check. That's very affordable and very easy to do. You have to get the permission of the person whom you're hiring, however, it is worth it to do that. It's very unlikely the person you're hiring will be insulted and if they want to be honest with you, they can tell you if there's anything in their background that you should be concerned about. Now, of course, many people might not be comfortable asking their new employees to submit themselves to a background check and not all of these recommendations are for everyone. You should know what will make it most likely that you will not have a problem with the people whom you're hiring regarding security issues and you will greatly increase your likelihood of not having a problem if you do a background check before you hire the person who will work on your QuickBooks.

Credit checks are absolutely the same idea. It might not seem important for a person to have good credit before they can work on your QuickBooks however, our goal is to make it the most statistically likely that you will not have any kind of issue and statistics show that you are much less likely to have a security problem with an employee if this person has good credit job reference. Checks can sometimes be helpful but you cannot completely depend on them. Sometimes past employers can be friends with a worker even if they're a problem and they give them a good reference. The opposite is also true; sometimes a person is a reliable trustworthy employee and might have some falling out or some issue with a boss so it's something additional that you could do to send a signal to the person you're hiring that you're serious about security. Our goal is to make it as likely as possible that the person whom you're hiring won't give you a problem and all these things make it much more statistically likely that you will not have a problem.

After you hire, there are specific steps that you should take. Most people don't think about bookkeeper insurance. Bookkeeper insurance is very affordable. You could pay as low as 300 dollars a year to some reputable and stable insurance companies and be covered up to 300,000 dollars for any kind of fraud or even bookkeeping mistake that your employee might accidentally make.

The most important thing you can do to keep your money secure is to make sure that the bookkeeper you hire is never able to physically write checks. If the same person who's keeping records has access to the checks, they may write themselves a check and put it down as a typical business expense and you may never know. The person who's doing QuickBooks should never go to the bank to make deposits or withdrawals; they may make a deposit into their account and simply leave it blank in QuickBooks and you may never know that the money got there. They may do other funny business to cover themselves and keep the money for themselves; it's not always the easiest thing to do but again you want to make it as safe as possible and unlikely as possible for your employee to steal from you.

The person who's doing your QuickBooks should never be able to log into your bank account online; that's the same thing as handing them access to your bank account. Now it is true that some banks give users accounts with different levels of access and different levels of permission and if you're in a situation where the person who does

272

your QuickBooks must be the person who logs into your bank and you feel you have no choice, you might be able to ask your bank to give this person a separate username and password with limited permissions but again it's better to separate it.

Different bookkeepers should not know each other. You might have a person coming on Monday and Wednesday who does the bank reconciliation and does some other part of QuickBooks and you might have a different bookkeeper who comes on Tuesdays and Thursdays who does the payable part and some other part of QuickBooks; you should not have them working together and it's best if they don't even know that the other exists. This will help prevent something called **collusion** which means employees team up to steal from you and cover their tracks.

Also, if you have a physical office for your business where your company files are kept, you should limit access to the office. Make sure whoever goes in there has a key and that person is authorized. Ensure nobody can simply come in and out of the office or get to your computer without your knowledge or consent and of course, it always helps to be present physically in the office as much as possible. This tells employees that you might walk in the door at any moment and again it makes it much less likely that they will try to steal from you or falsify anything in QuickBooks.

As we proceed, you will see how to create usernames and passwords just to get into the computer and these sections will also show you how you can permit specific users to change the date and time in the windows clock. The Windows clock is the most important thing you have. To set up users and passwords for Windows, you have to make it so that only the owner and/or the tech person should be the administrator because the administrator controls everything that happens as well as what other employees and other computer users can do. The computer technician must be the most trusted person in the company next to the owner, this means that the same scrutiny in the same background and credit and reference checks that you would do on the bookkeeper you must do on any computer technician you hire. A computer technician who does not know QuickBooks is just as able to steal money and falsify information as a bookkeeper.

You may be wondering why all of QuickBooks' security depends on the windows clock. Well, it's very simple; when QuickBooks records an event and stamps it with the date and the time, the date and the time that QuickBooks will stamp the event is based on whatever is in the clock in Windows or let's say the clock in the computer at the moment that the item is recorded. If a QuickBooks user can change the Windows clock, then they can change the date and time that events are recorded making it easier for them to falsify records and possibly steal from you so do not let them have permission. You must make sure that before you even set up your QuickBooks you limit the windows permissions.

Setting Closing Date for security access

In this section, we will learn about a very important security feature which is setting a closing date. The Closing Date is the date when no transactions before this date may be added, changed, or removed unless, of course, you have the closing date password. Anything before the closing date should not be changed because those numbers have already been submitted to the government and different departments of government like the IRS. Anything you recorded after the closing date is no problem and you can edit, change, add or delete anything you want.

Setting a Closing date and Password

To make a closing date, the administrator must use the Preferences window and set up a closing date password. So, the administrator decides what the closing date is and also decides the password. You don't have to set up users and passwords to put on a closing date password. You're automatically logged in as the administrator if you did not set up users and passwords so that means just create the file, don't even deal with usernames and passwords, and go ahead and go to the Preferences window and put in a closing date and a password. You're automatically logged in as the administrator if you did not set up users and passwords.

Let's open a file where users and passwords are not set up and we'll put a closing date and a password. Let's make the closing date July 31 and the password 500 dollars. This is a very famous password for a closing date because accountants will tell their clients that if they change something before the closing date, they'll be charged 500 dollars to come out there and fix it.

So, let's take a look at how it would look. First, we have to be sure that in the open file we have no usernames and passwords set up. If you go to "**Company**", "**Set up users and passwords**" and click "**Set up users**" you'll see right now you only have the admin.

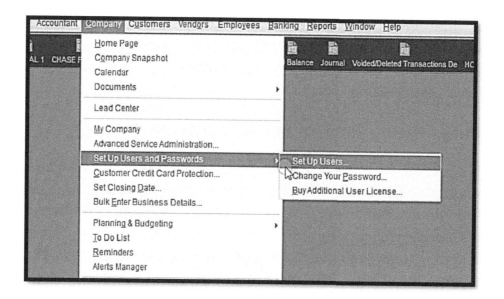

So, you are logged in because you've never set up users and passwords.

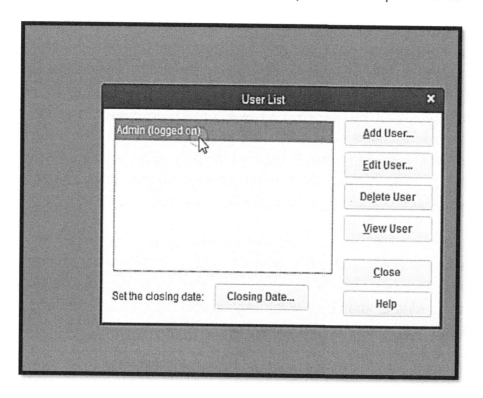

If you click "**Edit user**", you can see a password was never given which means you've never set up users and passwords.

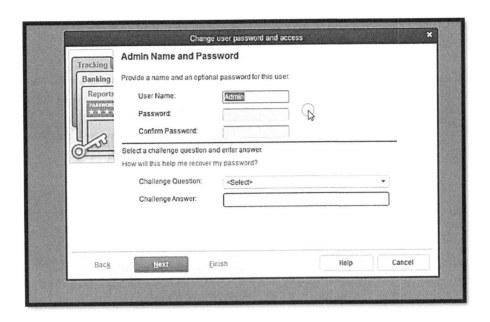

Now let's go ahead and put in the closing date and password. From the top left of the main menu go to "**Edit**" then "**Preferences**."

Now the preferences for the closing date are in the accounting category in the Company Preference tab. Go down to the bottom of the window and click "**Set date and password**".

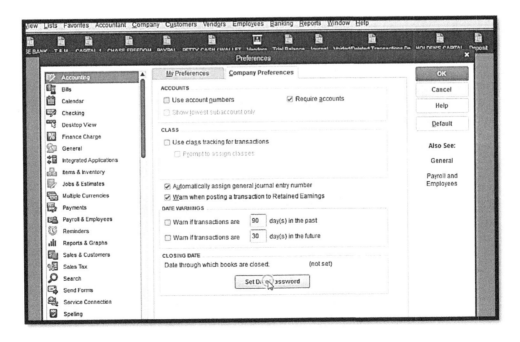

Remember for this illustration the closing date will be July 31 and the password will be 500 dollars (which is entered twice for confirmation purposes) then click OK.

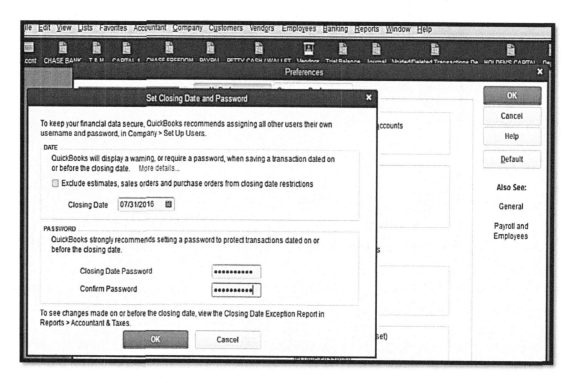

Next, you'll get a pop-up window that is only warning you that you did not set up users and passwords but it will still allow you to put a password on the closing date. You're going to click "Yes" and then close out the window.

Changing Transactions Before a closed date

Now we have set up a closing date with a password, let's see if it works. We're going to open one of the registers and we'll try to delete something that was entered before July 31. Go to "**Edit**", and navigate to "**Delete deposit**."

Immediately, you'll get a popup window from QuickBooks notifying you that you cannot do this without the password but if you type in the password 500 dollars and then click OK, you can now confirm if you want to delete the transaction or not.

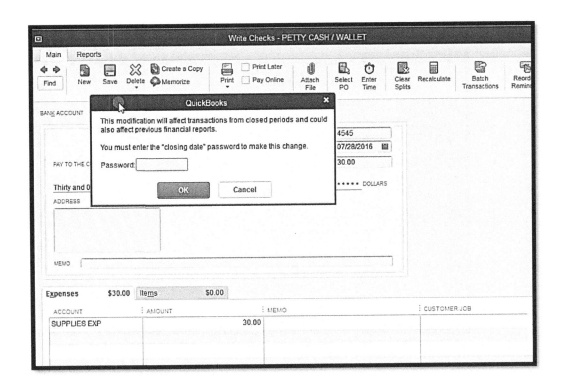

So, it does allow us to change something but only if we have the password and as you can see that's true even if there are no usernames or passwords set up because by default we're logged in as the administrator. Now you know that only the administrator can set up or change the closing date password, which means that if you're not the administrator you'll need permission to change any transaction before the closing date, and then you'll also need the closing date password.

As a further illustration, we have already set up a user named Jill and in the last stages of setting Jill's username and password we told QuickBooks that she does not have the ability or the permission to change closed transactions (that's transactions before the closing date). Now let's see if Jill can change one of the transactions in July.

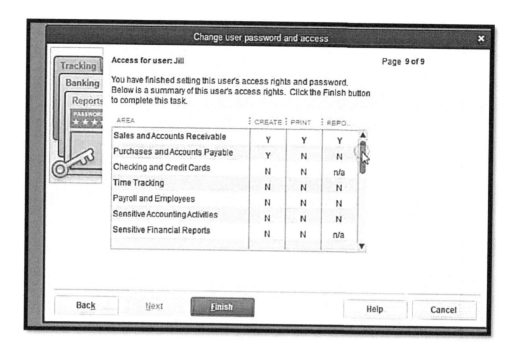

Currently, let's say we are logged in to the same file as Jill. Let's open one of the transactions during July that Jill would normally have access to for example a transaction on July 28th. When we try to delete it, you can see that we got a warning that says we cannot perform this action because the transaction date is before the closing date and that we need permission to modify transactions before the closing date for which we have to ask our administrator.

So, QuickBooks did not even ask us for a password because this particular user was not permitted to change anything before the closing date even if she had a password.

Changing User permissions

Now let's permit Jill. We're logged back in as the administrator and now we're going to alter Jill's permissions. It's a very simple setup. Simply go to "Users and passwords" again, put in the administrator password and we're going to edit the user, Jill. We're going to fast-forward to the end where it asks if this user will be allowed to change transactions before the closing date. Now we're going to say "Yes" and click "Next" and you can see Jill now can change transactions before the closing date. We're going to click "Finish" to save our changes.

Now we're logged back into the same file as Jill, let's see if we can delete that July check. We'll go to "Banking," "Write a Check," go back to the checks that are in July and if click to delete, you can see it now allows us to do it but even though jill has permission to change it she still has to type in the password after which she has to confirm that she wants to delete that transaction and if she has, the transaction has been deleted.

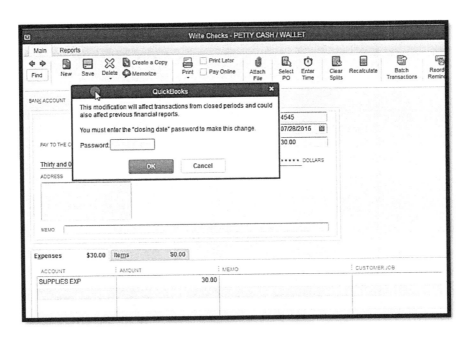

The Closing Date Exception Report

A great security feature that goes along with the closing date is the Closing Date Exception Report. The Closing Date Exception Report shows every change to every transaction before the closing date. It will also show the date and time of the change and exactly who changed it. Now even though the format is somewhat similar to the Audit Trail, this report sorts all the changes by the user so it may look like it's repeating information because it might be that two separate users change the same transaction.

From the main menu go to "Reports," "Accountant & taxes" and then "Closing Date Exception Report."

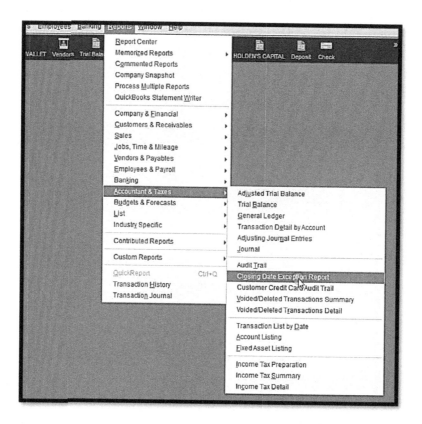

You'll notice all the transactions listed here are transactions entered or modified by the admin's actions. Below there are the transactions entered or modified by the user and in both sets, there's only one. You can see, July 1 was when this particular check dated July 28th was originally entered by the administrator and then on July 7th it was deleted by the user. Now that's the information about what the administrator did and who else changed the administrator's information. Below that it looks like a repeat but it's not, it's the user's information because if the user was involved in any of the changes it'll be listed down here even if it's listed in another user's section of this report.

So, the very same check that the administrator entered on July 1st, the user deleted on July 7th, and that information is also shown in the section of the user.

Setting Up QuickBooks Usernames and Passwords

Usernames and passwords are the foundation of security in QuickBooks. When you first create the file, you're logged in as the administrator or admin for short. Anyone who uses the file right after it's created is logged in as admin and the admin has access to everything in the file. Once you make an admin password you cannot open the file without inputting the password so if you're not going to use security features, it might not be a good idea to make an administrator password because once you do that you will always have to put in a password every time you open up the file.

It's the administrator who gives all the other users their usernames and their passwords and it's also the administrator who gives the other users whatever permissions they might have. You're going to see how to put a password on the administrator and you'll also see how to set up other users with different usernames and passwords and permit them but for now, let's just give the administrator the password.

Setting up an admin password

When we do this in our example, we'll leave the username as admin. You could change the username to something else but in our example, we'll keep it simple. When deciding on a password we will use conventional wisdom; we will take the typical common advice for setting up a safe password. That means the password will have at least one capital, at least one number, and at least one special character. We'll also consider a punctuation mark. So, for this example, we have decided that the admin password will be Jeremy12! with a capital J and an exclamation point after the number 12.

Let's take a look at what the file looks like both before and after we put in an administrator password. The image below shows the file for a company and it does not yet have an administrator password.

So now when we double-click on it, QuickBooks will open up the file with no problem at all and without asking us for a username or a password. Now we want to put a username and password for the administrator. Once we do this, we will never be able to open this file again without putting in some kind of username and password so make a backup copy before you do it.

From the main menu go to "Company" and go down to "Setup users & passwords". Come across to the right and down to click "Change your password."

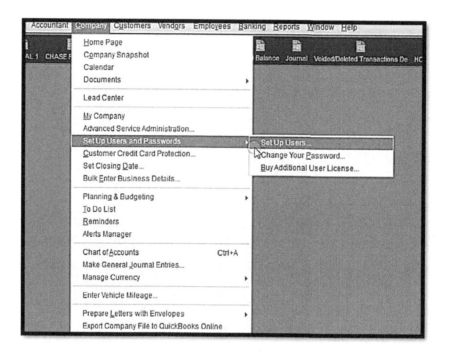

Now let's leave the username as admin (it's only five letters and only the A is capitalized). Now we're going to type in the password we want and select a challenge question, providing the answer as well. Then we will click OK to proceed.

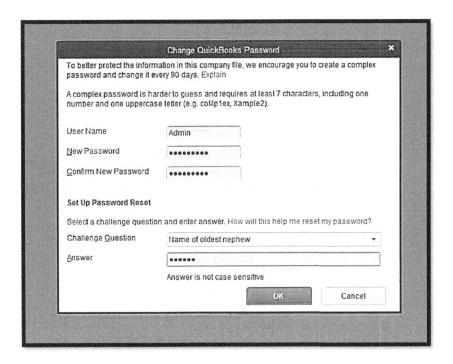

QuickBooks notifies you that your QuickBooks passport has been changed, recommending that you change it again in ninety days. Click OK and now you will not be able to open this particular file until you put in that password.

Now we're going to close out QuickBooks and try to open this same file. You can see that it's now demanding a password and if we don't put it in, we won't get in. Now if you type in the correct password, QuickBooks lets you back into the file.

By the way, if you click "I forgot my password" you can still recover your password or at least reset it if you type in the security question.

Setting up Users and Password

Now that we've made an administrator username and password, we're going to set up another user and give that user a password. After we do that, we'll give an example of how the administrator sets permissions. In this example, the user's name will be Jill and again we will follow the conventional wisdom when making a password (at least one capital, at least one number, and at least one special character or punctuation mark), in this case, it'll be "Allison22?" with a capital A and a question mark at the end.

From the main menu, we'll go to "Company," "Setup users & passwords," and now we're going to click "Setup users."

Before we do that, we have to make sure we put in the administrator password, then click OK and it allows us to add a user. We will now enter the username and password. Don't worry about the QuickBooks license issue just clicks "Next" to proceed.

When we click "Next," we are asked to confirm if we want to give Jill access to all areas of QuickBooks or just selected areas.

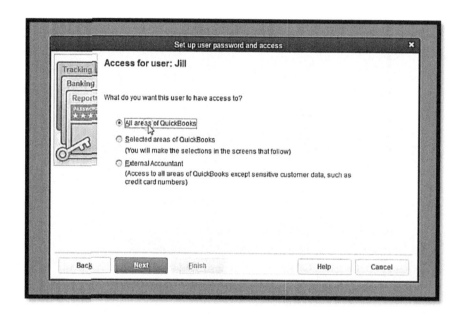

Granting the user access to all areas in QuickBooks

Here in our first example, we're going to click "all areas of QuickBooks" and then click "Next." This brings up a window confirming we are sure about our decision of which we're going to click "Yes."

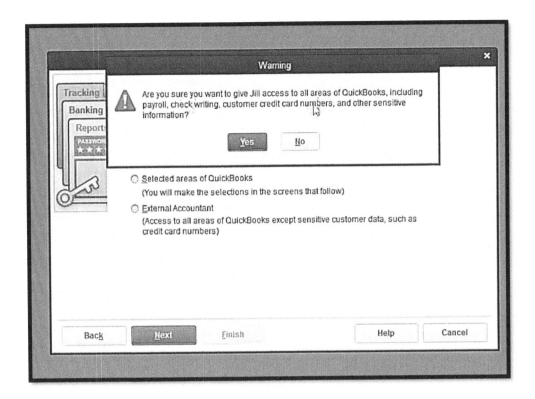

You'll notice it gives you a list of places and things within the file that our new user can do and you can browse this later to remember what Jill is allowed to do and what Jill is not allowed to do. Click "Finish" and now we have the administrator and we have Jill.

The best thing to do is to close this window and now let's make sure Jill can log in. Now when we reboot the program by double-clicking our company file it'll ask us for the username and password and instead of the admin, we enter the username as Jill and the corresponding password for this user. We're now logged in as Jill and not the administrator.

It is very important to remember that even though we did not restrict Jill in any way, it is still the case that only the administrator can add new users, delete existing users, change access privileges for other users, import and export data, change company preferences, change company information like the name and address in the file, set or edit closing dates, create accountants copy or clean up the data file. These are all things that only the administrator can do that Jill or any other user cannot do. Now you remember a moment ago we allowed Jill to have access to all areas of our QuickBooks file but even though we told QuickBooks to give her access to everything,

286

just the fact that she is not the administrator prevents her from being in these nine areas or doing these nine things.

Let's prove this to you by giving you two examples of having Jill try to do something and getting an error message that she's not allowed to do it. First, let's confirm that we're logged in as Jill: go to "Company," "Set up users & passwords" then "Set up users" and you can see Jill is the one that's logged in and we know she's not allowed to change Company Preferences.

Every area of preference has a "My preferences" tab and a "Company preferences tab." Recall that the "My preferences tab" can be changed by any user because that's the preference of a particular user and QuickBooks will remember each user's preference. If Jill enters the "Company preference" and tries to change something, she'll get a message telling her that only the QuickBooks administrator or external accountant can perform this action and that she must reopen the company file and log in as the admin or eternal accountant to do this. That's one example of what Jill is not allowed to do.

The other example is changing company information. From the main menu go to "Company" and then click "My company."

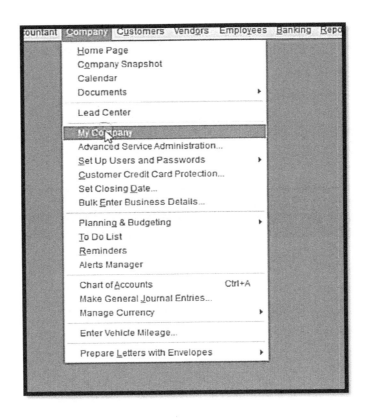

You can see this is where we would normally put the username and password but we're getting a warning message here and there's no pencil to click (normally there'd be a little pencil to click for us to edit the name and address of the company) but instead, we have this message that tells us that only the QuickBooks administrator or external accountant can view this information. So that proves as long as we've logged in as Jill and not the administrator there are these few things that Jill is not allowed to do.

Granting the user access to selected areas in QuickBooks

Now let's go even deeper; let's limit Jill's permissions so that she can handle all areas of receivables and customers and she has access to the vendors and payables transactions but not the reports. What would we have to do first? Well, first we have to make sure that we close the file, reopen it and log in as the administrator because only the administrator can do that.

288

After entering the admin's login details, we're now logged in as the administrator. Now we can go to "Company," "Setup users & passwords," and "Set up users." Now again we have to enter the administrator password, click OK and now we're going to click the user Jill and go to edit the user.

The username and password are fine (we're not going to change that), we'll click "Next" but this time we are going to give her access to selected areas of QuickBooks.

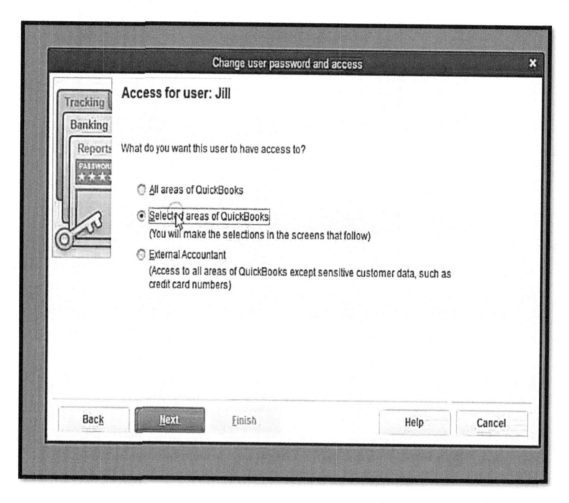

When we click "Next," it's going to ask us about each area one by one. For Sales and Accounts Receivable we'll leave it as full access, then click "Next."

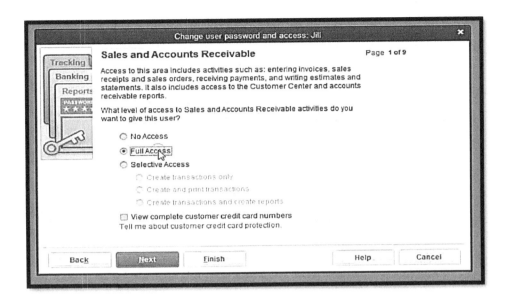

For Purchases and Accounts Payable, we'll click selective access and then we'll put "Create transactions only" which means she cannot print transactions and she cannot see payable reports.

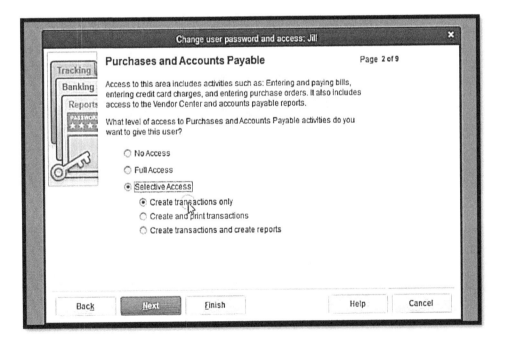

Now for all other areas, we're going to click "No Access." Finally, when it comes to deleting transactions, we can indicate if we want this user to have the ability to change or delete transactions in the areas, they have access to and if we want this user to also have the ability to change or delete transactions that were recorded before the closing date.

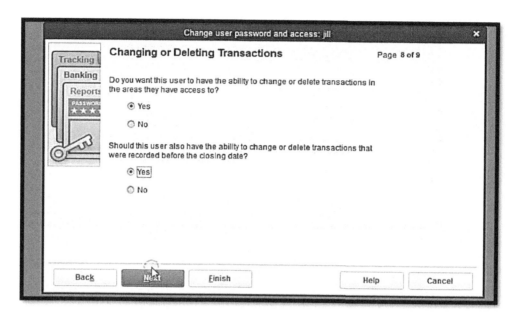

When we go to Next, we can see a summary of all the areas that Jill does and does not have access to and you can browse this on your own time. When we click "Finish" we have now set the permissions for Jill.

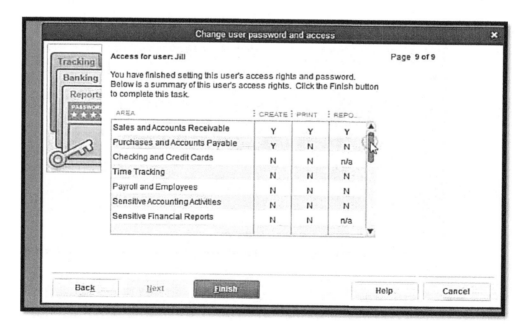

Let's now prove that they work properly and to do that we have to close QuickBooks completely, then reopen QuickBooks and log in as Jill and we will see if the permissions work.

Now we are logged in as Jill, let's see what areas we're allowed to use. If we try to write a check, we will get a warning from QuickBooks telling us that we need Checking and Credit card permissions to perform this action.

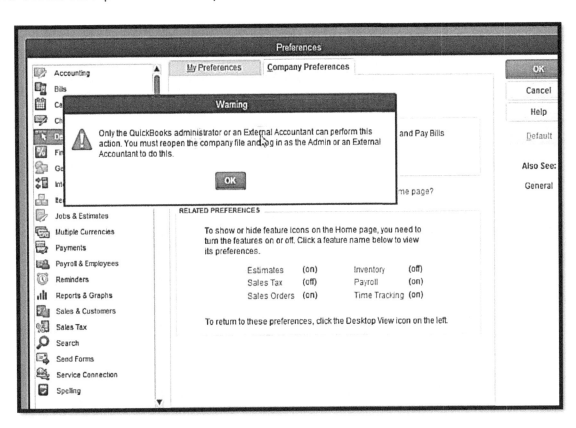

If we try the areas where Jill was given permission such as creating an invoice for a customer, we will have no problem there.

If we try to enter time using a weekly timesheet, we will get a warning again from QuickBooks saying we need time tracking permission to perform this action (remember we had told QuickBooks no when it comes to Jill having permission for this area)

292

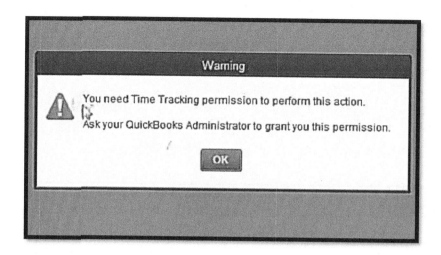

Also, if we try to enter a bill, we will have no problem there because the admin allowed Jill to record transactions in the Vendors and Payable section. However, even though Jill was allowed to enter bills and record transactions in the vendor area when she tries to view reports of unpaid bills, she'll get a message saying that she needs reporting permission to perform this action.

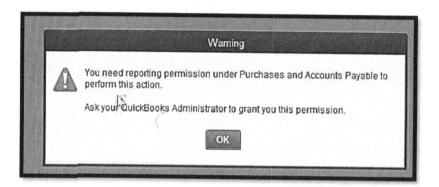

Review Questions

1. Mention 3 QuickBooks security measures that can be taken as an employer.
2. What differentiates an Admin from a user?
3. What are the functions of a QuickBooks admin?
4. What is a Closing Date?

CHAPTER 17

RESTORE AND BACKUP FILES

In this chapter, we will look at how you can restore and back up data files. We're going to be opening up the two locations where we'll be putting these files, noting that you want to keep these things distinct in that the software for the data files and the backup files will be distinct files in and of themselves. So, you should be able to track when you're restoring these items onto your desktop or into a file as you have to know where they are located.

Creating a company backup file

First, you'll go to open the company file. You're going to be putting that file then into your data files because this is going to be a "qbw" file (the data file).

Then when you go there, you can see that you now have the data file versus the actual software. Note that you have to put that into a folder because you've got all this other junk that comes along with it and if you just put it on your desktop, you're going to get a lot of junk on your desktop so putting it into its folder would be the best practice.

Now you're going to go to the File drop-down, the "Backup Company File" and you're going to create a local backup.

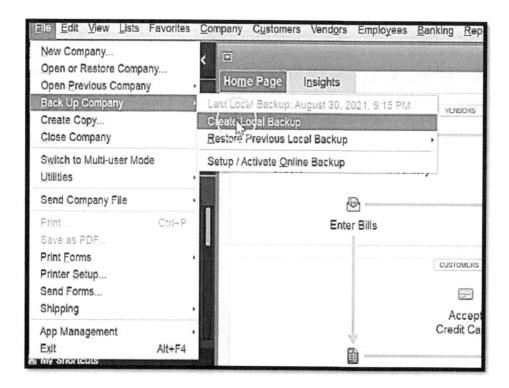

To practice the backup process, in the next window, you're going to be picking the local backup instead of the online backup. Remember that as you back up the software you do not want to know what your purpose of backing it up is and if it's to just back up the data then you want it on a separate drive from the drive that you are using for your data file in case the whole computer crashes; you want the backup somewhere else. Then you could browse here and explore the options you have here. One of the options will limit the number of backups in a folder (so you don't have too much in one particular folder), you have a reminder option and typically you want the default most of the time for the complete verification recommended.

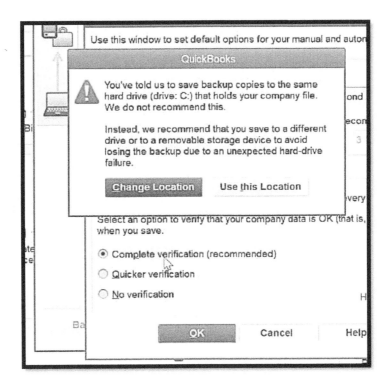

The next screen for the backup process is to save it. So, then you're going to save it to a location which is a new location and now you're going to have a backup file which is going to be another file added to it.

Now you have your icon to open the software, the backup file which is a qbw file as opposed to the data file which is the one that you open up into the software. They both look similar (the backup file and the data file) but you want to keep them distinct in your mind.

Restoring a company file

Now we're going to show you how to restore the backup file. First, you'll go to the File drop-down and click the option to restore the backup file.

If you are opening up a backup file you can't just double-click on it; you have to restore the backup file to unzip it.

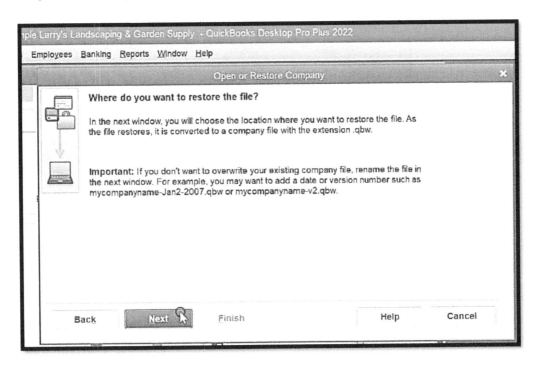

Now you'll go through the "**Restore a backup file**" to practice the restoration process.

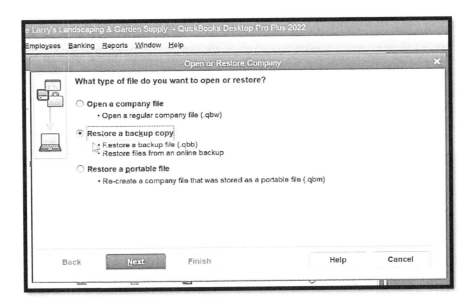

You need to locate the backup and you must know where it's at, remember this is part of the problem and you have to make sure that you know where the backup is. After locating the backup file, you're going to select that file to restore it.

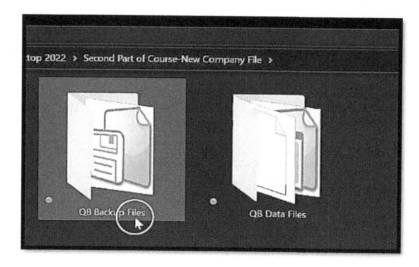

Now when you restore it, you're going to also have another location because when you restore the backup file, you're not just opening up the backup file, you're restoring it and putting another file somewhere else which will be the actual data file. Now when you restore the data file, you're going to have another data file that will be located on your computer. So, as you're using the backups or if you're using them to practice, then you want to make sure that you're organizing your backup files and your data files so that you know where you're at and that's good practice for a client based bookkeeping system as well because you want to make sure that you have an idea of where the backup files are, what the data files are and the difference between the two.

Review Questions

1. What is a company file?
2. What is the difference between a data file and a backup file?
3. How can you create a backup file?

CHAPTER 18

TROUBLESHOOTING COMMON ISSUES IN QUICKBOOKS

The focus of this chapter is how to troubleshoot common issues with QuickBooks. You are going to see some common issues you may likely come across and how to resolve them.

When you can't open the program

What happens if you can't even open the program? What do you need to do? You simply reset the app. To do so, just hold down the shift key on the keyboard while opening the program. So, you continue to hold down the shift key until the program comes up and then you will see the sign-in screen

Getting a white screen after you sign in

Sometimes after signing in, you may get a funny-looking white screen, what do you do? Simply go to the File menu and refresh your QuickBooks app and that will take care of some of these issues.

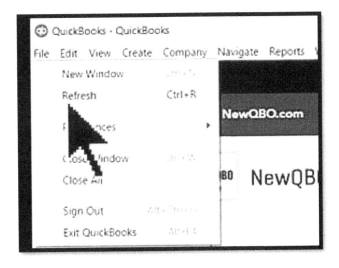

If after refreshing your app you're still getting that white screen, you have to go to the "Help" menu, "Reset App Data" and that should solve the issue.

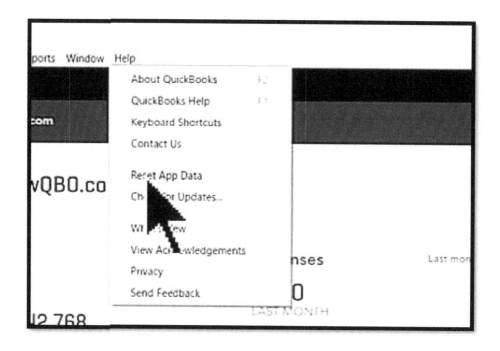

If nothing else works

After trying the method above and it doesn't work, then you have to uninstall your app and reinstall it again. To do that go to the official website of QuickBooks after uninstalling your existing app and then reinstall the QuickBooks app again.

Review Questions

1. When do you need to troubleshoot your QuickBooks?
2. What do you do when you can't open the QuickBooks program?
3. When do you need to reinstall your QuickBooks program?

Thank you so much for your order and for taking your time to read this book. We are constantly striving to improve our customer satisfaction, hence, we are curious to find out how helpful this book is to you, if you can spare us a minute to leave us a review, we'd be super grateful.

INDEX

303

305

X

Z

Made in United States
North Haven, CT
29 January 2023

31581470R00174